The Cornell Journal of Architecture

Fall 1987

Preface

In 1923, in *Towards a New Architecture,* Le Corbusier articulated a vision of the future as the modern movement in architecture ushered in the twentieth century. Modern architecture, as architects have profoundly discovered, affected our lives and built environment much more than we suspected. We hardly even stopped to take a look. Now we have taken a look, and in the words of Aldous Huxley, "You looks around you and you takes your choice."

If architecture changed and the world changed, there was no significant change in the way we educate architects. The Bauhaus tradition was added to the Beaux Arts tradition, which was added to the master-apprentice tradition, all of which boils down to studio teaching of architectural design: fifteen students on one end of a log and a professor armed with tradition on the other. It is a rather crude laboratory practicing hypotheses, trial and error, and, just as in science, mostly error. Unlike the scientist or engineer in his laboratory, the architect deals with several major conditions that are dramatically different. The architect is involoved in a creative search, his/her world is empirical at best and there are few questions with only one answer. There are fewer facts. There is, however, as in any empirical quest, experience, tradition, and most of all, logic. Other than these few things the architect is left with a patient search indeed. Probably the most frustrating difference is that the tools are crude. Architecture is one of the few hand-made products left in the world. The equipment is almost exactly the same as it was on the desk of Michelangelo (of course, he didn't do too badly, did he?)

If architecture changed in the twentieth century, the way we teach architecture and the tools we use will almost certainly change in the future. The computer has forced us to stand on a new threshold and whether it will destroy architecture or liberate it from the toil of the past lies in the hands of the educators, not the profession.

Although one cannot predict the future, the aspect of architecture that will probably be affected the most by the computer is the vertical surface. The computer's promise of instant three dimensional manipulation challenges the architect's propensity for plan fixation. The difficulty that the Journal staff had in extracting the manuscripts for this issue is testimony to the fact that architects are uncomfortable when they are asked to think about "The Facade". In fact there is not even an argument as to what a "facade" is as compared with mere elevation.

The computer will not solve this argument nor any other conceptual argument. Even as we enter into this new era of architectural design with our new powerfully equipped computer-aided design studio at Cornell, there is the realization by all that we will probably still have to make architecture the old fashioned way — with our minds.

Jerry A. Wells
Nathaniel and Margaret Owings Distinguished
Alumni Professor of Architecture
Chairman, Department of Architecture
Cornell University

Introduction

From our experience the issue of the vertical surface in architectural education is rarely addressed more than parenthetically and then it is encumbered with a set of notions whose critical contributions operate more out of habit than ideation. These received ideas, while serving to initiate discussion, are for the most part marginally beneficial and, because of their cognitive akwardness, also facilitate a quick exit. This Journal makes no pretense of being holistic in discussing the subject of the vertical surface, but rather is an attempt to take a significant hunk out of this cultural shell which tends to impede investigation of one of the most significant aspects of architecture.

Dominick LaCapra, in describing his own book *Rethinking Intellectual History*, writes, "This book is a collection of essays which, to the extent that they are successful, are essays in the etymological sense of the word.... [It is] my belief that the essay is the best 'form' in which to explore the interaction between unification and challanges to it. A series of essays will necessarily harbor tensions, 'internal contestations,' and even contradictions that are worth preserving insofar as they stimulate further thought about the questions at issue." These words could not be more accurately appropriated than for this Journal. The essays taken together are activated by a number of concerns. They do not argue one dominant thesis and at times even contradict each other.

Two of the authors, Thomas Schumacher and Val Warke, found it necessary to describe a history of ideas and develop a critical base before initiating a visual analysis. These articles are bipartite; verbal and visual—so much so that Schumacher has elected to present his as two separate essays. To a certain extent the other articles are informed by arguments set forth by these two and we have discovered that an interpretation is dependent on the order in which the articles are read. This is also true of the student projects; without too much difficulty the reader can align projects with articles though this was not explicitly planned, and yet less obvious combinations will yield richer interpretations.

We greatly appreciate the patience of the authors and students in responding to our requests and it is due to their tenacity and perserverance that this Journal is completed as you see it today. It is surely to the credit of the faculty and student body of the Department of Architecture that they continue to provide a poignant setting for the development of ideas. People too numerous to mention have provided a background for this Journal and there are certainly people to whom a debt is owed that we do not know. Contributors we would like to thank by name are: Colin Rowe, who will not recognize this Journal as being the result of his suggestions and Daniel Kaplan who provided its seminal dialogue. We would also like to thank John Coyne who is certainly the Journal's messiah and lastly, while we have thanked her elsewhere, Ruth Thomas who has been a patient contributor and friend, in every sense of the word.

Pamela A. Butz and Jeffrey L. Klug
Editors

Contents

Staff

Editors
Pamela A. Butz
Jeffrey L. Klug

Associate Editor
John P. Coyne

Copyright Editors
Philip A. Carhuff
Gloria Civantos

Advisory Board
Martin Kubelik
Christian Otto
Colin Rowe
Val Warke
Jerry Wells

Editorial Staff
Pamela A. Butz
John P. Coyne
Milton S. F. Curry
Patrick R. Daly
Daniel Kaplan
Jeffrey L. Klug
Alexander J. Ware

Staff
Bryna Bearman
Timothy Downing
Mark Klopfer
Stuart Muller
Rosie O' Grady

Journal Class
1985
1986
1987

The Skull and the Mask:

The Modern Movement and the Dilemma of the Facade

Thomas L. Schumacher

1

A building is like a soap bubble. This bubble is perfect and harmonious if the breath has been evenly distributed and regulated from the inside. The exterior is the result of an interior.

Le Corbusier

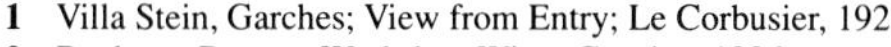

1 Villa Stein, Garches; View from Entry; Le Corbusier, 1927
2 Bauhaus, Dessau; Workshop Wing; Gropius, 1926
3 Werkbund Exhibition Pavillion, Cologne; View; Gropius and Meyer, 1914

3

The Skull: Internal Needs and External Wants

The term, *facade*, as applied to architecture in this century, has taken on the same negative connotation that it has when applied to people. Modern-movement theory shunned the facade and gave us the *skeleton* or the *skull*. Post-Modernism, though not single-handedly, gave us the *mask;* the rhetorical facade that caricatures reality via hyperbole, sometimes employing grotesque elements.

This characterization is admittedly oversimplified. It describes tendencies and not individual buildings or architects. There are so many exceptions that it might be difficult to find *any* architects to fit it perfectly (it is possibly as difficult as finding an example of Venturi's 'orthodox' modernist). Nonetheless, it is a characterization of a tendency, a theoretical position, and a set of aspirations.

My purpose in this essay will be to explain how the alternative of skull/mask came about; how historical change and architectural principles 'conspired', around 1920, to create an attitude according to which *face* became an impossible choice between the expression of the internal skeleton and the cosmetic applique of artifice; and how that attitude persists.

The argument concentrates on construction (as compared to structure) in relation to function, space, and surface. Over the past two hundred years, the design of the exterior surface, the identification of the building program, and the creation of interior space have each been liberated from construction and have come to be viewed as independent variables in the design equation. This independence has changed the way architects have viewed the design of facades more than it has affected any other aspect of the design process. Confusion over these variables has, in my view, been the real contributor to modern architecture's cop-out in facade design.

The Liberation of Surface from Construction

> No mouldings, no frills, were permitted to distract one's attention from true architectural values: the relations of wall to window, solid to void, volume to space, block to block.[1]
>
> Nikolas Pevsner

> Before all else the wall must be shown naked in all its sleek beauty, and anything fixed on it must be shunned as embarrassment.[2]
>
> H. P. Berlage

The decade between Gropius and Adler's Werkbund Pavilion in Cologne (1914) (fig. 3) and Bauhaus in Dessau (1926) (fig. 2) witnessed as great a change in mass and surface as can be chronicled in the history of architecture. These two buildings by the same architects display some overt similarities of massing and construction system but they are worlds apart in terms of the architects' attitude toward surface. The details of the Werkbund Pavilion are still rather traditional; they articulate the construction process, for example, pilasters and window sills. In the Bauhaus the details have been ironed out and all the 'frills' (Pevsner's term) are gone. Only the metal mullions holding the glazing remain, and one imagines that they too might have been eliminated had Gropius had the budget or the technology to do so. Gropius' later building (while not the first of its type) emphatically represents the liberation of surface from the building process, from construction.

Because traditional facades represented traditional building assembly, the decorative parts were acceptable to a modern sensibility as integral with traditional methods of construction. But because modern buildings were to be produced by the technical process of an industrialized society and assembled in the factory, the addition of ornament was believed to be insignificant and spurious. The notion of the registration of details, what Frampton has called "the ligaments of the construction process",[3] in the final product was seen as hopelessly craft-oriented. The work could no longer appear to have been manipulated after it was in place. The idea of ornament, conceived of as the element of detail invented to cover a joint or to make the building watertight (although that was obviously not always the case in the past), was eliminated as much because it was not a constructive necessity as because of any Loosian moral proscription.

Moreover the exterior surfaces were to be as abstract and seamless as possible in imitation of the de Stijl exercises of the preceding decade; they were icons of a benign and magical future, where no seams or joints would be needed. That is not to say that the elegance of smooth, unbroken, well-crafted surfaces is the exclusive province of the modern architectural sensibility. A smooth, unrelieved surface is 'proof' of the solidity and quality of materials and workmanship, whether handcrafted or machine produced. The sixteen monolithic polished porphyry columns of the Pantheon, rough-cut in Egypt, shipped up the Tiber to Italy, dragged up over the fall line, and polished to a reflective finish are the ancient embodiment of a variant of Mies' dictum: Less *costs* more.

Parallels to building design abound. In *haute couture* of the 1960's, for example, women's dresses were made without darts on the bodice, separating high fashion from ready-to-wear. Or we can also cite Italian coach work from the same period, when the sides of Ferraris and Maseratis were plain, with no creases to prevent "oilcanning" and with no moldings to make the car look lower. The car *was* lower, the metal *was* thicker.

Roland Barthes eloquently expressed the aesthetic patrimony of this style in his short article on the Citroen DS, written in 1957, when the automobile was introduced: "Christ's robe was seamless, just as the airships of science-fiction are made of unbroken metal."[4] To "less is more" we may add "seamlessness is next to godliness."[5]

In traditional architectures distressed surfaces (for example, rustication) represent the difficulty of carving an expanse of stone perfectly smooth. A smooth surface will also show any deformation caused by injury. In modern design however this norm has resulted in a necessary irony when modern objects are presented as having articulated parts. The advertisement for the Audemars Piguet watch (fig. 5) is a good case in point. The caption reads, " 'A price like that' he teased 'and they don't conceal the screws?' "

It is not surprising, then, that modern architects in the1920s should have looked to a streamlined aesthetic for buildings. Buildings that would have been manufactured in the factory if those architects could have had their way.

In the European avant-garde, when by the 1920s construction had been generalized into pure white planes (or pure colored planes) and glazed voids, the only variables left to the architect to manipulate were massing and solid-void ratios. Functional identification and scale were assumed to be the results of this process. For Siegfried Giedion, the historian and apologist of the Modern Movement, to have practiced in the late twenties and *not* to have used white planes was most certainly a transgression. Why else would he condemn W. M. Dudok, an architect whose basic compositions are as "modern" as those of Rietreld and Van Hoff but who built in brick and often used pitched roofs?

Pevsner's assumption that 'true architectural values' are abstract is a reflection of Le Corbusier's definition of architecture as "the masterly, correct and magnificent play of masses brought together in light"[6] and the abstractionist theories of Van Doesburg. These are attitudes that allow the separation of the act of building (and even the act of habitation) from the desired result. (The Grand Canyon may also be considered the magnificent play of volumes seen in light, and while it may be metaphorically called architecture, it *literally* is not.)

The abstraction of surface, however, does not preclude a symbolic reading for form in the more general sense. On the contrary, by simplifying the surface, functional expression (that is, function considered as the expression of programmed activity or an institution) might be more transparent. By conventionalizing the surface *so that the surface itself is not an index to pragmatic differences*, the variables can be reduced. The index to program variations then resides in solid-void relationships and massing.

Between the middle of the eighteenth century and Pevsner's expression of modern values quoted above, stands two hundred years of philosophical, social, cultural, and technical changes in the history of ideas that deeply affected architectural theory and practice. These ideas did not converge in the early twentieth century to produce a wholly abstract architecture, but within the avant-garde of the 1920's and in terms of the *vertical surface*, the dominant themes perfectly reflect Le Corbusier's definition and Pevsner's values.

The Liberation of Space and Volume from Structure

A comparison of two facades by Le Corbusier may serve as an entree into the problem of the relationship between interior space and exterior surface. In the unbuilt house for M. X in Brussles (fig. 4), the front facade displays the internal volumes explicitly. The great room at the top of the house is covered by a huge window-wall, while the more modular and smaller-scale windows below express the modularity of the rooms behind.

In the facade of the Villa Stein at Garches (fig. 6), no such telegraphing of internal volume occurs. The ribbon windows of the *piano nobile* are identical in height to those of the less important floor above. Nor do these windows vary in width to distinguish differences in the rooms behind. The kitchen on the *piano nobile* receives the same window treatment as the library and stair landing. Further, the one element that is accentuated on the facade is rather low in programmatic hierarchy—a bathroom. This room presents itself in the center of the facade as some latter-day equivalent—albeit at vastly reduced scale—of Louis's bedroom at Versailles, occupying as it does the center of a major visual axis that penetrates the house and goes on to the garden behind.[7]

The facade of the Villa Garches is obviously telling us something very different about its contents (and content) than the house for M. X. It is referring back, via its format if not its style, to the tradition of *piano nobile* houses of the Italian Renaissance and French Rococo.[8]

The important question is which aspect of the inside is reasonable to bring to the outside, and what are the various ways in which inside and outside can be interrelated.

The opposites implied by the above comparison are an analogue to opposite methods of design fostered by two of the most influential teachers of architecture in America in the twentieth century: Mies and Gropius.

For the student of Gropius the design process starts with the program. He takes the space requirements and makes little squares to scale, arranges them according to reasonable adjacencies and connections, raises up the walls, and adds fenestration to taste.

For the student of Mies the process is reversed. The analysis of the program gives him the structural module. He then chooses column sections, develops the horizontal members and encases the volume (usually a simple object) with an appropriate number of units to fit the space needed.

The 'method' I am ascribing to Gropius was characterized by Reyner Banham as the method of design common to most avant-garde architects of the 1920's. Banham traced the origins of this idea to the influence of Guadet's theories of elementary composition stating, "...it may be taken as a general characteristic of the progressive architecture of the early twentieth century that it was conceived in terms of a separate and defined volume for each separate and defined function, and composed in such a way that this separation and definition was made plain."[9]

While many recent critics, historians, and architects have leveled attacks on modern architecture's "Miesian sterility" or the boring repetition of steel curtain-wall towers, I would like to examine the tacit doctrine in the profession, and in American schools of architecture, that the internal organization of building spaces ought to provide the norm of external expression and that any variatrion from this norm is understandable (and justifiable) *only* as deviation. The concept finds its paradigm with the Bauhaus-influenced projects of the 1950's and 60's commonly referred to as the exploded cube. The exploded cube is composed of elements of a functional program, more or less abstractly structured, either in a preformed envelope (urban, party wall contexts) or as a picturesque assembly of wings or pavilions (for open sites).

The exploded cube was made possible by technological advances in structure combined with an interest in abstraction. Only when volume (liberated from construction), program (liberated from shelter), and

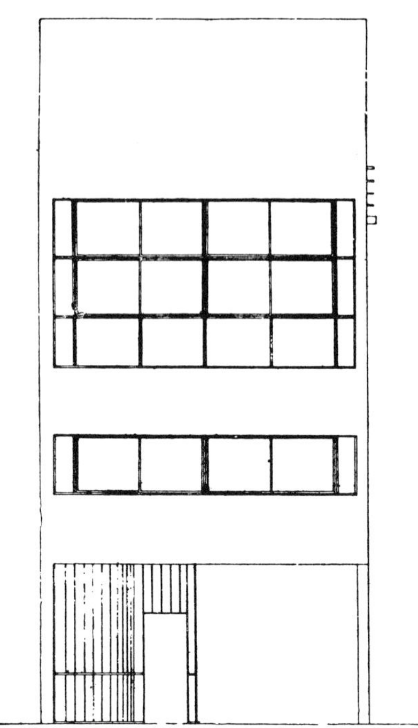

4

5

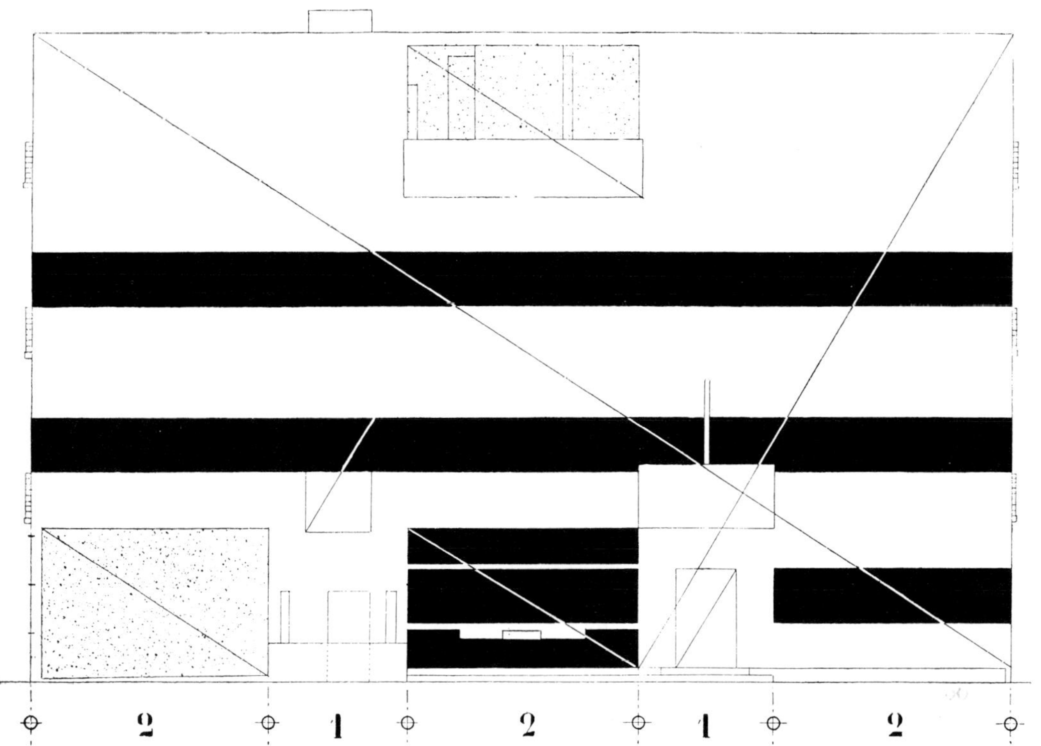

4 Maison de M. X., Brussells; Facade; Le Corbusier, 1929
5 Audemars Piguet Advertisement; New York Times Magazine, 1980
6 Villa Stein, Garches; Regulating Lines; Le Corbusier, 1927
7 Casa del Fascio, Como; View; Terragni, 1932-36

space (liberated from structure) could be viewed abstractly—with each an independent variable in the design process—could the exploded cube be developed.

Space, before the turn of the twentieth century, was itself an idea subsumed under structure. As Peter Collins suggests, whereas the Rationalists, such as Violet-le-Duc, could conceive only of the structure of churches as providing the archetype for a new way of building, Wright took *space*. It is this that distinguishes Wright from the other great architects of his generation...henceforth, space was regarded as the twin partner with structure in the creation of architectural composition.[10]

But even for Wright, an architect working within a craft tradition and consciously rejecting the overt machine aesthetic of the International Style (until perhaps Falling Water in 1936), space remained dependent on structure, despite his rhetoric. In his early work the articulation of the various elements of construction never forsook their expressive place. Nor was Wright particularly interested in the articulation of program as were many Europeans in the 1920s. While the various wings of the early houses vaguely represented division of functional zones, all the external surfaces were articulated in the same manner, that is, based on ideas of construction, not function. Though he achieved clear functional separation in the plan, Wright was more interested in expressing Democracy than kitchens or livingrooms.

For the architects committed to the expression of program function, however, both space and structure could now operate in the service of that function. By the early thirties, it was possible, within the International Style, even imperative, to abjure the societal hierarchy to which the pre-Modern programs deferred (suddenly it was absurd that a Town Hall could resemble a Court House): pre-Modern hierarchy derived from ideas of permanence, the difficulty of construction, and of spanning great distances, all created changes in scale. Long spans meant thick walls, buttresses, or side aisles. The exterior surfaces of buildings, when they registered anything of the internal organization, registered the struggle to create the clear span.

With the advent of the International Style the constructive constraint faded. Now it was possible to span virtually any distance with a flat ceiling and enclose the volume with thin membranes. No longer did the intermediate element of construction intervene to give concrete form to the expressive intent; construction was generalized.

Italy was perhaps alone in the twenties and thirties as an exception to the above argument as is explained by the almost pathological use of the frame as a decorative motif (fig. 7). The Italian rationalists never quite abandoned the idea that architecture is, in part, a decorative art and that much of traditional decoration derives from construction. Hence in Italy, more than anywhere else the frame became the ornamental equivalent of the column.[11]

Hitchcock and Johnson characterized this shift in expressive intention as the difference between expression of mass and expression of volume.[12] In American architectural education after World War II, *program* expressed through *volume* was one of the more consistent theoretical assumptions (outside Chicago and the ambiance of the Illinois Institute of Technology). Students were given exploded cube projects in beginning design courses. One of the rules of the game was to maintain the volumetric correspondence between inside and outside. This, coupled with the idea of continuity between inside and outside, further specified the architects' attitude toward the exterior surface. This kind of assumption is questioned by Venturi in *Complexity and Contradiction in Architecture.*

Perhaps the boldest contribution of orthodox Modern architecture was its so-called flowing space, which was used to achieve the continuity of inside and outside. Flowing space produced an architecture of related horizontal and vertical planes. The visual independence of these uninterrupted planes was scored by connecting areas with plate glass: windows as holes in the wall disappeared and became, instead, interruptions of wall to be discounted by the eye as a positive element of the building.[13]

To the generations of architects educated in this manner, terms like *transparent plane* replaced *window*, and *glass line* replaced *doorway*.[14] To this day, if one asks a student to account for some aberrant opening on the facade of, say, a Renaissance building, the answer is inevitably that the architect must have been trying to express internal volume on the outside wall.

Le Corbusier is often held to be influential in having created the common wisdom that the *norm* of facade expression be internal volume, and his distinction between *free facade* and *ribbon window* (two of his five points for the New Architecture) seems to support this interpretation. Both of these elements are made possible by the separation of structure and enclosure, which is in turn made possible by the concrete or steel frame. Both elements clearly denote the existence of this frame behind, whatever surface is hung on it. The ribbon window announces the existence of the frame by the visible absence of vertical support on the exterior, the free facade, more inchoate and abstract, might seem to imply some other expressive intent. But Le Corbusier described both the elements in precisely the same manner in the *Oeuvre Complete*: "The windows...can run from edge to edge."[15] Le Corbusier had never specified that his *soap bubble* analogy meant that the volume of air in the soap bubble is the perfect equivalent of the volume of the rooms of the building. Even in the most plastic of his buildings, such as the Shodan house in Ahmedabad, the volumes of the interior are never literally projected onto the exterior. Rather, the plasticity of the facade is a more general adumbration of the idea of the frame.

That so many architects have misinterpreted Le Corbusier's theory is perhaps a testament to the seductiveness of Van Doesburg's formal exercises and Hitchcock's and Johnson's definitions.

The expression of volume that the house for M. X displays is also related to the idea of the expression of program, independent of other variables. Only when function could be seen as potentially independent of the more general idea of shelter could it be assumed that functions were directly accessible in the design process and directly expressible in the facade of the finished work.[16]

The Liberation of Function and Program from Shelter

To the architects of the seventeenth and eighteenth centuries it was common to contrast a regular exterior, expressive of the function of constructive and environmental control, with an interior of great variation in room size, scale, and proportion. Starting with Carlo Maderno, at the beginning of the seventeenth century,[17] and then moving to France in the eighteenth century, arrangement of space for increasingly specific uses (called the art of *distribution*, in French) was beginning to overtake composition as a primary activity of the Architectural design process. We see this in the theories and practice of J. E. Blondel, an architect at the forefront of the development of modern distribution and hierarchy in the plan. To Blondel the facade did not express this hierarchy directly but rather supressed it. As Richard Etlin explains:

> Blondel had to manipulate two distinct systems of organization which had to be coordinated together at the same time that each satisfied different and sometimes opposing demands. While the decoration of the interior required an individuality for each type of room as well as a hierarchy between the sizes of rooms, the decoration of the exterior prescribed uniformity along the facade. The difficulty resided in combining a facade with regularly spaced windows all the same size with correctly proportioned rooms of different dimensions.[18]

As the variety of room types proliferated in the eighteenth and nineteenth centuries, the capacity of architects to reconcile an interior with a regular exterior (or at least an exterior not determined by interior arrangement and volumes) began to be taxed. Happily, the same romanticism that reveled in images of a classical past also relished the picturesque. In asymmetrical picturesque architecture the combination of rooms of wildly different contour, size, and shape was easier to accomplish.

But while the picturesque tradition made it easier for individual rooms to assert themselves without destroying a regular envelope, this did not mean that bulges, wings, pavilions, and protuberances regularly corresponded to the specific spaces behind. Sometimes they did, and sometimes they didn't.

The route to an architecture that seeks to express program-function via abstract surface treatment and massing relationships was a slow one throughout the nineteenth century. There were many reasons for the shift but among the most important are the increase in the number of institutions and building purposes, (implying a need for a greater variety of communicative expression), and the gradual separation of the architect from the engineer and the artist in the late eighteenth and nineteenth centuries. This separation created a void in the way an architect rationalized his mission. Simply stated, the engineer took the technical expertise, and the artist took the aesthetic expertise. Architecture, left dangling, borrowed from social theory and began to be viewed as the environmental independent variable on which behavior depended.[19] A corollary to this idea was that one of the primary expressive intentions of buildings should be social identification.

The increase in importance given to the social realm over the tectonic may be seen in a comparison of two seminal theorists: Laugier, writing in 1753,[20] and Semper, writing exactly one hundred years

8

8 Guaranty Building, Buffalo; View; Louis Sullivan, 1894-95

later.[21]

Laugier imagined a wholly constructive rationale for the origins of architecture. He assumed the programmatic need for shelter to be pervasive but generalized. For him the manipulation of the primary elements to make that shelter—the column and the architrave—was the first act of man the architect.

Gottfried Semper wrote his treatise in 1853 after the intervention of the seminal social ideas of the Enlightenment and their application to architecture by Ledoux, Fourier, Pugin, and others. Semper was strongly influenced by the biologist George Cuvier, whose scientific innovation "was to shift emphasis from description by the identifiable members of an organism, and classification by description, to classification by the function performed."[22] This led to a classification of building by social, not formal or constructive criteria. As Rosemarie Bletter has exlained, Semper "insists that style be seen as the reflection of socio-political conditions."[23] Semper divided the primary elements of architecture into four independent forms: the hearth, the platform, the roof (including the vertical structure), and the enclosure (or infill). The hearth was the first and most elemental of his forms. "What is exceptional in Sermper's schema of classification," Bletter continues, "is that he begins with a *non-architectural* element—the fire—an element without spatial dimension but one that bestows *social significance* on the site (Italics mine.)."[24] Further to this, Semper's "roof with its supporting member is read as a continuous unit"[25] thereby unifying two of the discrete elements of all previous architectural systems. (including Laugier's)

Both of these theoretical changes: (1), the introduction of the anthropological setting as the architectural determinant and (2), the destruction of one of architecture's most lasting structural conventions (the clear distinction of vertical and horizontal members), were to be influential in the further abstraction of traditional and conventional architectonic 'parts' during the post-Bauhaus period of the Modern Movement. *Program* was not to take its place alongside *structure* (with construction having slowly split off) and *space* as the generators of architectural form and surface.

Sir John Summerson explains the sequence of changes to theory in his seminal essay "The Case for a Theory of Modern Architecture," in which he states, "The source of unity in Modern Architecture is in the social sphere, in other words in the architect's programme."[26]

Summerson then traces the routes toward twentieth century function/program expression.

> From the antique (a world of form) to the program (a local fragment of social pattern): this suggests a swing in the architect's psychological orientation almost too violent to be credible. Yet, in theory at least, it has come about; and how it has come about could very well be demonstrated historically. First the rationalist attack on the authority of the antique; then the displacement of the classical antique by the mediaeval; then the introduction into mediaevalist authority of purely social factors (Ruskin); then the evaluation of purely vernacular architectures because of their social realism (Morris); and finally the concentration of interest on the social factors themselves and the conception of the architect's program as the source of unity—the source not precisely of forms but of adumbrations of forms of undeniable validity. The program as the source of unity is, so far as I can see, the one new principle involved in modern architecture.[27]

The slow and arduous development of the art of *distribution* that began in Italy and France then, finally, reached a high point in the post-Bauhaus architects of the 30's, 40's and 50's. Its paradigm was perhaps given by Christopher Alexander in his influential book, *Notes on the Synthesis of Form.* For Alexander in the early 60's and for the 'user needs' architects wedded to social concerns the task of the designer was assumed to reside solely in space arrangement.[28]

While I am substituting Semper for Summerson's example of Ruskin as an agent of the anthropological model, the important point is that the anthropological view of function has come to dominate architectural theory, and together with ideas of abstraction, it has often eclipsed the expression of construction on the vertical surface.

The Mask: Post-Modernism and the Rhetorical Figure

> A certain violation of truth to function and materials is a condition of architecture. Only such violation allows a building not just to be, but also to mean, to represent architecture. But instead of speaking here of 'lies', it would be better to give truth a different meaning. Truth in architecture is the truth of representation.[29]
>
> Karsten Harries

For many recent architects the term *meaning* has replaced the modern-movement term *function*, and the idea that a building may 'talk about' this or that aspect of culture, class structure, the *Zeitgeist,* or the *genus loci* is one of the most predictable constants of contemporary theory.

This attitude is possible only through the abstractions described above. When the elements of architecture are viewed abstractly, they become interchangeable, so much so that architects and theorists often find themselves in positions that lack logical parallelism. This is reflected in the description, sometimes attributed to Paul Rudolph, of the dwelling unit as the twentieth century brick.

By substituting a program element for a construction element by way of metaphor, Rudolph (and others of his generation) paved the way for projects and buildings where glazed cylinders containing elevator shafts 'support' cornices of ranges of rooms. Like such late modern examples, the tripartite division of a Sullivan office building would appear to reflect the same abstraction: occupiable space is divided into a base, shaft, and capital. But in the Sullivanian office building the structural members themselves are "believable" (truthful in Harries' terms) in terms of weight distribution, etc. Conventional elements like cornice or column (whether literal or representational) remain within the domain of construction. Conventions of use, like mezzanine or attic, remain within the realm of function (fig. 8).

For those architects of the 1970's who strive to create an architecture of illusion and the rediscovery of metaphor, symbol, and the traditional kit of parts of the Graeco-Roman styles was sufficient. Filtered through a syntax of abstraction, the rediscovered parts might be collaged together without regard to their past compositional rules. Indeed, the bizarre new syntax could even justify the use of such elements since it separated those architects from the reproductionists.

Charles Jencks, often an apologist for a libertine attitude concerning sources, recognized an incipient problem when he wrote, "Possibly because metaphor and symbolism were suppressed by the modern movement their re-emergence now at a time of unsettled metaphysics is bound to be over-emphatic."[30]

To the architect trying to transform a style based on the assumption that the most basic unit of design is point, line, and plane into a style whose most basic unit is a 'window,' 'aedicule ' or 'loggia,' the fine-grained distinctions of an elemental typology might still be out of reach. A classical column, for example, to be useful to the modern (or Post-Modern) architect, must necessarily be viewed abstractly. Were it to be viewed literally, it would be absurdly out of context with modern compositions. A classical element can be integrated into a modern building most easily as a fragment in a collage. It makes its point precisely in the same manner as the piece of newspaper in a Cubist collage or the ship's cab in the Ozenfant studio by Le Corbusier.[31]

Like any quotation, the use of the found object imparts an authority and association to the composition. It is a badge. It is instantly recognizable. It represents the *idea*. Like the *Carnevale* mask held on a stick, the collaged element calls attention to its fiction and therefore separates itself from the true 'reality' of the composition. Its affectation is a kind of knowing wink, and as such it can be acceptable to even the most stringent of modernists. Ruskin, from whom so much of the morality of modern syntax derives, could conceivably have accepted Post-Modernism, if only because it declares its own falsehood. The immorality of deception, for Ruskin, lay in the believability of the fiction: "When the imagination deceives it becomes madness. It is a noble faculty so long as it confesses its own ideality; when it ceases to confess this, it is insanity. All the difference lies in the fact of the confession, in there being no deception."[32]

But the believability of the fiction is the very underpinning of the classical system and its own fictions.[33] When Alberti overlaid the image of the temple front and triumphal arch onto the facades of the *Tempio Malatestiana* and S. Andrea in Mantua (fig. 9), he was careful to imitate accurately the arrangement of the constructive elements of those models, even though his applied structure was not literally self-supporting.

The classical system of conventional elements takes account of this difference between literal and figurative structure. The truth of representation often contradicts the material realities or logic of construction. For example, in the canons of intercolumniation, when the columns are freestanding (fig. 10), they must be spaced closer together than when they are applied to a wall (fig. 11). Yet when the columns of the Colosseum (the seminal building for Western Architecture's column-wall relationships) were "applied" to the wall, the visual span of the entablature was greater than the span of the arch. All things being equal (or literal in this case), because of its inherent structural ability, the arch ought to span a greater distance. But in the conventions of the classical all things are *not* equal. If they were, perhaps Ledoux's Maison Guimard (fig. 12) would better represent the paradigm of expression than the Colosseum. The convention itself is thus based on a fiction. It is a fiction that the entablatures are supported by the columns; it is a fiction that the engaged column is added to the wall. In many cases in ancient architecture the applied column and the pier are cut from the same stone.[34]

If we remember that the entablature may act as a molding when applied to a wall without columns, and that the column may act as buttress on the wall when applied without entablature, and that these elements have the same form when they are engaged together to make an 'order', then the idea of the conventionality of the system—with its attendant rules—becomes unavoidable. The 'breaking of the rules' in the Post-Modern collage is not a contradiction of structural logic. It is a contradiction of conventions in a system that owes its origins to the logic of compressive structure but is not a slave to that logic.[35]

The desire to go out from the simplicities of construction to an expressive system that can 'fool' the casual observer and fool the system as well is evident in Mannerist and Baroque architecture, as well as the architecture of early twentieth century Italy.[36]

But revivals like Post-Modernism are indeed different from the continuities of a living tradition. It is the archaeologically identifiable element that is often the first to be revived, whether or not it is archaeologically accurate. And while all precious revivals of antiquity from the Renaissance of Brunelleschi to the 'American Renaissance' of McKim, Meade, and White sought to imitate carefully the syntax as well as the profiles of the revived elements, Post-Modernism has sought to place the found object in a contemporary compositional mode. At the very least, a certain anxiety over breaking rules before they are obeyed has plagued contemporary architects at least since the late thirties.

Berthold Lubetkin's Highpoint Number Two (fig. 13) is a good example. This building is self-consciously in costume. The caryatids are, to be sure, actually supporting the canopy in a literal sense; the pragmatical role of the element is being fulfilled. We cannot, therefore, argue that an idealism of form has eclipsed the materialism of function. The element is not rhetorical; it is *real*. For a modern-movement architect like Lubetkin there could be no other reason to revive such an element than to use it instead of a modern equivalent. Indeed, Lubetkin concocted an elaborate explanation why the caryatids were the only solution open to him. He seemed to exude sufficient embarrassment (or is it dissimulation?) over this move, adding the disclaimer, "The caryatid casts have been temporarily made use of as standard objects to adorn the entrance, pending the creation of their modern equivalent."[37]

The caryatids look to the future with unconscious prescience and

9

9 Sant' Andrea, Mantua; View, Leone Battista Alberti, 1470
10 The Ionic Order; *The Four Books of Architecture*
11 The Ionic Order Applied to an Arcuated Wall; *The Four Books of Architecture*, Andrea Palladio
12 Maison Guimard, Paris; Elevation; C. N. Ledoux, 1771
13 Highpoint Number Two, London; View; Berthhold Lubetkin, 1938

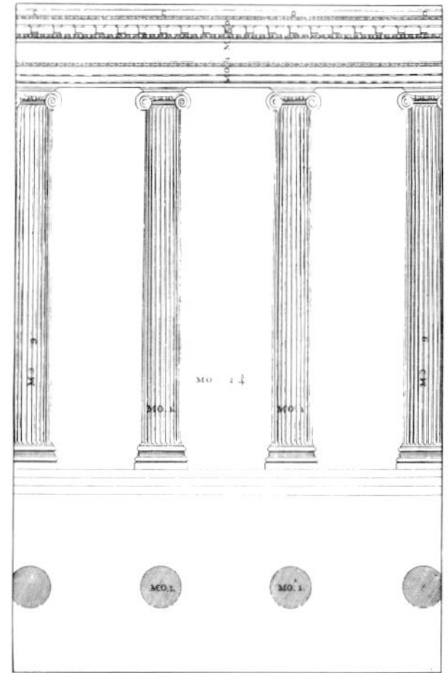

10

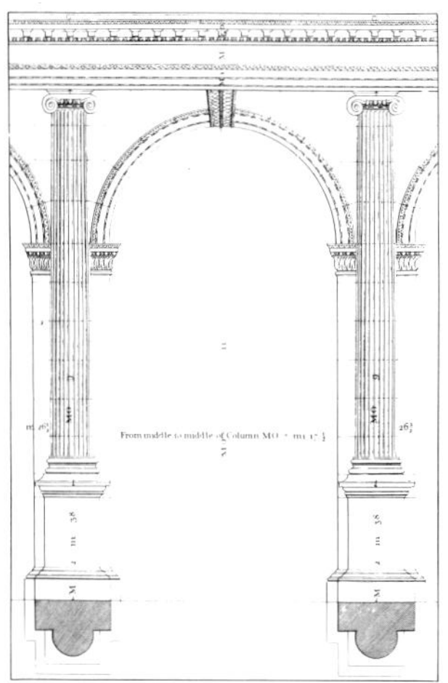

11

12

13

to the past with nostalgia. Highpoint Number Two, if not the first, was certainly one of the earliest revivals of the idea of the *figure*, the element that Alan Colquhoun has termed "a configuration whose meaning is given by culture, whether or not it is assumed that this meaning ultimately has a basis in nature."[38]

An element of rhetoric, the 'figure' in architecture occurs when all the brute facts of construction, all our perceptions of gravity, and all our dispositions toward spatial enclosure are 'humanized' and become the signs of other things. In the architecture of the Middle Ages and the Renaissance we find a limited number of basic elements which are thus turned into signs: walls and their penetrations, columns, beams, arches, roofs, and so on."[39]

Lubetkin's caryatids were a gesture toward a new figure for modern architecture: an element that could become the sign of another thing without losing its literal sense in the composition. It is significant that postmodernism had abandoned the search for such elements as soon as the Zeitgeist-grounded proscription against the literal revival of detail forms was lifted. This is because collage could justify any lack of a literal sense for the otherwise allegorical element.

In prose, the idea that a literal sense is simply a cypher for an allegorical sense, and has no value on its own, is known as gnosticism. It is also often called the 'allegory of the theologians' and compared to the 'allegory of the poets'. For the theologians (presumably) the literal meaning may not be as important as it is to the poets, since the purpose of scripture, unlike poetry, is assumed to reside in the unambiguous aiding in our quest for salvation. If exegesis (like scripture) is an agent of that purpose, it may be accepted that the literal sense is the servant of the allegory, merely provided for those who might have trouble deciphering higher meanings without the aid of a story. But the same cannot be said for poetry, whose purpose is less certain and more elastic. By relying on an 'allegory of the theologians', Post-Modernism often eliminates this multiple set of meanings. Its mask is immobile, inelastic, incapable of nuance. The search for the 'face', however, may very well require of the facade what is required of the human being, that is, a polysemous reading from the literal to the allegorical and other higher senses of meaning. ■

The Palladio Variations:

On Reconciling Convention, Parti, and Space[1]

Thomas Schumacher

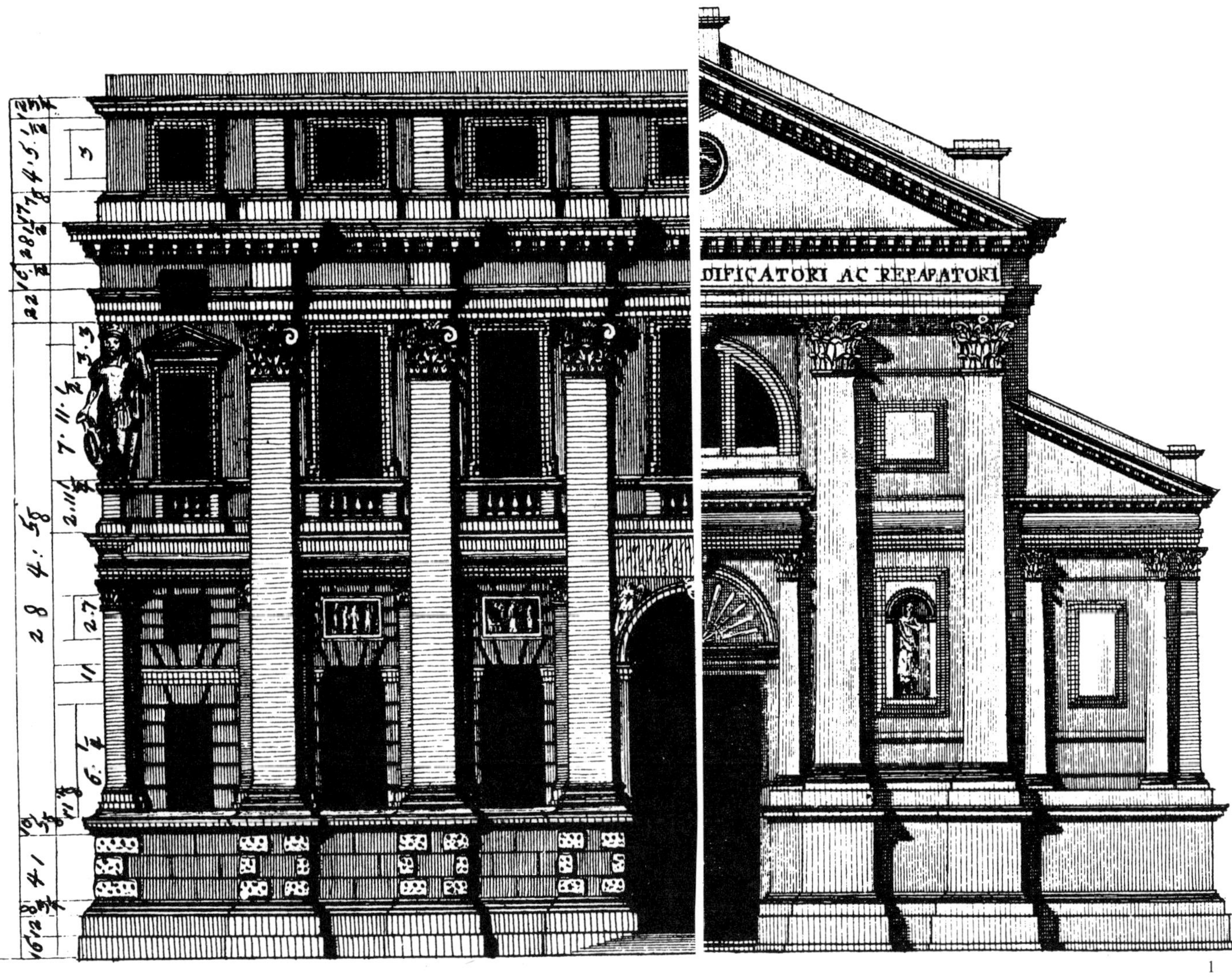

1

1 Palazzo Valmarana-Braga and San Giorgio Maggiore; Palladio

The relationship of the skin to internal spaces of most modern buildings of accepted quality is usually assumed to be reasonably direct. Even a Miesian office block 'expresses' the modular and flexible nature of the interior spaces behind a taut steel and glass skin.

While adherence to the expression of structural technique may conflict with an equally rigorous display of internal volume or function, many modern architects have succeeded in opting for the one while allowing for the other. Louis I. Kahn's Exeter Library is a building that, through its massing, subtly telegraphs its grand internal space and scale while maintaining rigorous repetition of elements in terms of the traditional conventions of masonry construction.

That there be a reasonably direct relationship between volume and cladding is one of the few axioms of the Modern Movement. But, like lawyers debating the fine points of constitutional jurisprudence, most architects would doubtless disagree on 'which what' of the inside should seep to the exterior surface. Yet among the more orthodox of International Style modernists, few would allow that the outside surface ought to determine interior distribution, Le Corbusier's maxim that the exterior is the result of the interior still holds sway, even if architects find it difficult in practice to stick to the straight and narrow.

Further, when observing the architecture of the past, most orthodox modernists (Venturi's term, and a rare bird to find in pure form) take great delight in discovering inside-outside relationships that appear to portend modernism.[2] Vernacular buildings, ancient archaeological remains stripped of their revetments, and doggedly plain buildings (like Cistercian Abbeys) often are cited as buildings worthy of the contemporary value of 'truth' so lavishly expounded by Ruskin.[3] The Italian historian, Bruno Zevi, has gone so far as to claim that all buildings, no matter how old, could be considered 'modern' if we only look at them with a modern lens.[4]

In addition to a penchant for plain walls and the use of the same material on the inside as on the outside (and presumably all the way through), many modern architects have come to appreciate those historical examples in which the interior volume relates to the outside wall, where the spaces are 'projected' onto the facade.

In pre-twentieth-century architecture, however, the more important the facade, the less it related to the building it covered and the more it related to the space it faced. In the Renaissance, as in antiquity, the most important and grandest facades displayed an architectural form that "was not that of the solid volume whose facades suggested [the] internal structure, but a cubic void whose facades are the enclosing walls."[5] The idealized versions of this type may be found in the stoas of Greece, the fora of Rome, or in the arcades of Vigevano, the Procuratae of Venice, or the Loggia dei Banchi in Bologna, to cite but a few.

These buildings are admittedly deep, porch-like structures, where the spatial depth may be imagined to be 'properly expressed' in the repetition of the deep bays. They are also relatively nonhierarchical in terms of volumes behind the walls. Yet the persistence of the same highly repetitive, nonhierarchical facades, covering buildings that display greater hierarchy of volume than the above examples, requires note. The Pal. Massimo and the Pal. Farnese are buildings in which the facade rather deftly hides a 'discrepancy' between internal void and the outer wall (figs. 3–6). In these two palaces the tension between the inside and the outside poses a dilemma for the 'orthodox' modern architect. Confronted with a similar situation deriving from contemporary functional distribution, the modern architect would most often allow the inside to determine the outside. He would probably make every effort to exploit the condition as well.

Given the historical context, and the jarring asymmetries that would result, most contemporary architects would doubtless agree that Michelangelo and Peruzzi were prudent to favor the consistency of the wall surface. But they remain a little uneasy. They would prefer not to be put in that situation, and they prefer historical examples that don't require them to make these choices.

The Basilica Church, with its high central nave and lower side aisles, is a good example of the spatial-structural format preferred by this sensibility, and the Romanesque version of the type often is the most beloved. S. Zeno, in Verona (fig. 10), is typical of the format. The spaces and structure of the interior appear to be directly projected onto the facade. Even the details of the facade seem to intensify the reading. The modern sensibility that I am describing here sees 'truth' in this spatial projection and a 'lie' in the facade of S. M. in Via, in Rome (fig 11). Detached from the body of the church, this facade projects itself well beyond the limits of the block. Yet for the historical and architectural context of the late Renaissance the convention of structural expression (albeit figurative structure) overshadowed inside-outside correspondences.

The very convention of the two-story church facade developed from images and ideas that are unrelated to internal volume, it is the flattened projection of a real one-story porch onto the facade. As if the facade of S. Lorenzo Fuori le Mura (fig. 12) had been flattened to become S. Miniato al Monte (fig. 2). The latter also recalls the two-story colonnades of antiquity, and in the early Renaissance the literal double-story colonnade was resurrected as a facade type. Ss. Appostoli (fig. 7) and S. Marco are two examples of this type. The applied fictive structure on the flat facade, however, remained the norm.

Other examples of the 'truthful' projection of interior volume and function onto a facade can be found in vernacular buildings and the high-style progeny they often spawn. The Venetian Palace type of the late Middle Ages, itself a direct descendent of the *architettura minore* (vernacular achitecture) of Venice, is often cited by teachers of architecture as one of the best examples of the close relationship of inside and outside in the entire history of architecture. The great central room, the *portego*, is projected onto the facade as a screen wall while the side bays are considerably less porous, presumably to express the serial nature of the rooms in the outer bays (figs. 8 and 9).

But two questions must be asked of this building: First, is the Venetian Palace as pure an expression of correspondence as we often assume, and second, was such expression a conscious intent on the part of builders in the late Middle Ages, the Renaissance and the Baroque?

The history of the development of this palace type leads us to question the interpretation of an intentional inside-outside correspon-

142

2

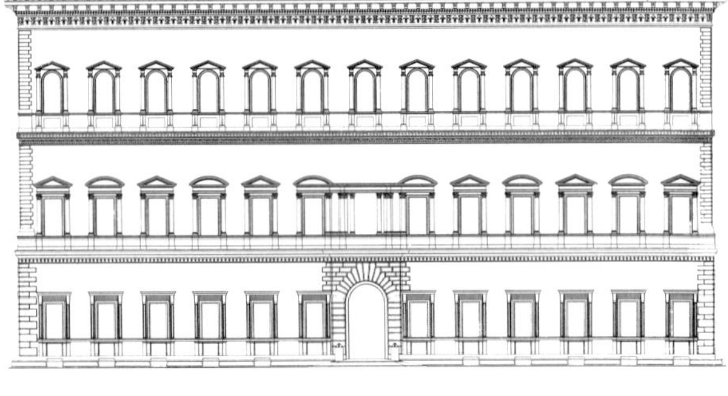

3

5

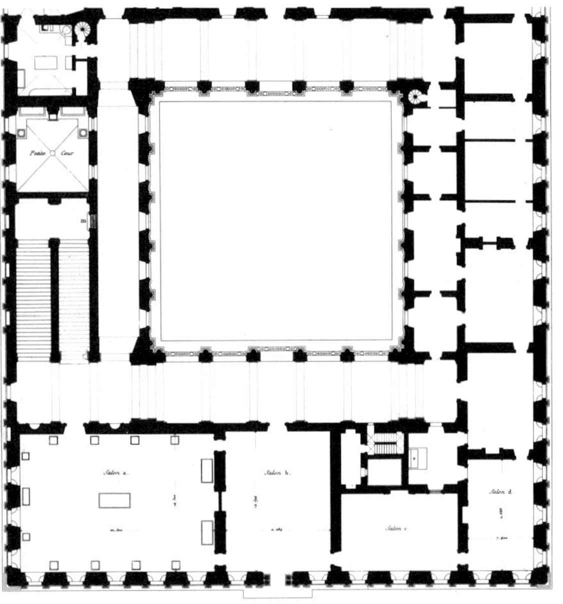
Petite Cour

4

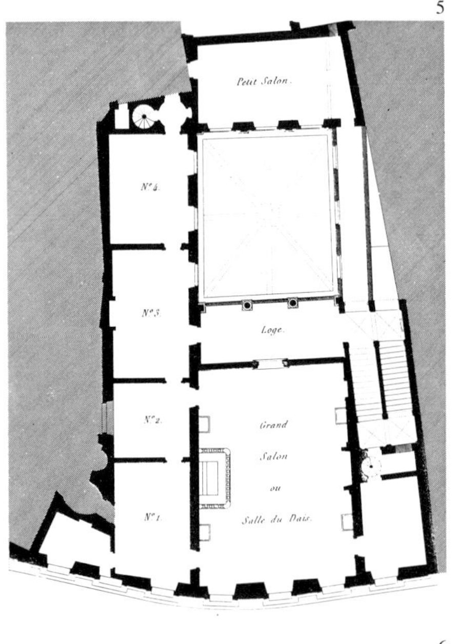
Petit Salon
N°4
N°3
Loge
N°2
Grand
Salon
ou
Salle du Dais
N°1

6

7

8

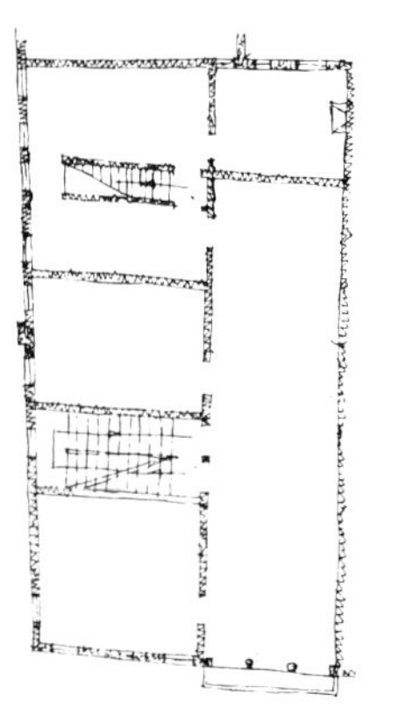

9

10

11

12

2 San Miniato al Monte, Florence; 1018-62
3 Palazzo Farnese, Rome; Facade; Sangallo and Michelangelo, sixteenth century
4 Palazzo Farnese; Plan
5 Palazzo Massimo, Rome; Facade; Peruzzi, 1525
6 Palazzo Massimo; Plan
7 San Appostoli, Rome
8 House in Fondamenta del Traghetto, Venice; Facade
9 House in Fondamenta del Traghetto; Plan
10 San Zeno, Verona; Facade; twelfth century
11 San Maria in Via, Rome; Facade; Martino Longhi, 1594
12 San Lorenzo fuori le Mura, Rome; Reconstruction, circa 1227

dence. Indeed, we immediately see that repetition and continuity, not hierarchy, were often important intentions of the architects and clients of these buildings. Moreover, during the Baroque era, the palace facade became even more consistent across its breadth, despite the fact that the plan-form remained largely the same and the palaces of that period grew in size.

Among the earliest palaces, and models for the future, were the Loredan and Farsetti (figs. 13–15), each with its *piano nobile* loggia in imitation of the *"grandezza secondo l'use Tedesco* (German Romanesque style)."[6] Paolo Maretto describes these two palaces as:

> Rich Byzantine house-warehouses, inserted in a slot of the Grand Canal...predominantly Gothic, with numerous Byzantine traces...in these buildings the structural, distributive arrangement is clearly announced on the principal facades: the central hall slot is widened towards the canal in a porch on the ground floor and a loggia on the piano nobile, a loggia that is contained within the central zone in Ca' Loredan but seems to involve the entire facade in Ca' Farsetti.[7]

In Venice, where space is a premium commodity, to sacrifice interior volume to a porch was a great extravagance. Later families, perhaps more penurious, were loathe to engage in such lavishness, yet the desire to stretch the reading of the *portego* persisted. The internal organization of the type shows rooms in the side bays marching back from the canal in *enfilade*, connected by doors close to the side facade and lighted (and ventilated) on the front by edge windows at the corners, lining up with the doors. The logical place to put another window, thereby creating a symmetry on the *inside* wall, was on the edge adjacent to the *portego*,

This interior window pairs closely with the loggia of the *portego*. In some instances, as in the Pal. Priuli (fig. 17),[8] the window is detailed to make it appear as one of the windows of the *portego* itself. In the Pal. Boldu (fig. 20), the pairings of windows place emphasis on a group of four windows, only three of which light the *portego*.

The Florentine-Roman classicism that came to Venice with Coducci, Sansovino, and Scamozzi had little use for the highly differentiated facades of the existing palace type. The Florentine type, by contrast, presented equally spaced windows which could inhabit a wall with or without benefit of superimposed structure (fig. 18). Under this 'foreign' influence the Venetian palace developed in the sixteenth and seventeenth centuries. Its facade developed from uncomfortable compromises between regular repetition and hierarchical projection toward almost complete regularization and the successful disguising of the differences between central *portego* and adjacent rooms. In the Pal. Corner-Spinelli (fig. 19), one of the earliest examples of Florentine influence, Coducci seems to have accepted the condition of discrepancy and simply allowed the inside to seep to the exterior even though the window surrounds are all detailed in the same way. But in the Pal. Grimani (fig. 21), Coducci added pilasters with interstitial decorations, thereby partially disguising the discrepancy.

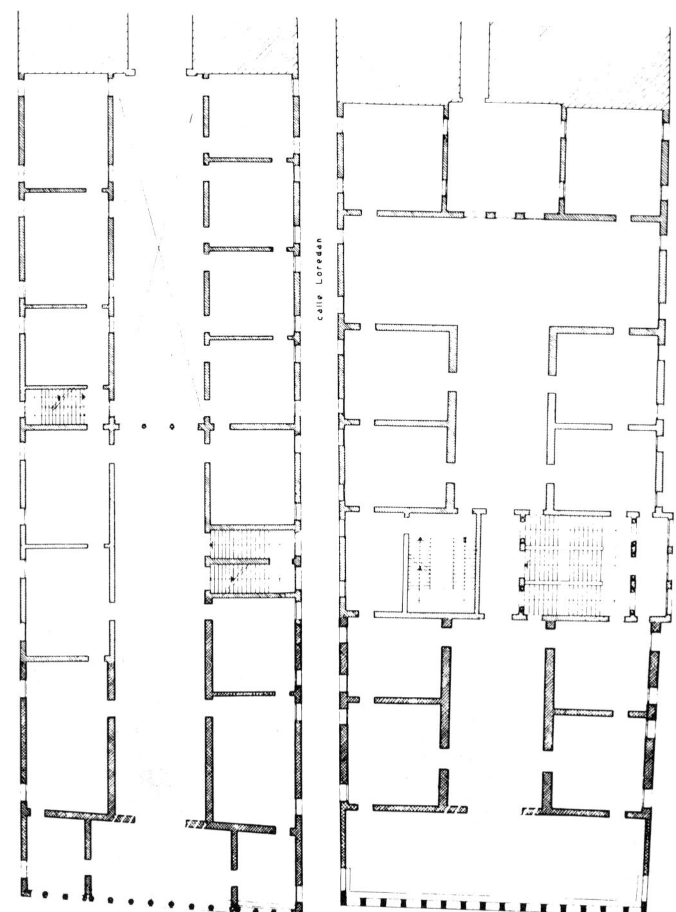

13

14

15

16

13 Palazzo Loredan and Farsetti; Plans; twelfth and thirteenth centuries
14 Palazzo Loredan; Facade
15 Palazzo Farsetti; Facade
16 Mint and Library of San Marco, Venice; Sansovino, 1537, 1536 respectively
17 Palazzo Priuli, Venice; fifteenth century
18 Palazzo Pandolfini, Florence; Raphael
19 Palazzo Corner-Spinelli; Mauro Coducci, late fifteenth century
20 Palazzo Boldu, Venice; fifteenth century

17

18

19

20

Many of the public buildings that were erected in Venice in the sixteenth century, such as the library of S. Mark, and the Zecca (fig 16), both by Sansovino, are unconstrained by the form of the Palace plan. They display none of the variation between edge and center shown in the palaces, and these buildings became models imitated by architects of the later sixteenth, seventeenth, and eighteenth centuries.

In the sixteenth century the scale and size began to change, and by the early seventeenth century, the palaces grew to truly Roman proportions. Their facades became far more plastic, with engaged columns rather than flat pilasters. Many of the later facades tended to be much more consistent across their entire width; they returned to the paradigms of the Pal. Farsetti and Loreden in format if not in style.

I will show just a few examples. In the Pal. Corner a San Maurizio (fig. 22) Sansovino seems to have slurred over the differences between central *portego* and side bays by simply overlaying the entire facade with a dominating array of paired columns between all the openings. The eye is distracted from the change in wall surface between edge and center.

Three immense Baroque palaces may complete the argument. Pal. Rezzonico (1660), by Baldassare Longhena, (figs. 23 and 24), Pal. Pesaro (1662), also by Longhena (fig. 25); and Pal. Corner della Regina (1724), by Domenico Rossi (fig. 26).

An early version of the Pal. Rezzonico (fig. 23) shows a widening of the *portego*. Inserted between the central four bays and the side bays are the same paired columns that terminate the facade. In the built version (fig. 24), the portego is about the same width as the side rooms (it is likely that this change was due to construction pragmatics); it is faced with only three arched bays. The piers are all faced with single columns instead of pairs of columns. The discrepancy between the center and edge is once again 'slurred', this time by a slight narrowing of the central arches, stilting them, and by covering all the arches with elaborate decorative relief.

The Pal. Pesaro (fig. 25) is quite similar to the original version of the Rezzonico. Paired columns separate the central zone from the sides. These paired columns take up the thickness of the bearing wall between the *portego* and the side rooms, leaving only enough wall to barely frame the window and upsetting the expected axis of the enfilade relationship of the doors to the windows in the seaside rooms. I suspect that this ungainly interior relationship (to the sensibility of the Baroque) was performed for the sake of making the facade appear as regular as possible.

The Pal. Corner della Regina (1724) (fig 26) may serve to close the argument. The facade is seven bays wide, as usual, and the facade connects five bays in a loggia that resembles that of the Loredan. A two-four-two division would be more natural. The five bay center is accomplished by the creation of a sort of interior ambulatory loggia. Here, the facade appears to have indeed sponsored change in the plan.

The Venetian palace type, with its doggedly consistent plan, (a parti determined by site, program, and structural limitations), furnishes a good laboratory for testing variations of style and expression. We find subtle variations on the themes of repetitive continuity vs. hierarchical

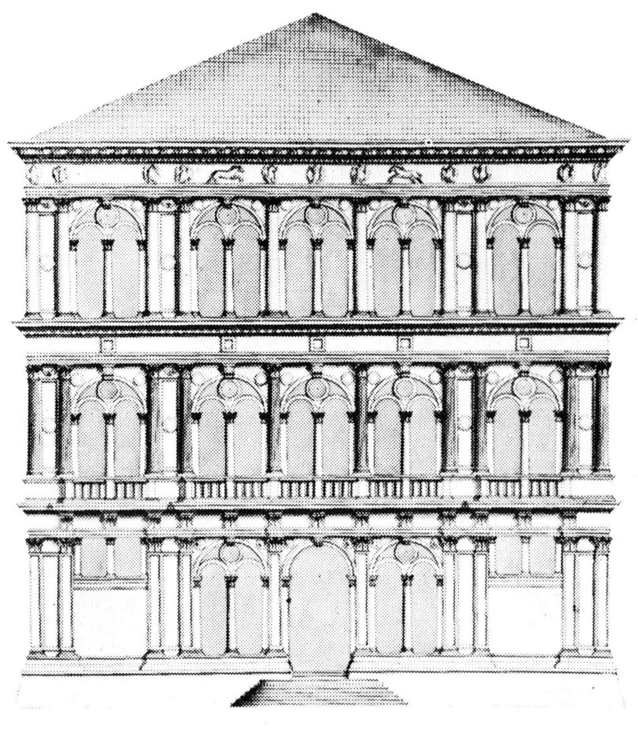

21

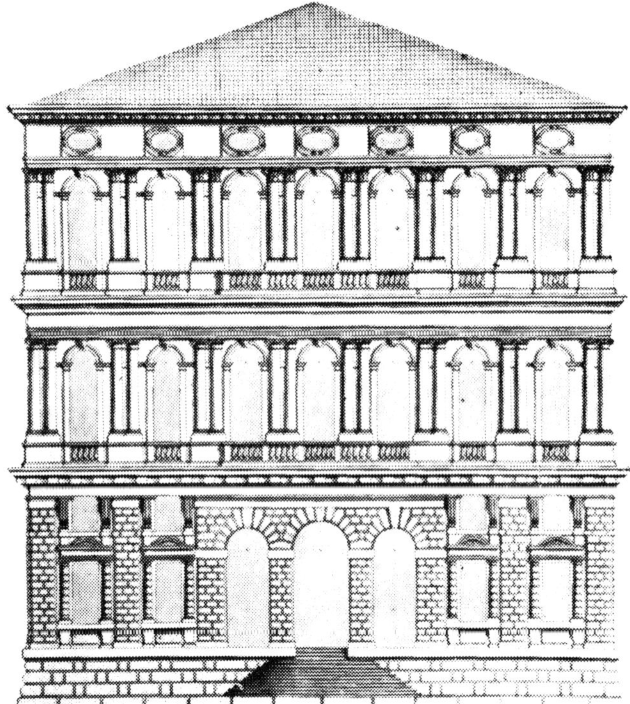

22

21 Palazzo Grimani; Mauro Coducci, 1470-1504
22 Palazzo Corner a San Maurizio; Sansovino, 1530's
23 Palazzo Rezzonico; Preliminary Scheme; Baldassare Longhena, 1660
24 Palazzo Rezzonico; Final Scheme; Baldassare Longhena
25 Palazzo Pesaro; Baldassare Longhena, 1662
26 Palazzo Corner Della Regina; Domenico Rossi

23

24

25

26

gradation. The architects' concern, as in the case of the Renaissance-Baroque church facade type, was to reconcile a desired effect based on a constructive convention and precedent—with the 'reality' of spatial and structural conditions.

II. Palladio and the Inside and the Outside

Palladio's architecture also provides a good laboratory for above-mentioned ideas because, almost alone among Renaissance architects, Palladio's buildings were often completed. His intentions were realized, or at least realizable, and we have ample proof of his intentions in the form of his books. He had reasonable control over the plans, sections, and elevations of his projects and was one of the few architects of his age who drew all three drawings.[9]

Palladio's church facades for S. Francesco della Vigna, S. Giorgio Maggiore, and the Redentore (figs. 27, 29, and 39) are textbook examples of Renaissance solutions to the aesthetic problem posed by the section and resultant elevation: roughly an inverted 'T' shape. Ancient Temples and Triumphal Arches did not easily fit the format of the Basilica facade. Rudolf Wittkower traced the evolution of these solutions from Alberti through Peruzzi to Palladio.[10] I would like to propose some further interpretations of readings that extend those of Wittkower and other scholars.

Palladio's superimposed temple-fronts differed from Peruzzi's in the important respect that each was 'complete'. If one could remove the upper temple front, the lower temple in all three of Palladio's Venetian churches would be reasonably believable as a fictive structure, give or take a few feet on the intercolumniations. Palladio, ever aware of his relation to antiquity, created an architecture whose individual parts 'worked' as they had in antiquity.[11]

The logic and consistency of Palladio's Venetian church facades may be established by posing alternate solutions in the form of interventions onto those facades. Along with analysis, these interventions are speculations on *possible* conditions, solutions, and partial solutions that help to establish a reasonable design process model. (They are not intended to simulate Palladio's presumed design process.)

The struggle to resolve difficult conditions, i.e., the awkwardness of the Basilica facade—the inverted 'T' of the section, did not end with S. Francesco della Vigna, Palladio's first Venetian church and a building he inherited from Sansovino. Palladio's solution left many unanswered questions concerning the adaptation of the language of Ancient Roman forms and elements. Among the compositional irresolutions is the manner in which the entrance door seems partially sunken into a basement formed by the pedestals of all the orders across the facade (fig. 27). The condition can be 'corrected' by trimming off the pedestals (fig. 28), a solution obviously not open to Palladio. The problem was partially resolved in the S. Giorgio Maggiore facade (fig. 29), where he had full control over plan, section, and elevation. Here the pilasters supporting the lower temple-front spring directly from the base molding, and the door is placed in a 'believable' location in relation to the wall. The upper temple-front, its columns set up on high pedestals, has been described as awkward by some scholars, including Wittkower.[12] Palladio seems to slur over a solution to the two ground planes portrayed here by giving the aedicules in the side bays enormous pedestals the same height as the column-pedestals. While a transition is implied, the 'preferred' solution for Palladio was most likely the one contained in his sketch (fig. 30), a drawing that appears to be intended for a church with a true, detached portico.[13] But whether Palladio is the architect responsible for the facade as we know it or not, *he could* have solved the problem easily in the manner of the sketch.[14]

Here it is opportune to examine some of the possibilities that might have been open to Palladio. Using Ottavio Bertotti-Scamozzi's drawing of the facade of S. Giorgio and beginning with the actual facade (fig. 29), the transformation to fig. 31 shows that the central temple-front would be considerably wider than the body of the church were the orders and the pediment simply enlarged to reach the ground. If Palladio had simply enlarged the orders alone (fig. 32), they would not have been in proper proportion with the pediment (figs. 33, 34, and 35). Equally difficult would have been a solution that lowered the entire pediment in the manner of the Redentore. At S. Giorgio this would have produced a truly jarring effect (fig. 36) to say nothing of the fact that Palladio had not yet conceived of the Redentore, and the solution implied by its design.

Many observers consider the Redentore facade the solution to the problems partially solved in the first two churches. It is the most harmonious of the three facades, in part because the figure of the facade itself tends to minimize the inverted 'T' of the section, but perhaps also because the two temple-fronts rise from the same base. On first observation it would appear that the easier solution for Palladio would have been to extend the gable end into the pediment and raise the columns up on pedestals in the manner of S. Giorgio (fig. 40). Yet, when compared to many other temple-fronts, both the S. Giorgio and Redentore porticos are rather squat. Figures 41 and 42 show how the Redentore might have absorbed a gable-height portico derived from that of S. Giorgio. Figure 43 shows how Palladio's own drawing of the Temple of Fortuna Virilis, in Rome, with its Ionic portico (naturally lower than a Corinthian portico), might be overlaid onto the Redentore,

Wittkower's note that the Redentore, like Alberti's S. Andrea, in Mantua, possessed a nave that "was too high to be covered by one Temple front; the attic was therefore a necessary expedient"[15] must therefore be questioned, and another motive for the lowered temple front and attic must be sought. The S. Francesco-S. Giorgio solution, while scenographically resolving the problem of the inverted 'T', does not totally destroy its reading. Palladio could have extended the facade well beyond the body of the church, as did many of the Roman architects of the sixteenth and seventeenth centuries (that is in the manner of S.M. in Via mentioned in the previous article). But this would have been uncharacteristic of him: a purity of form was his trademark. Moreover, if Staale Sinding-Larsen's thesis is correct,[16] and Palladio would have preferred a centralized church for the Redentore, there is reason to believe he would have made an effort to supress the inverted 'T' in the building as it was built. One of the ways to

27 San Francesco della Vigna; Palladio, Drawing by Ottavio Bertotti-Scamozzi
28 San Francesco della Vigna, pedestals removed
29 San Giorgio Maggiore; Palladio, Drawing by Ottavio Bertotti-Scamozzi
30 San Giorgio; Palladio's sketch, RIBA XIV/12 right, overlaid onto San Giorgio facade
31 San Giorgio; when columns rise from the base, the portico is oversize
32 San Giorgio; oversize columns support the portico
33 San Giorgio; Portico Comparison, columns are too short for the building
34 San Giorgio; Portico Comparison, columns are too big for the pediment
35 San Giorgio; Portico Comparison
36 San Giorgio; portico lowered in the manner of Redentore

27

28

29

30

31

32

33

34

35

36

accomplish this reading would be to emphasize the Temple-in-Antis reading of the facade (fig. 44). But further questions remain unresolved by Wittkower's and Singing-Larsen's theories.

Among these questions is the problem of the buttresses above the side aisles, particularly those in the plane of the facade. Sinding-Larson states, "Whether the existence of the buttresses sustaining the nave is due to technical or aesthetic considerations cannot be determined."[17] If the buttresses were built for aesthetic reasons, why would Palladio need buttresses in the very plane of the facade even if he needed them alongside the nave?—speculation as to his reason(s) is warranted.

On the side façade of the church the buttresses which appear in pairs (fig. 37) are a necessary means of extending the vertical thrust of the pilasters. Palladio might have avoided the buttresses in the facade itself, and he could have increased the reading of the Temple-in-Antis, by eliminating the small rooms at the very front of the side bays (fig. 38). This would have eliminated the need to create the lower temple-front (fig. 45), or would it? Another possibility would have been to eliminate only the foremost buttresses, making the Redentore similar to S. Giorgio and S. Francesco (fig. 46). This intervention retains the inverted 'T' of the Renaissance basilica church and poses the most interesting questions as to Palladio's possible intentions.

By building up the temple-front motif in stages, including the suggested portico motif on the buttresses, Palladio neutralized the inverted 'T'. The hip roof, a motif that Sinding-Larsen calls "another problem"[18] now may be seen as an ingenious device to (1) avoid the need for a double pediment covering the gable (fig. 47, a kind of architectural hiccup), (2) allow Palladio to use the same proportioned porch as he did in the facade of S. Giorgio, and (3) thrust the dome forward visually to simulate a centralized church. (While the Redentore dome is proportionally further back from the facade than that of S. Giorgio, it appears to be much further forward.)

Why, then, did Palladio retain the lower temple front at all? He could have easily solved the facade without it (fig. 48). The answer is iconographic, as Joseph Rykwert postulated. The lower temple is the "home of man," and the upper temple is the "home of God."[19]

Why, too, did Palladio decorate the buttresses as if they were pediments? The answer to this question requires a degree of speculation that relies on both Palladio's predilictions and on the formal preoccupations of Renaissance architecture, i. e., linear perspective. Most scholars have acknowledged the influence of the Pantheon on Palladio's churches,[20] but usually they rely on Palladio's own elevation of the Pantheon (fig. 50). Visiting Rome Palladio would have seen the Pantheon in perspective, not in elevation. His view would have been much like the view we get today (fig. 51), where the upper cornice of the Rotonda disappears into the attic and the lower cornice disappears into the drum. Looking again at the Redentore (fig. 49), is it just possible that Palladio was creating a kind of flattened Pantheon in the very plane of the facade?

37

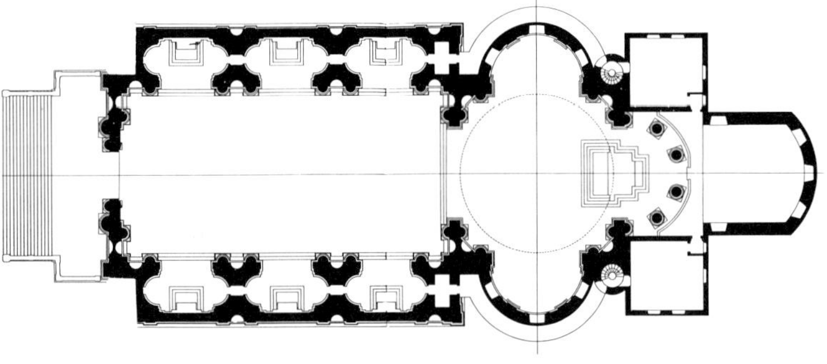

38

37 Redentore; Side Elevation
38 Redentore; Plan with front rooms omitted
39 Redentore; Palladio, Drawing by Ottavio Bertotti-Scamozzi
40 Redentore; San Giorgio portico is overlaid onto facade
41 Redentore; San Giorgio portico, without pedestals, overlaid onto Redentore
42 Redentore; Palladio's sketch for San Giorgio, overlaid onto Redentore
43 Redentore; Palladio's drawing of Temple of Fortuna Virilis, overlaid onto Redentore
44 Redentore; Temple-in-Antis version
45 Redentore; Facade with lower temple front omitted
46 Redentore; Facade with buttresses omitted
47 Redentore; Facade with double pediment
48 Redentore; Lower order is replaced by an order the same height as the central portico order

39
40
41
42
43
44
45
46
47
48

The Palazzo Valmarana-Braga

The apparent Mannerist qualities of the Pal. Valmarana in Vicenza, 1565–71, (fig. 57) have intrigued architects and scholars from Temanza to Wittkower, Murray, and Ackerman.[21] In the words of Wittkower: "Language and patience have limits when describing a mannerist structure;"[22] and Ackerman: "The abrupt shift in scale in the end bays where the giant order is abandoned and all the apertures are altered, is carried out with an irony learned from mannerists like Giulio . . . who like to play architectural jokes on the purists"[23] we find both frustration and intrigue.

Palladio inherited this building, and while it is uncertain how much control he had over the discrepancies in the plan (fig. 52), it is possible that Palladio simply adapted a villa plan to a palace site. (In the case of the Pal. Antonini, in Udine, he simply designed a Villa for an urban site.) Whatever the impetus, he was confronted with a building that had five stories on the ends and three in the middle.[24] None of Palladio's palace projects displayed such a discrepancy between the center and the edge, even though the villas often possessed facades of great hierarchical differentiation.

If we therefore approach the Pal. Valmarana in the same way as the churches, through interventions, we discover some interesting characteristics. Figure 53 shows the solid-void relationships of the facade (not unlike those of many modern buildings). If we assume that Palladio was attempting to minimize the differences between edge and center through additive detail (like the Venetian palace examples cited above), then each 'successive move' can be interpreted as abetting that intention. We must, I believe, view the Pal. Valmarana as a composite type after Sinding-Larsen's Redentore analysis.[25] This leads us to see some of the details as expressive of such hybrid and vestigial qualities.

As we build up the facade with window frames (fig. 54), rustication, moldings, cornices, and aedicules (fig. 55), we can discern how these moves tend to reconcile center and edge.[26] The mezzanine relief plaques behave like windows; the aedicules over the windows of the end bays on the *piano nobile* help to increase the window's scale and make them appear closer in size to the windows of the center-bays; the upper mezzanine windows in the end bays are quietly cut through the cornice as if they were added later. Just as the plaques and the mezzanine windows relate, so do the moldings and arches above the windows. (It is curious that Bertotti-Scamozzi neglected to draw the segmental arch over the molding in the outer bay. The arch tends to make the molding look as if it is a free-beam, thereby further extending the vertical thrust of the window.) The implied capitals at the top of the center-bay windows of the ground floor are of the same profile as the molding over the outer-bay windows and the impost block of the entrance arch. It appears as if the molding had been removed from the wall in intervals and could very well be put back.

Were it not for the need to place a mezzanine floor level where it would interrupt the ground floor center-bay windows, Palladio could have extended those windows to the end bays.

The addition of the lower order of pilasters (fig. 56) helps to

49

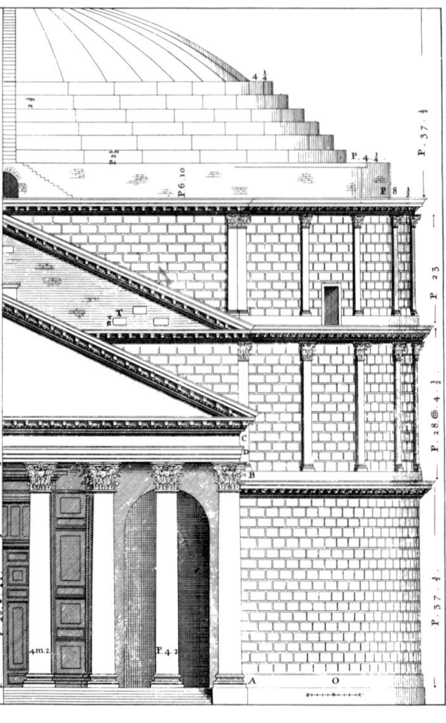

50

51

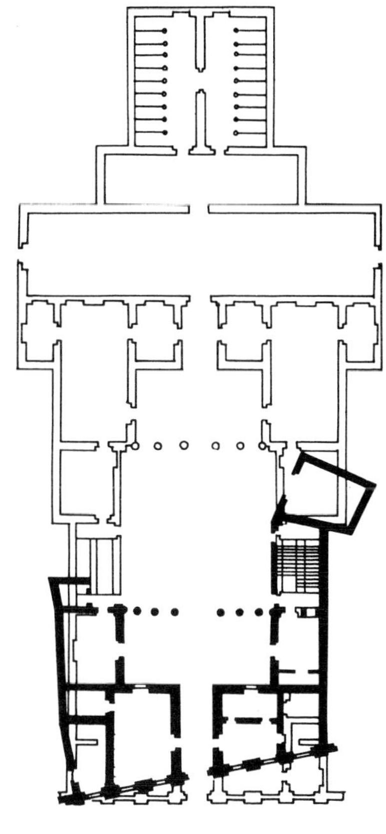

52

53

54

55

56

49 Redentore; View
50 Pantheon; Elevation; Drawing by Palladio
51 Pantheon; View
52 Palazzo Valmarana; Plan
53 Palazzo Valmarana; Facade Drawing with window openings only
54 Palazzo Valmarana; window frames added
55 Palazzo Valmarana; Facade with all its decoration except the lower and upper orders
56 Palazzo Valmarana; Facade with the giant order removed

equalize the facade further on the lower floor; this effect is enhanced by the molding added over the small windows in the end bays (fig. 57).

If the Pal. Valmarana had been designed with a plan more typical to Palladio's *oeuvre* (like Pal. Porto Festa, fig. 58), the problem of the end bays would never have surfaced. The facade would probably resemble the intervention in fig. 59.

The two most puzzling aspects of this facade, however, are Palladio's particular use of the giant order and the atlantic figures in the corners of the *piano nobile*. As Wittkower noted, Palladio got his giant order directly from Michelangelo.[27] The stringing together of two distinct floors was an act of revolutionary proportions in the sixteenth century and were Palladio to have terminated his building with a giant order, he would have been stringing together four floors. This act was not only probably beyond his sense of adventure but would have further complicated the system. The end-bay is narrower than those in the center, and either the end-bay window would have had to be moved, or even more camouflaging decoration would have had to be added to symmetrize this bay.

Another interpretation of why Palladio left the end-bay devoid of its 'normal' termination appears if we remove the giant order from the facade (fig. 60) and then add a pediment to it (fig. 61). Did Palladio conceive of this facade (like the plan) as a kind of villa imbedded in the street wall of Vicenza (fig. 62)?[28]

The final oddity of this facade is the atlante at each 'corner' of the *piano nobile*. Wittkower quotes Temanza as having condemned Palladio for a corner that was weakened where it should have been strengthened.[29] Is this figure the effete index to a major flaw or rather the brilliant solution to the problem of reconciling parti and convention? Why did Palladio use a human figure rather than some version of a column? Why not simply leave the wall bare (fig. 63)? Possibly there exists an iconographic reason, but certainly there is a reason related to the syntax of the classical system and the constructive logic of its fictive structure.

Once Palladio had overlaid the giant order onto the facade without removing the cornice at the end bays (fig. 63), the wall itself could no longer be seen as supporting the cornice as a molding. The endbay cornice segment would be visually cantilevered from the giant order, a condition that Palladio might have likened to the problems he would have seen in Peruzzi's Carpi Cathedral facade.[30] The problem, then, was how to support the cornice at the corner. A single pilaster in this position (fig. 64) would have no other pilaster within 'reach' with which to pair. There is no room to insert another pilaster next to the giant order in the end bay; and even if there were, the capitals of these two members would be at the same height, another 'mistake' in the system. The atlante then (figs. 65 and 66) becomes the solution of choice by (admittedly an invented) elimination. It requires no pairings yet allows the corner to be completed, even 'turned', making the building stand out illusionistically in a very narrow street. But is that all this corner is doing?

Interpretation of the corner becomes more important when we compare the Pal. Valmarana to the Loggia del Capitaniato, a later building that owes much to the Pal. Valmarana. In the set of interventions in figures 67 to 69 the palazzo is transformed into the loggia.[31]

The turning of the corner of the traditional triumphal arch gives plasticity to the Loggia. It also allows for the change in scale necessary to its context.[32] Is it possible that the same idea ran through Palladio's mind when he was designing the Palazzo some years before? Had the loggia preceded the Palazzo, this connection would be part of the common wisdom on these two buildings, yet Palladio was responsible for the interchangeability of elements of more remote connection than this. The Pal. Valmarana (fig. 70) is indeed a composite building: part Florentine palace, part Venetian Palace, part Palladian Villa in its plan and Triumphal arch crossed with Palladian villa crossed with Florentine Palace in elevation. The only building type left out of this amalgam is the Palladian church facade. Or is it?[33]

Interventions in figures 70 to 75 show how simply the Pal. Valmarana may be transferred into the church of S. Giorgio Maggiore.

Through the above speculation facades like those of Palladio may be viewed as less the mannerist aberrations of a period of transition than as the solutions to the problems of reconciling distributive necessity and form with the conventions of a chosen syntax. They are solutions, in my view, that display the resource fullness of an architect of genius. ■

57

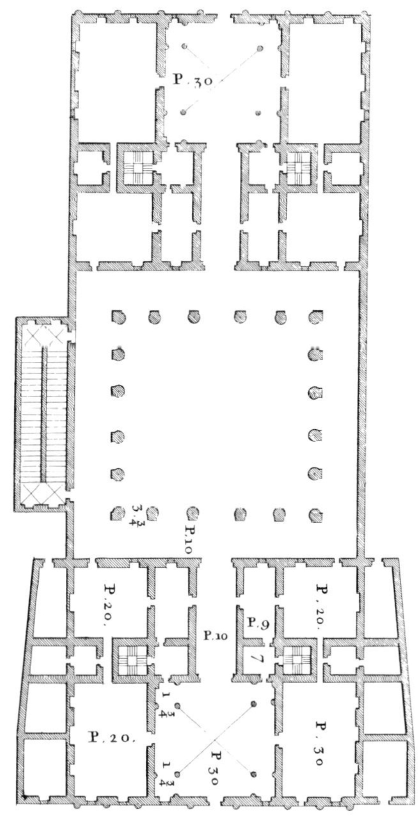

58

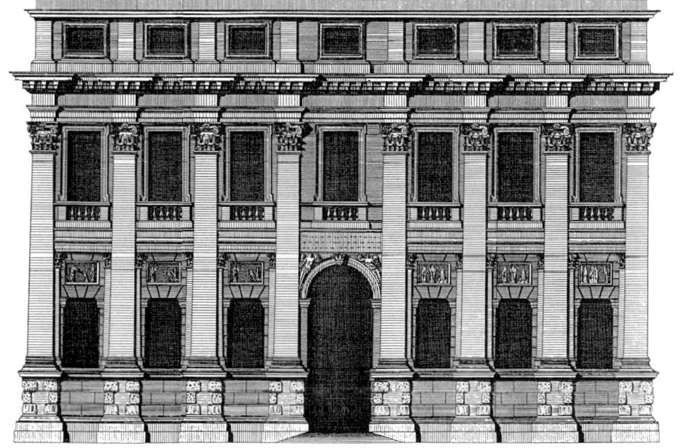

59

60

61

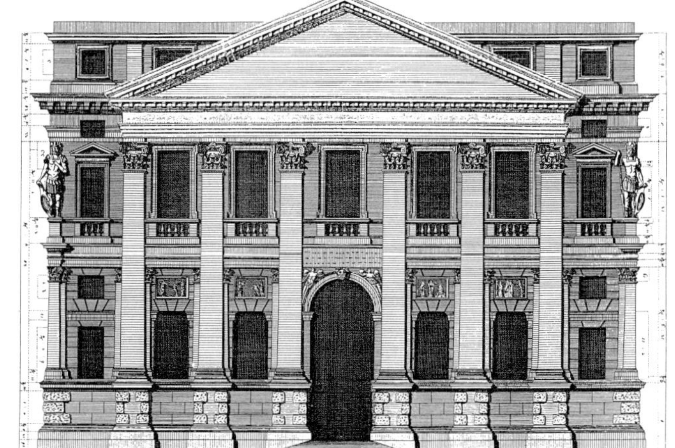

62

57 Palazzo Valmarana; View of Corner
58 Palazzo Porta Fest; Plan; Palladio
59 Palazzo Valmarana; Facade shown with seven equal bays
60 Palazzo Valmarana; Giant Order and its Entablatures
61 Palazzo Valmarana; Giant Order shown as a portico
62 Palazzo Valmarana; pediment added to the facade

63

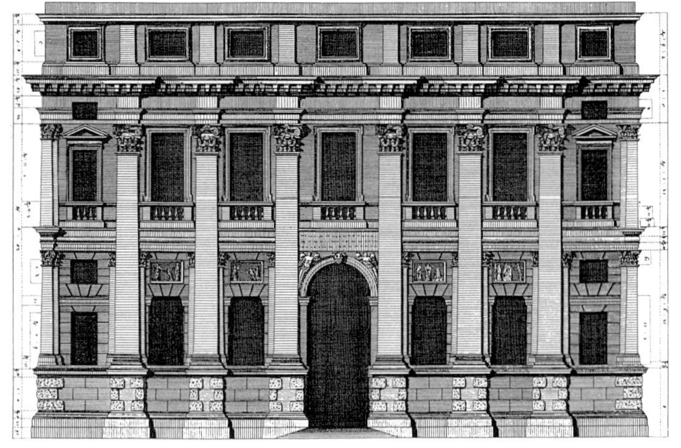

64

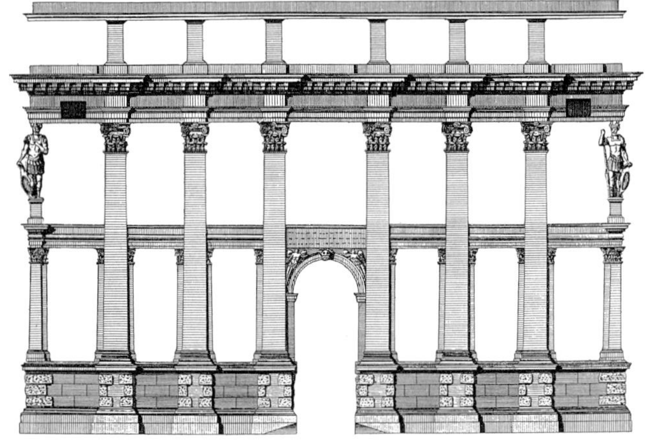

65

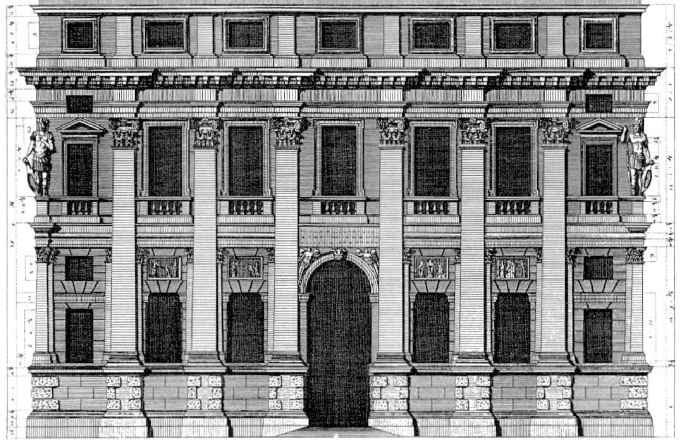

66

67

68

69

63 Palazzo Valmarana; atlante removed from the corner
64 Palazzo Valmarana; corners held up by a pilaster
65 Palazzo Valmarana; lower and upper orders shown seperated from the facade
66 Palazzo Valmarana; Facade as is
67 Palazzo Valmarana/Loggia del Capitaniato; end bay is collapsed, center bay replaces the others
68 Palazzo Valmarana/Loggia del Capitaniato; pilasters are replaced by engaged columns
69 Loggia del Capitaniato as is (Bertotti-Scamozzi, three bays only)
70 Palazzo Valmarana; Facade as is
71 Palazzo Valmarana/San Giorgio; step one
72 Palazzo Valmarana/San Giorgio; step two
73 Palazzo Valmarana/San Giorgio; step three
74 Palazzo Valmarana/San Giorgio; step four
75 San Giorgio Maggiore; Facade

70

71

72

73

74

75

The Interior Facade

Lee Hodgden

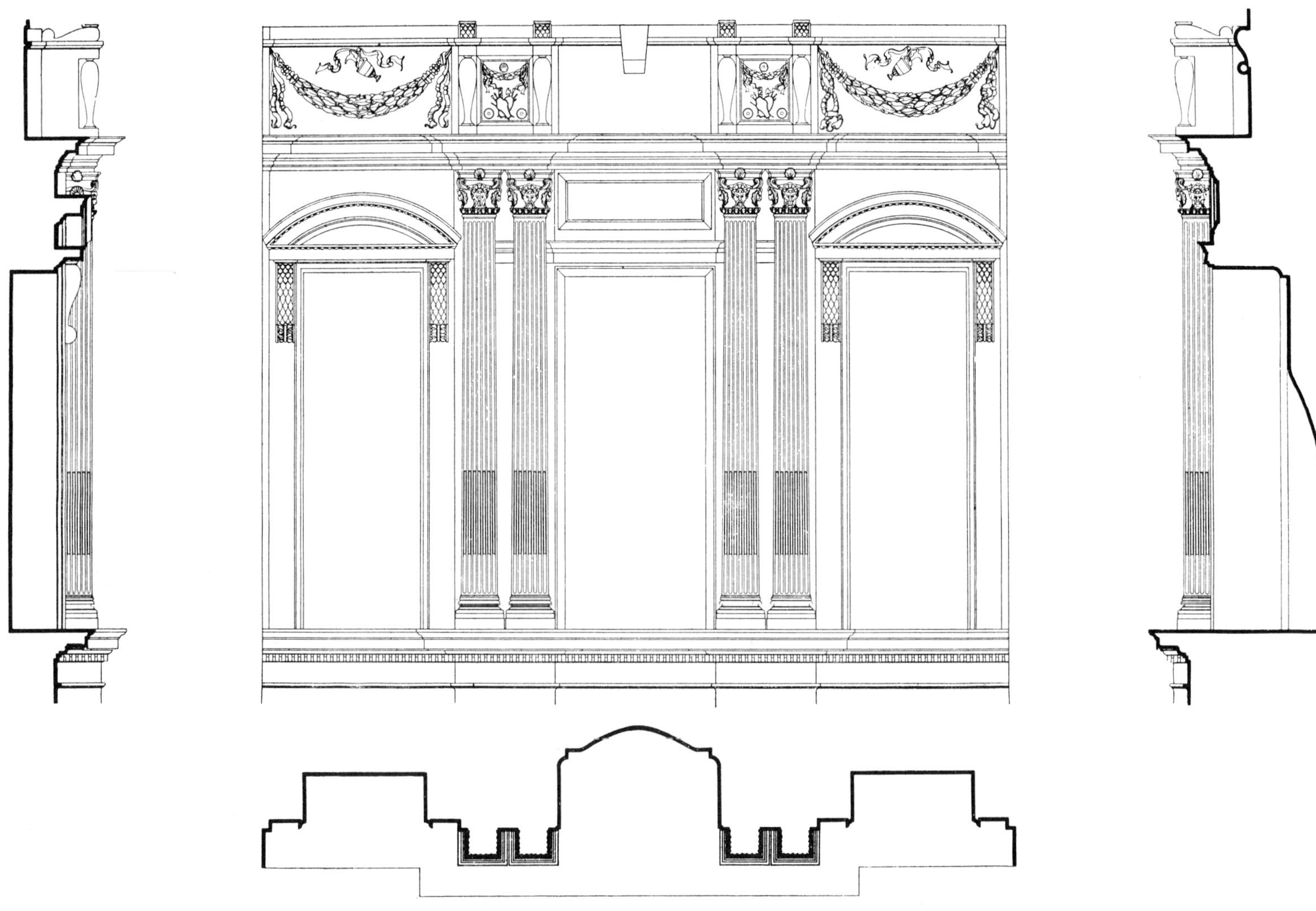

1 Medici Chapel, Florence; Partial Elevation and Sections; Michelangelo

In two essays published in 1950, *Composition in Modern Architecture* and *Function and Form*,[1] Matthew Nowicki, the talented Polish architect then working in the United States, percipiently observed that modern architecture was another architectural style, not intrinsically different from the other styles of the past. It was, of course, a style of revolutionary importance in reshaping our attitudes and our theory but, nonetheless, a style, and as Nowicki said, "A style as pronounced, as defined, more limited perhaps, and as legitimate for our times as the style of the Renaissance had been in its days. We can no longer avoid this term 'style' simply because it brings to our minds unpleasant memories. We cannot keep on pretending that we solve our problems without a precedent in form. We have to realize that in the overwhelming majority of modern design form follows *form* and not *function*." He went on to discuss some of the unfortunate architectural implications of the concept of function as flexibility, which tended to replace the earlier modern concept of functional exactitude: for example, function as flexibility tended to reduce a museum and a supermarket to the same level of significance. In the nineteen fifties, few architects would have agreed with Nowicki's observation, and even fewer would have admitted it. For we were still caught up in the dogma that modern architecture had rendered unnecessary any overt consideration of style. By now the state of the Emperor's clothes is evident to everyone, and we must examine the stylistic attributes of modernism and their implications.

It seems abundantly clear that a large part of the present climate of dissatisfaction with modern architecture is attributable to its seeming inability to produce a good room. This observation does not necessarily reflect nostalgia for the excesses of the high eclectic period, which modern architecture displaced in the nineteen twenties, for I think that anyone even moderately literate in architectural history, on seeing a good building of whatever period of the past, often asks: "If these rooms are so interesting, why must our rooms today be so dull?" Of course it is possible that the early modernists, in their revolutionary fervor to throw out eclecticism and anything associated with it, also threw out some things that might later have proven valuable to the development of their own architecture; for example, the consciousness of history necessary to eclectic theory. My intention is to discuss those theories of modern architecture that, whatever their merit in other respects, tend to undermine the concept of the room as a primary unit of architectural composition. Even though some fundamental theories and concepts of modern architecture have tended to devalue and to ignore the room, I maintain that it is still possible to produce well designed and interesting rooms while staying within the canon of modern architecture.

In speaking of a 'good' room, I mean a room that is animated by an architectural concept of sufficient merit to command our interest, in contrast to a room inscribed in a plan conceived with minimal architectural ambition. Of course, as we well know, that architectural concept might be that of a minimum of elements to define a room. I might add that not all rooms in a building need to be architecturally elaborated, for some may be merely stuffing, necessary but not really part of the architectural experience. The interior facade of the title refers to one or more of the walls of a room; I use the pretentious word facade to indicate the possibilities of a wall that is somehow more compositionally well conceived than the wall as a simple rectangular plane or a plane with some casually disposed doors and windows in it. I also use facade to call attention to the fact that, spatially, the wall may sometimes be a picture plane or some sort of referential plane for various elements of the composition, as the word facade implies frontality in its derivation. While it is possible to discuss an exterior facade as an independent, isolated element, one must always bear in mind the interior facade's relationship to the other walls, ceiling, and floor and to the more general considerations of space and the ensemble of the room.

A relatively pure example of an interior facade that is strictly comparable to an exterior facade is provided by a shopping arcade or *galleria*. The galleria typology implies the concept of a covered street. Its facades are like street facades that confront one another across the principal space. Similarly the interior of any great church, whether centralized or basilican, offers interior facades that are analogous to exterior facades. Examples are St. Peter's in Rome, St. Paul's in London, or any Gothic cathedral. Any good Renaissance courtyard in a palazzo also serves as an example. Clearly, a courtyard is an interior space; if one were to provide a glass roof, it would become a room. The principal difference between a courtyard facade and a true exterior facade is that in a courtyard the facades continue around the corners to make four facades in dialogue with one another, as do the walls of a room. A truly exterior facade, even in a freestanding building, may be seen to have continuity around the corner with only one other facade for we can see at most two faces of the building at the same time.

I have given examples so far of spaces of very great dimensions. In such large spaces it is easier to see that we may legitimately regard the walls of the room as analogous to facades; their very size seems to demand compositional structure and hierarchy in order to be in scale. However, size is not the critical factor in determining whether we see an interior facade or not. Much smaller rooms, such as the principal rooms of a palazzo, or even those of a more humble house, may also be regarded as having facades. Modern architecture, on the other hand, offers all too many examples of interiors of truly monumental size that have interior elevations, but that do not suggest the concept of the interior facade. One example is the "Crystal Cathedral," built by Johnson and Burgee. In this case, it is not the fact of the complete glass wall that prevents one from entertaining the idea of facade as much as the whole concept of space and the non-hierarchical detailing of the building: only the two great wooden pipe organ enclosures flanking the altar provide any semblance of an interior facade. There certainly exist large glass walls having only the most tenuous and linear structure that convey the idea of facade: Joseph Paxton's Crystal Palace had facades, and his "conservation wall," or wall of camelia cases, at Chatsworth is an elegant facade of extreme length. The dominant concept in modern architecture of the curtain wall as a sheer surface of glass having only the most tenuous and repetitive divisions possible has obviously tended to devalue the idea of facade. Some greenhouses, while being almost totally glass buildings, must be considered as having not only exterior facades, but also interior facades. A particularly attractive example is the conservatory at Syon House, designed by Charles Fowler in 1820. Fowler's conservatory has stone walls but, except for the pediments, they are completely reduced to a frame of entablature and supporting pilasters. Through this stone frame is threaded a system of wrought iron divisions of the glass, giving a layered effect to the wall. On the interior, the elegant glass dome is supported by an independent system of slender cast iron columns. The residue of the stone and glass walls together with the wrought iron system make interior facades that divide the spaces of the conservatory.

One of the great concepts of modern architecture is that of the continuity of interior and exterior space: it may, in fact, be the only really new contribution to architectural composition as it implies a redefinition of the elements of composition. I shall discuss two formulations of this idea: the Wrightian version and the De Stijl version. The problem to overcome is our perceptual predisposition to see objects rather than space: as space is incorporeal, and architectural space is more a concept than a thing, it can be 'seen' only when it is delineated by suitably disposed defining elements. Owing to this secondary and derived character of volumetric space, it is quite natural that we are biased in favor of seeing objects rather than relationships that imply space. The prototypical space is a room, a completely defined space. A multi-room building, such as a palazzo, may internally be a collection of rooms, but when we view it from the outside, we tend to perceive the building as an object defined by facades, or by one facade if it is part of a row of buildings on a street. There is no intrinsic connection between the individual room and the exterior except the window. The classic problem of composition is to arrange the windows and doors in a satisfactory manner on the facade and simultaneously to dispose the windows properly within the various rooms. Of course, it is possible to make the room manifest on the exterior as an articulated form, but if all rooms are expressed this way, they not only compete with one another, but the part tends to dominate over the whole, and unity of the facade becomes difficult. We thus arrive at the uncomfortable realization that the architecture of the exterior and the architecture of the interior may be totally at variance with one another. We may, in fact, find interiors done up in a variety of conflicting styles that have little in common with the architecture of the exterior, the only connection being memory: the architecture of the room evokes memories of the exterior, and vice versa. Given that the compositional problems of a room are quite different from those of the exterior, it is evident that it is not easy to overcome the dichotomy between interior and exterior architectures; it is possible only if we can find some common denominator between the two. Clearly, it would be a great advance in conceptual elegance if we could reduce the two architectures to one system of composition, to one architecture for the building both inside and out.

Wright and the De Stijl theorists saw the concept of space as the means to accomplish this unification of the interior and exterior. Space is a medium that pervades all aspects of architecture; if one could employ the same system of space-defining elements for both the interior and the exterior, unification would be achieved. Both correctly saw the wall, the solid corner, and the 'hole-in-the-wall' window as the ene-

2

3

4

5

6

7

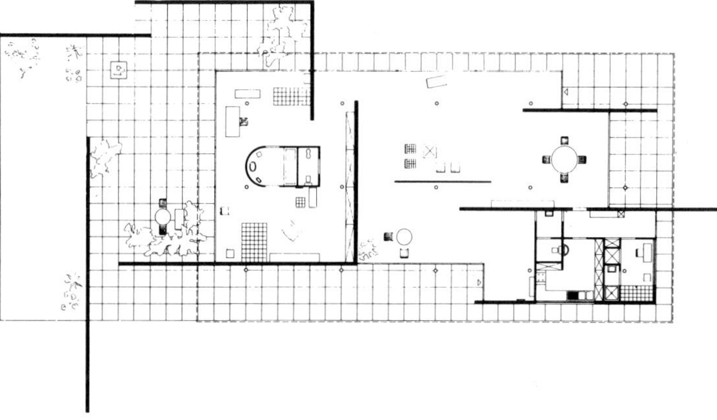

8

2 Palazzo Farnese, Rome; Courtyard Elevation; Michelangelo 1547
3 Conservation Wall, Chatsworth; View; Joseph Paxton
4 Conservation Wall; Detail
5 Syon House; Interior View; Charles Fowler
6 Syon House; Exterior View
7 House, Berlin Building Exposition; Living Room; Mies van der Rohe
8 House, Berlin Building Exposition; Plan

mies of the desired continuity of space, for the wall separates space, the solid corner reinforces the perception of the exterior as an object, and the traditional window fails to achieve spatial continuity. Neither succumbed to the simplistic notion that to make the wall totally of glass would achieve their aims, although van Doesburg sometimes seems to flirt with the notion. That glass houses do not achieve the objective should be evident from the previous discussion of greenhouses; greenhouses are still object-like on the exterior, albeit crystalline objects.

While one cannot make an interior into an exterior without destroying the house, it is possible to conceive of an exterior composed of open or exterior room-like elements: courtyards, porches, overhangs, balconies, reentrant corners, and so on. The elements that define interior space are thus extended to define these transitional exterior spaces. The concept is one of gradation, or vignetting of the space-defining system: one proceeds from the room, the completely defined space, via a less defined exterior equivalent of a room, to undefined exterior space. Moving from the outside to the inside, one reverses the sequence. It is difficult to avoid completely the perception of the house as an object seen from the outside, but one can at least establish a frame of reference for conceiving the whole spatially.

Theo van Doesburg proposed that all defining elements be considered as abstract planes, ignoring all differences that might exist between floors, walls, and roofs (although he later revised his manifesto to say that these planes should be sustained by a system of columns, relieving the walls of the necessity to be supporting elements). Augmenting ideas from Wright's early work with ideas derived from his experience of modern art, centering on Cubism, he specified that these architectural defining elements be the most neutral (non-object-like) forms possible: namely, rectangular planes, preferable unencumbered by windows. Thus the corner is made by articulated planes and the window is ideally reduced to being the gap that articulates planes. Recognizing that some rooms need to be separated or partitioned off for reasons of privacy, he proposed two categories of wall: exterior walls, or walls of closure, which would be glass, and partitions, or walls of division, which would be considered as extending to "infinity." Each room would share a wall (extended by passing through the glass wall of closure) with an implied exterior space, which would be in the nature of an overhang, a platform or balcony, or a courtyard, either actual or implied. Perhaps the most complete realization of these ideals is to be seen in Mies van der Rohe's brick country house project of 1923 or his Berlin Exposition house of 1931. One can easily see in these examples that the ideas of continuity of space, which have been persistent in modern architecture, imply the impoverishment of the vertical surface (Mies compensates for this by using rich materials, such as onyx, polished granite, or travertine for some wall surfaces) and the virtual elimination of the room as an entity.

Frank Lloyd Wright's resolution of these problems of continuity of space, in his early houses, is much less hostile than that of De Stijl to the concept of the room, perhaps because he had his origins in the nineteenth century and retained a certain degree of respect for the integrity of the room and a concern for its compositional necessities. His spatial development of the room outward normally involved extension of the horizontal surfaces—floors and ceilings—to form porches. This one-way extension of space required relatively modest glass areas, such as glass doors onto the porch, while on the bedroom floor he extended the ceiling through a band of windows to become the soffit of the roof overhang. His celebrated 'destruction of the wall' was accomplished by reducing the wall to three-dimensional, linear elements—spandrels and piers—in contrast to large rectangular areas of wall surface; the mullions between windows became merely the smallest in a hierarchical set of piers. While it is true that a spandrel is literally a rectangle of wall surface, when one dimension of a rectangle is stretched to become very long relative to its width, one tends to perceive it as a linear element; thus the spandrel is perceived as a horizontal band penetrating the piers (which are themselves vertical elements). Such a band accomplishes horizontal integration of the facade, and also may be extended outward to define exterior spaces. The perceptual effect of this redefinition of the elements of the wall is to avert expression of the wall as a large area of frontal surface. The windows are seen merely as the spaces between the smallest piers, a residue of use of the defining elements, rather than as positive figural elements in a surface. In much of traditional architecture, windows and doors are elaborated with brackets, pilasters, pediments, and so on, to the point that they become aedicules, or small buildings in their own right. When given minimal elaboration, as in the architecture of Claude-Nicholas Ledoux, windows may appear as simple rectangles incised in the surface, but they retain their figural character as elements on a background surface. Only when Ledoux strings his openings together, do they become spatial slices across the facade, anticipating Wright to some degree.

The traditional way of relating rooms to one another spatially has been to create an enfilade through a range of rooms, lining up the doors, windows, etc., of the various otherwise autonomous rooms along an axis in such a manner that one may experience a perspective view through the rooms to the farthest reaches of the range. Sometimes the definition between rooms, or parts of a room, may be reduced to merely implicit walls, such as screens of columns supporting only an architrave. Wright's stated preference for an open plan on his principal floor is accomplished by nothing more drastic than a slightly exaggerated version of the enfilade; we can thus observe that the concept of the open plan is not inherently antagonistic to the concept of the room as an entity, if only an implied entity. His famous 'interpenetration of spaces' for the interiors of his open plan relies heavily on wide flat moldings, both applied to walls and ceilings and standing free in space, to delineate the implied volumes that interpenetrate. Neither the idea of interpenetrating implied volumes, nor the use of prominent moldings to delineate space were particularly new, except perhaps for their application to such humble interiors as those of the Wrightian house, for the historic use of interpenetration of implied space is mainly to be found in the great, one-space interiors of the past, such as churches. The Wrightian use of these devices produced singularly well-composed interior elevations, for his prominent moldings were excellent promoters of continuity around the room and integrators of the room facades.

9

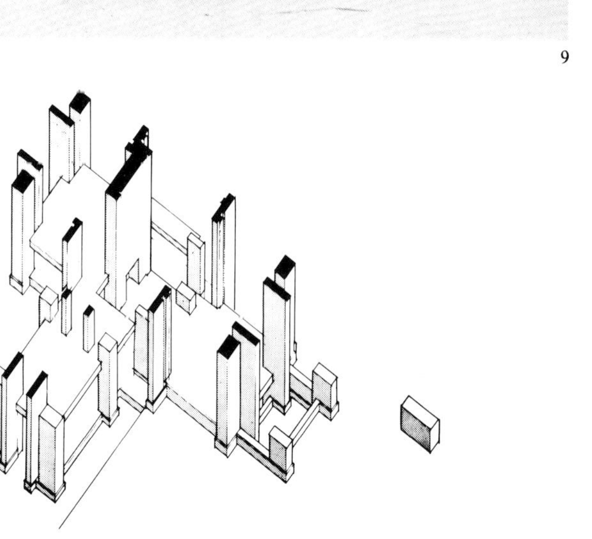

10

11

9 Palazzo del Podesta, Verona; Aedicular Portal; Michele Sanmicheli
10 Ullman House; Frank Lloyd Wright; Analysis, Lee Hodgden
11 Little Thakeham, Sussex; Hall; Edwin Lutyens
12 Pazzi Chapel, Florence; View from Lantern; Filippo Brunelleschi, 1429
13 Robie House, Chicago; Living Room; Frank Lloyd Wright
14 Martin House, Buffalo; Dining Room; Frank Lloyd Wright
15 Maison de L'education; Elevation; C. N. Ledoux
16 Maison de M. de Lanzon; Elevation; C. N. Ledoux
17 Chateau de M. de Barail; Elevation; C. N. Ledoux

12

13

14

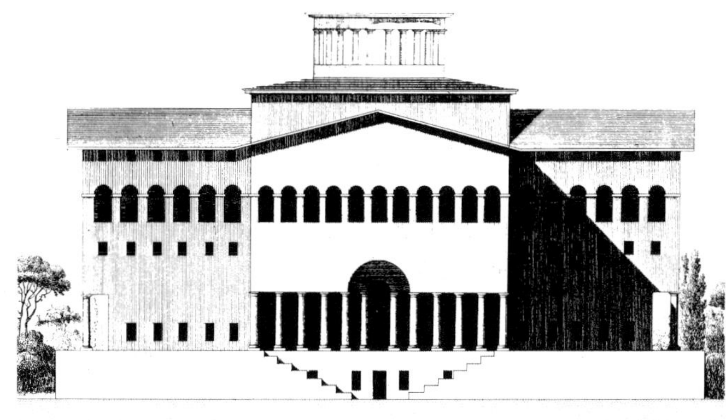

15

16

17

Le Corbusier, the great didactic exponent of modern architecture, produced his "Dom-ino" model in 1914. The Domino concept demonstrates his precocious insight that a future, industrial society would be obliged to build with some sort of structural frame, in most instances, rather than the more labor-intensive mass bearing wall. He outlived all of the shortcomings and restrictions imposed by bearing wall construction and, in his "five points of the new architecture," drew certain corollaries implicit in the adoption of frame construction: the free plan and the open plan, the free facade and the *fenêtre en longueur,* and so on. In houses of the Domino model the floor planes are sustained by a grid of columns, permitting interior space, or the room, to be the entire interior volume of that floor, conditioned only by certain object-like or figural elements, as in his plan for the speculative house at Vaucresson. His other early dwelling model, the Citrohan type, double-height rooms permit space to be continuous in section between parallel vertical surfaces, which are potential party walls for townhouses. As Colin Rowe has pointed out, in the work of Le Corbusier and his followers, space tends to be conceived as a 'slice of space' between two parallel planes: horizontal space between the floor and ceiling planes of the Domino model and vertical space between the party walls. In some instances, he later employed a 'giant order' of the Domino in which the principal floors occur at double the usual ceiling height, with a partial mezzanine interpolated to provide the height of subordinate rooms. He thus overcame the limited choice of height implied in the original Domino scheme, as in the Governor's Palace at Chandigarh and the Palais de Congrés in Strasbourg. A simplistic adoption of these notions, of which we can hardly accuse Le Corbusier himself, can have disastrous consequences for the design of interior spaces. While Le Corbusier's Domino 'slice of space' may in theory extend to infinity, it is in sober fact necessarily bounded by the walls, even when the walls are of glass. Yet some architects naively seem to think that the model has disposed of the problem in such a way that they do not have to devote very much thought to the design of the walls. A persistent residue of the Citrohan concept is encountered all too often among architecture students, who sometimes think that they have created an important or noble room simply by making it a double-height space, disregarding its poverty of architectural concepts in all other respects. In fact, it often seems that they can conceive of no alternative way to make a room more signifant than others. Thus the traditional concern of architects to endow each room with appropriate proportions, including noble proportions for especially significant rooms, has been impoverished to a very limited set of options, that is, to make the ceiling either one standard floor in height, or to make it two, regardless of the floor area of the room.

Neither the De Stijl concept of space, nor the Wrightian idea of interpenetration challenged the intuitively obvious, conventional view that architectural space, being three-dimensional volume delineated by defining elements, is seen in a perspective view, as perspective corresponds very closely to the way the eye actually perceives three-dimensional things. Yet there exists a very different and important conceptual model for seeing space, one that involves the idea of frontality. This model assumes that, in certain works of architecture, there are

18

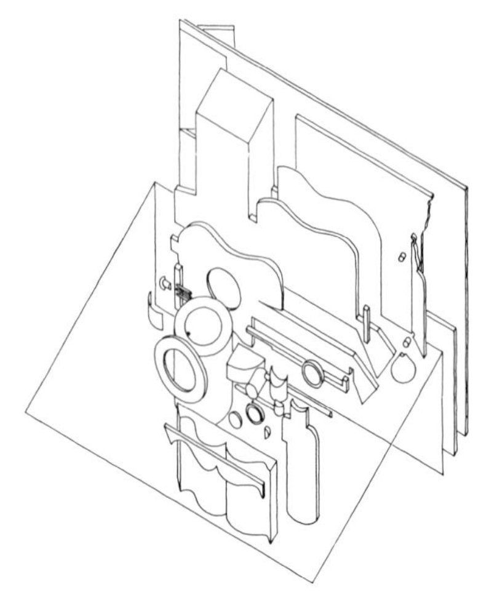

19

20

21

18 Still Life Composition; Le Corbusier, 1920
19 Still Life Composition; Analysis, Bernard Hoesli
20 Palais de Congrés, Strasbourg; Section; Le Corbusier, 1964
21 Villa á Vaucresson; Perspective Sketch; Le Corbusier, 1922
22 *The Accordionist*; Pablo Picasso, 1911
23 *The Dice*; Juan Gris, 1922
24 Villa á Vaucresson; Plan

22

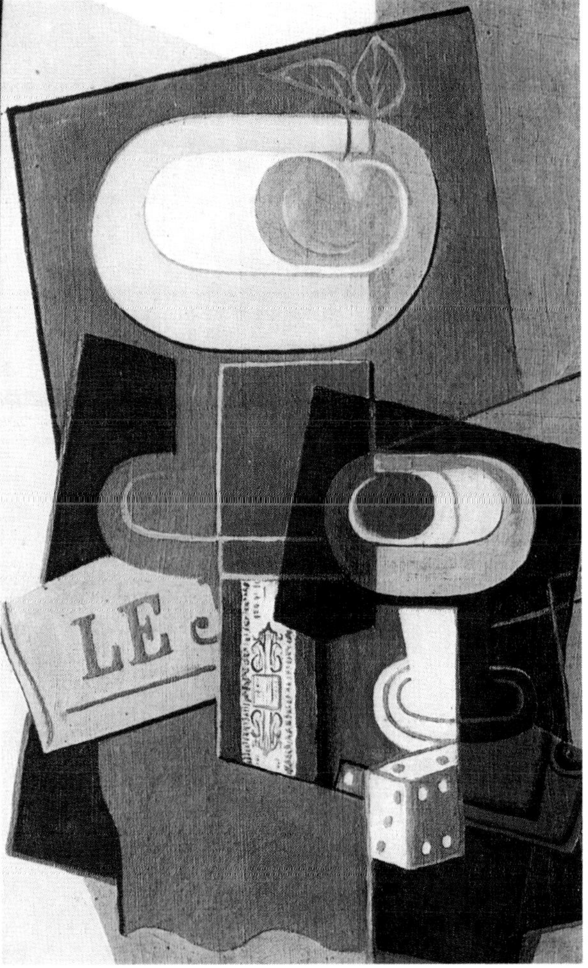

23

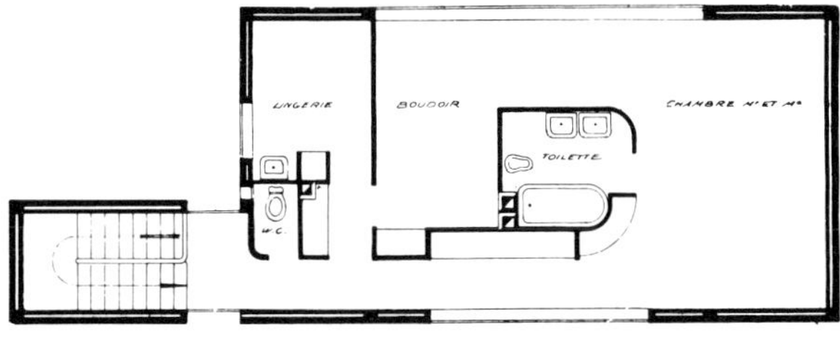

24

significant reference planes that the mind accepts as generating frontality. Le Corbusier, the architect, was at the same time Jeanneret, the purist painter, and he was thoroughly familiar with the innovations in spatial representation that had been introduced by the Cubist painters.

A crucial problem in painting concerns the duality of perception that one experiences in viewing a picture between the awareness of the two-dimensional composition on the surface and the representation of three dimensions in the picture. One of the greatest intellectual accomplishments of the Renaissance was the solution of the problem of the geometry of linear perspective by Alberti and Piero della Francesca. Since perspective provides the most compelling illusion of depth that one can have in a picture, it seemed for a very long time that the problem of representation had been solved. But the Cubist painters, by investigating nonperspective ways to represent space, revolutionized the way we visualize space. They found that at least a small sort of space could be created by much more primitive pictorial cues to depth than linear perspective, such as overlapping, figure-ground cues, transparency, and gradations of value, color, and texture. While these cues, which are local and autonomous, give a perception of depth that is a much less compelling illusion than perspective space, experimentation with their use led to some significant discoveries. One of these discoveries was that pictorial space no longer had to obey the holistic geometry of linear perspective, as it was created by independent local cues that, being autonomous, could be made to contradict one another as the eye shifted its point of fixation on the painting. This led to the celebrated Cubist iridescence, prominent in Picasso's and Braque's paintings from 1910 to 1914, in which eye movement promotes frequent reorganization of one's perception of the structure of space. More important for architecture was the concept that pictorial space in this kind of painting had to be assembled, or built, cue by cue. When the major Cubists, including Juan Gris, turned to a more hard-edged kind of painting, many of their former ambiguity-inducing devices were eliminated. The interrupted contour, the vignetted contour, and vignetted shading are no longer possible when one employs flat-painted color planes, which inevitably have complete closure of the bounding contour. For the most part, ambivalent readings of space can be created by contradictory overlappings and implied transparencies of composition. This restriction of the possibilities for spatial ambivalence produces little of the iridescent effect, but it allows for the reintroduction of vivid color that was excluded in iridescent painting.

If the fundamental painter's paradox is the simultaneous reading of the painting as surface composition and depth, the architect's possibly more profound paradox may be that, in an art of three literal dimensions, he or she may have to revert to lessons learned from the two-dimensional art whenever he wishes to call attention to the spatiality of his concept. The reason for this is that, however banal it may be in terms of spatial concept, any room whatever is perceived in perspective space because it is three-dimensional; therefore, perspective reading and three dimensions are not, in their own right, sufficient to signify a concept of particular spatiality. Hence, really spatial architecture may need to learn from the Cubists how to build space with primitive perceptual cues.

The Cubist concept of building pictorial space by means of local cues was not lost on Le Corbusier, who proceeded to apply it to architecture. As a painter-architect he adopted a frontal attitude toward space, in which the vertical surface is seen as the equivalent of the picture plane in painting. Given the two dimensions of the picture plane, the problem of space reduces to establishing depth with regard to the frontal plane. The canonical example of frontality in his work is, of course, the De Monzie/Stein Villa at Garches, which demonstrates at least two ways of establishing a dominant reference plane for a three-dimensional building: on the front facade this is done by the traditional frontal approach, typical in site plans for villas. The side walls are effectively solid party walls, denying spatial extension in this direction, while the frontal plane is pushed forward to the end of the Domino cantilever and articulated from the side walls by a vertical slot of glass. The screen-like character of the facade is made evident by use of the strip window across the facade. This picture plane is then agitated by certain elements that are pulled forward (for example, balcony fronts), while through the openings in the plane certain objects are seen to push closely up to the plane from behind (stairwell, columns, bathroom form, and so on), creating a shallow space similar to that of a Cubist painting. This scheme of things has long been familiar to us through Colin Rowe's writings about Garches. On the garden side of Garches, one can see another way to establish layering and frontality. Here, the end walls establish a sort of frame, or proscenium, around a prominent plane at the back of the outdoor room of the terrace. It may be considered as the ground plane of Cubist space, with the various planes of the facade building forward in layers, rather like the way that flats build layers of space on a proscenium stage.

Maison Cook demonstrates that a similar concept of the picture plane and of frontality may be applied to an interior facade as well. The front facade of Maison Cook is like a simpler version of the facade of Garches; when one moves inside and arrives in the two story principal room, one finds the space of those floors bisected by a plane at right angles to the facade. This central plane is penetrated by two major openings to the dining room and to the library above, permitting the space to be read all the way back to the party wall of the house as a ground plane, and a similar agitation of this plane by layers and objects (such as stair and fireplace) takes place. In my opinion, it is this painterly consciousness of frontality that distinguishes Le Corbusier's work from that of many architects who have taken the Domino concept as an article of faith without recognizing the necessity of composing the vertical surfaces as an unstated corollary of the idea.

Another useful and stimulating concept in architecture that derives from Cubism is the collage plan, although in unskilled hands the technique may be disastrous for interior space. To use collage plan composition successfully, one must always bear in mind that there are significant differences between the perception of a picture and the perception of a plan. The picture is seen frontally, so objects and shapes in a *papier collé* are seen with the simultaneity of transparent organization, and even quite incongruous and arbitrary figures may be superimposed with some compositional success, for each element retains its individual iden-

25

26

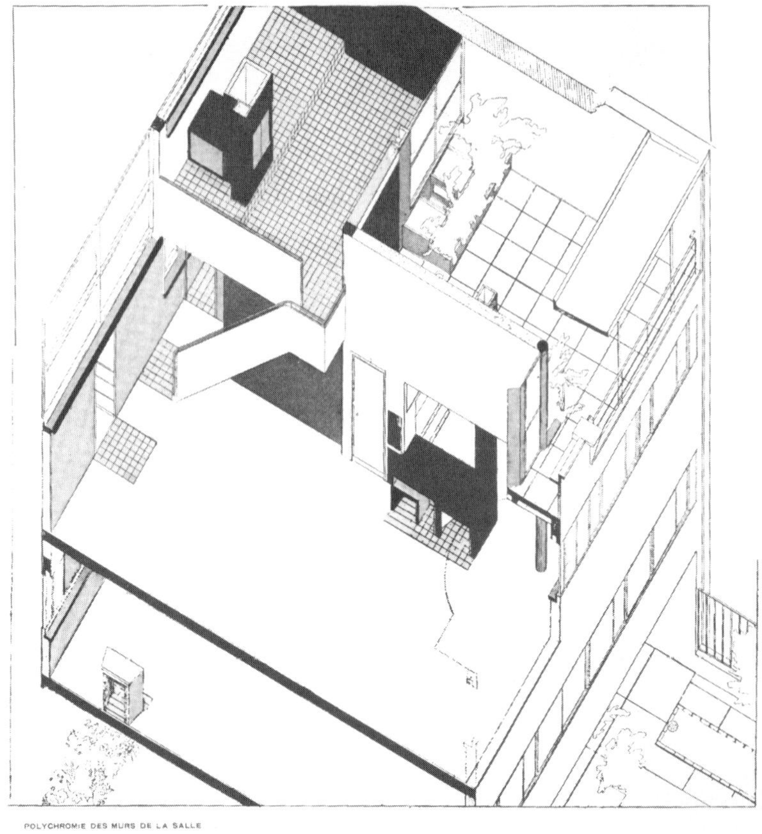

27

25 Villa Stein, Garches; Front Axonometric; Le Corbusier, 1927
26 Villa Stein, Garches; Garden Axonometric
27 Maison Cook, Paris; Living Room Axonometric; Le Corbusier, 1926
28 St. Mark's Tower, New York; Project; Frank Lloyd Wright
29 The Governor's Palace, Chandigarh; Guest-Apartment Floor; Le Corbusier, 1950-1957

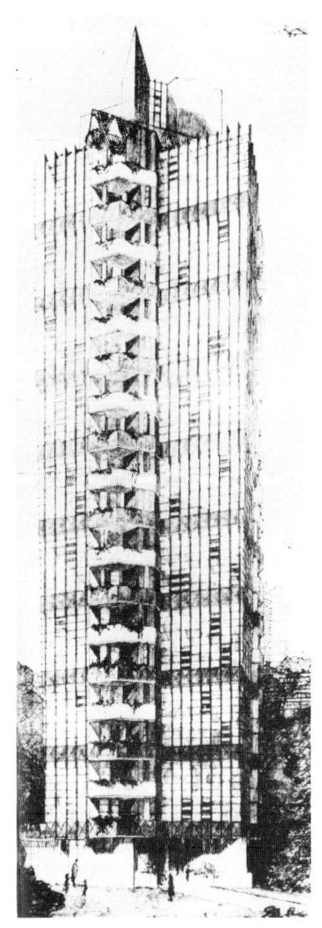

28

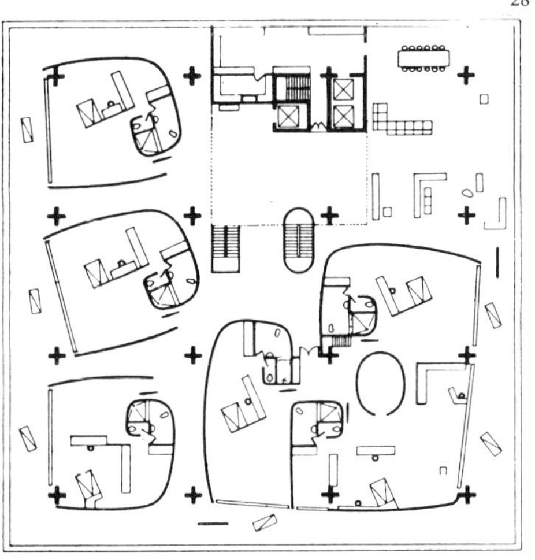

29

tity when montaged together with other forms. A floor plane, however, unlike frontally viewed walls, is seldom seen as a picture plane in any significant sense. We normally have a highly oblique view of the floor, so that transparency and simultaneity yield to opacity and isolation of forms. If too many arbitrary forms are collaged together the result may be total incoherence of the logic of the space. If, like Frank Lloyd Wright in his St. Mark's tower or in Taliesen West, one superimposes only two systems of form, comprehensibility is not lost, for each element may be readily associated with its generating system, even if the choice of systems of form is somewhat gratuitous. It seems to be critical to the success of plans that collage together two systems of form that the systems be clearly differentiated, and not merely the commonly seen angularly shifted grid plan in which the systems are not expressively differentiated. In Wright's St. Mark's Tower, for example, one system is generated by concrete structure while the other system is given primarily by the glass closure walls. In such freely collaged plans as the guest-apartment floor of Le Corbusier's Governor's Palace, free-form closure is contrasted with the square geometry of the column grid.

Apart from the form as aspects of architecture that I have commented on, I should not neglect to mention that modern architecture was revolutionary in more ways than one; it was also intended to be a social revolution with a strong ideological content of colial utopianism. The central social issue was to provide adequate housing for the masses, a task at which traditional architecture and traditional methods of building had so signally failed, and many of the devices that we have been discussing have their origins in addressing the problems of mass social housing. Beaux-arts architecture and its bourgeois orientation was clearly an anathema to these theorists. In Adolf Loos' famous phrase, "ornament is crime," the CIAM convened to discuss the "Existenz Minimum" and the minimal dwelling was a primary concern in architecture for many decades. Even today, when social issues do not seem to be in the forefront of architectural concerns, the residue of this long indoctrination exerts a strong influence on our thinking and inhibits us from making good interior spaces, because the concept of the minimum is a serious impediment to the design of a good interior facade. Few architects today, for example, when faced with something as remote from social concerns as the problem of designing a board room for a large corporation, can think of any way to make the room special or significant except to veneer the ordinary office space with expensive materials.

It is not merely the bias against lavish ornament that prevents us from designing significant rooms; a much more insidious corrupting influence that flows from concept of "Existenz Minimum" is the habit of regarding rooms only pragmatically. As long as the primary issue of the room is to achieve as many square feet as one can as cheaply as possible, composing the wall architecturally becomes an unaffordable luxury; openings and divisions of the wall occur where necessary, and nobody really cares. Yet we know from history that austere but noble rooms can be designed with little more than an idea of proportion and a concept for aligning the openings spatially in the room and arranging the openings in the wall as a concert of surface and void. The important thing is to have a concept of the room that transcends the totally casual ignoring of the problems of composition that ultimately results from the banal and profoundly untrue notion that whatever functions is automatically beautiful. It is a sad degradation of the concept of functionalism put forward by some adherents of the *Neue Sachlichkeit,* about whom Le Corbusier complained when they attempted to co- opt his lapidary phrase, "a house is a machine for living in."

Architects practicing in an industrial society today must increasingly face the fact that building costs have experienced great inflation, both in terms of labor and materials, and that industrialization has been accompanied by a serious decline in craft. It is increasingly difficult to meet any reasonable budget, and few buildings are built by patrons who have unlimited budgets. The architect is under continuous pressure to accept inferior alternatives in every aspect of building. Examples of this abound, so I will cite only one or two. On a recent visit to Finland, I heard architects complain that, while only twenty years ago they could rely on a face brick wall to be impeccably made, today it has become an unacceptable choice, as the skill of the average bricklayer has declined so much. In this twenty year period, Finland has progressed from being a marginally industrial country to full industrialization. In another example, I noted a recent catalogue which offers attractive *machine-carved* ornamental moldings made in India, but the price for a piece six inches wide and six feet long is in the hundreds of dollars. Industrialization has brought us better products, if they can be mass produced by automated processes, but where craft is required we have seen a steady decline. Craft requires skill and many hours of careful work, a luxury that few can afford today. Thus, while we may have better cars and better computers, very few benefits of mass production and modern technology have reached architecture and the art of building, which remains predominantly labor-intensive. Perhaps we have some industrially made curtain wall components, but if we want anything custom designed for the one-of-a-kind building—which most architects design—we shall have to pay a great price. These economic realities have an important influence on architectural design, and until now this influence has been a mixed blessing for architects. I do not advocate that architects can reasonably expect to solve the problems of their interiors by increasing the elaboration and expense of the design but, on the contrary, only by exercising diligence and inventiveness in their design concepts. Whatever design lessons we learn from history must be interpreted in terms of contemporary possibilities.

Architects of a pre-industrial age, not limited by such severe constraints on craftsmanship and labor, could design interiors as elaborately as they wished; history provided them with an extensive repertoire of elements with which to compose interiors as well as exteriors, primarily the classic orders. The orders provided not only the parts, but a system of composition guaranteeing horizontal and vertical concatenation. As the classical orders could be used hierarchically, the system provided a tremendous range of compositional possibilities. On the interior, the orders could be used for doors, windows, bookcases, and so on, or for whole screens and walls. It would seem that today we sorely need some kind of compositional equivalent of the function of the classic orders. In most instances we cannot use correct orders very extensively, even if we want to, for reasons of economy. Some architects have used pastiche orders for iconographic reasons, but this seems to be a limited and basically unsatisfactory answer, one that has contributed to the fact that postmodernism has so quickly become a pejorative term for most architects. An alternative is to use a completely abstract system of concatenation and hierarchy without capitals and entablature: one exterior example is Ammannati's use of shallow layering on the facade of the *Collegio Romano*. With this simple device, Ammannati could convey subtle compositional messages of conceptual frame and wall, rhythmic grouping of windows, horizontal and vertical concatenation, and so forth. Similar simple and abstract layering is to be found in the work of Guarino Guarini. In modern architecture, Wright's use of moldings and Theo van Doesburg's panelling of the Festival Hall of the Aubette perform a similar integrating function. I offer these as counter-examples to the uncomposed wall of the *existenz miminum*; the layered wall can certainly be as functional, even if it expresses not the actual structure, but only the compositional and conceptual structure.

If shallow layering of the wall is useful compositionally, why not deep layering? Traditional architecture commonly used thick walls of necessity, because it normally employed bearing-wall construction. Such thick bearing elements create poché in the plan, the positive figure of the solid elements. These thick walls may have niches, pilasters, and so on, that constitute deep layering and penetration of the wall. Deep walls are useful for containing bookshelves, fireplaces, and so on. After the Domino concept partitions became thin to demonstrate that the structural function was in the frame, walls were reduced to non-bearing screens. In 1930, Le Corbusier introduced a thick, bearing-wall typology for rustic country houses (De Mandrot, Mathes, Errazurris): thus thick walls became permissible in modern architecture, as long as they were bearing walls. Why not, apart from strict economy, thick non-bearing walls, which produce poche and deep layering? Actually, today nearly any gratuitous gesture or caprice is accepted in modern architecture in practice, except perhaps the serious use of the orders. In terms of the proscribed and the permissible in modern architecture, I am referring to the residual inhibitions that are common in our thinking and arise from the serious puritanism inherent in the initial theory of the 1920's. One of these is the imperative for honest expression of structure, or apparent structure: hence, no thick non-bearing walls. But this is not a sufficient reason for the prohibition, as honest structure is not always our primary objective in designing, and it is too frequently a rationalization for bad design.

We should also consider here the three-dimensional ramifications of a room, and not only the isolated wall as facade. As Wright demonstrated, there needs to be continuity around the room, not only around the corner but also spatially between opposite walls. Floors and ceilings are a linking part of the continuity, particularly ceilings, because ceilings are highly visible and not obscured by furniture as floors normally are. Thus, painted ceiling ornamentation, such as Robert Adam and many others used, can be highly effective in enriching a room. If such decoration is considered unacceptable, one might consider a chastely plain,

30

31

30 Festival Hall in the Aubette, Strasbourg; View; Theo van Doesburg, 1928-29
31 Williams Wynn House; Second Drawing Room; Robert Adam
32 Maison Jaoul, Neuilly-sur-Seine; Dining Room; Le Corbusier, 1955-1957
33 Maison de Mandrot, Le Pradet; Plan; Le Corbusier, 1931
34 Collegio Romano, Rome; View; Bartolomeo Ammanati

32

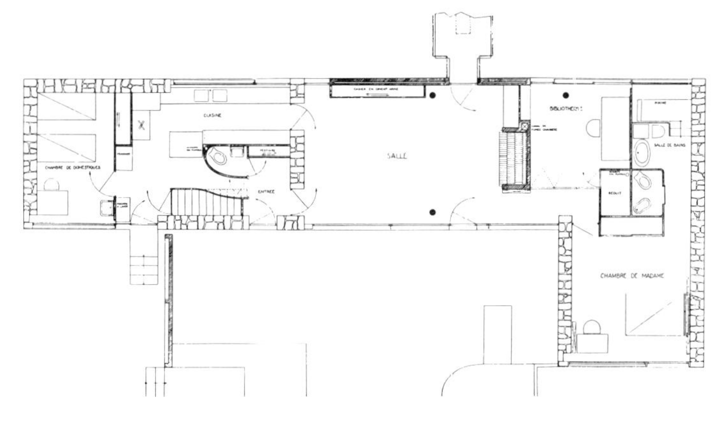
CHAMBRE DE DOMESTIQUES
ENTREE
SALLE
SALLE DE BAINS
REDUIT
CHAMBRE DE MADAME

33

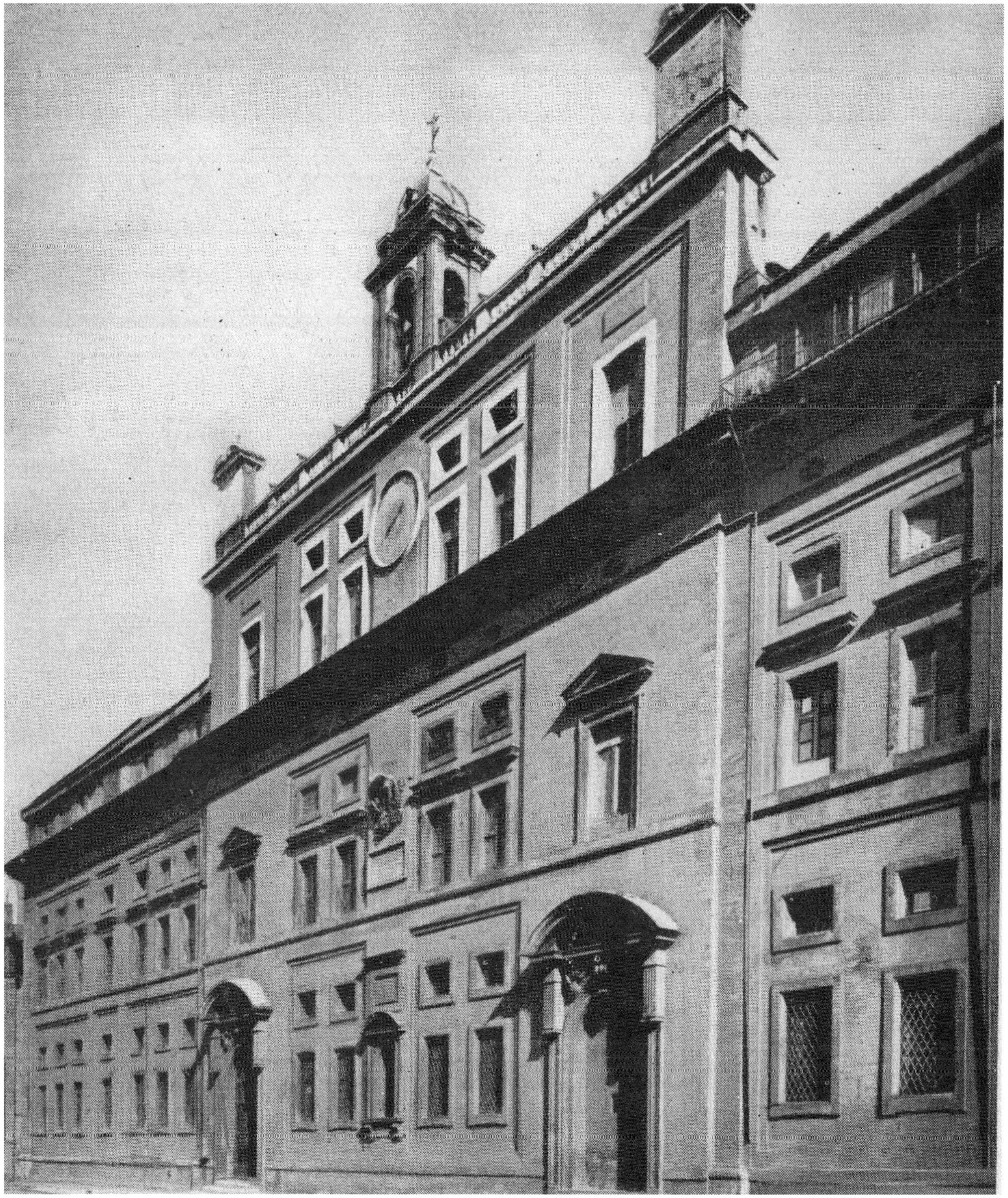

34

three-dimensional ceiling. We are long accustomed to vaulted ceilings in some of the best rooms in modern architecture, such as Le Corbusier's Villa Sarabhai and his Maisons Jaoul, or Louis Kahn's Kimball Art Museum. The work of Alvar Aalto provides many examples, as he exploited every aspect of the curved ceiling with elegantly disposed surfaces, from the symbolic function of vaulting in churches (Vuoksenniska), to the manipulation of acoustics (Kulturritalo Concert Hall) and lighting in many libraries and museums. Apparently, the permissible modern occasion for three-dimensional ceilings has been the engineering necessity of long spans, and engineers such as Torroja, Felix Candela, Pier Luigi Nervi, and Frei Otto have given us many examples. Vaulting for smaller, more intimate spaces is more difficult to construct and more expensive than slab construction and thus harder to rationalize. But one asks, "Does the curved ceiling have to be structural?" Aalto demonstrates that the functions of lighting and acoustics can provide rationalizations for non-structural curved surfaces, but generally the inhibition about honest expression of structure is still in force, however questionable the concept of honesty in architecture has been shown to be. I do not know why this should be of concern to us, because the hung ceiling to conceal ducts and wiring is certainly a commonplace in our architecture.

In the Bank of England by Sir John Soane, the important rooms are primarily very simple rectangles in plan, but they become very interesting spaces in three dimensions as they are ingeniously vaulted and domed to admit light from above. Soane's style in the Bank of England is particularly modern in the sense that its architectural expression depends on the concept of space and lighting and not on the orders and ornamentation. In his own house in Lincoln's Inn Fields, Soane employed to great effect many types of vaulted ceilings that are not necessarily structural. His work might provide an inspiration and a precedent that is totally acceptable to modern architectural thinking.

We are today accustomed to rooms of uniformly minimal height. If rooms are taller, they immediately suggest that there is a natural vertical order of scale based on the human stature: the lowest zone of the wall relates to the scale of furniture, reflected in chair rails and wainscoating; the next zone is that within the reach of an adult and concerns doors, pictures, bookcases, and so on (these elements may naturally provide horizontal integration of the wall); the upper zone of the room is associated with the ceiling. This upper zone presents possibilities for three-dimensional development; quite commonly in the eighteenth century, the room was coved with a plaster curve. While the cove may be only pseudovaulting, it is a relatively simple way to make the transition from wall to the zone of the ceiling: one does not have to incur the expense of vaulting to have a three-dimensional ceiling. There are many other ways of designing the ceiling to make the room a more interesting volume of space.

It appears to me that the present state of architectural thought, in the main, tends not to produce good rooms. I have tried to outline here some of the reasons for this state of affairs, and to suggest some alternative possibilities. Most of the inhibiting factors seem to derive from powerful didactic models adhered to even when they are not appropriate to the purpose at hand; Dom-ino, the free plan, the screen parti-

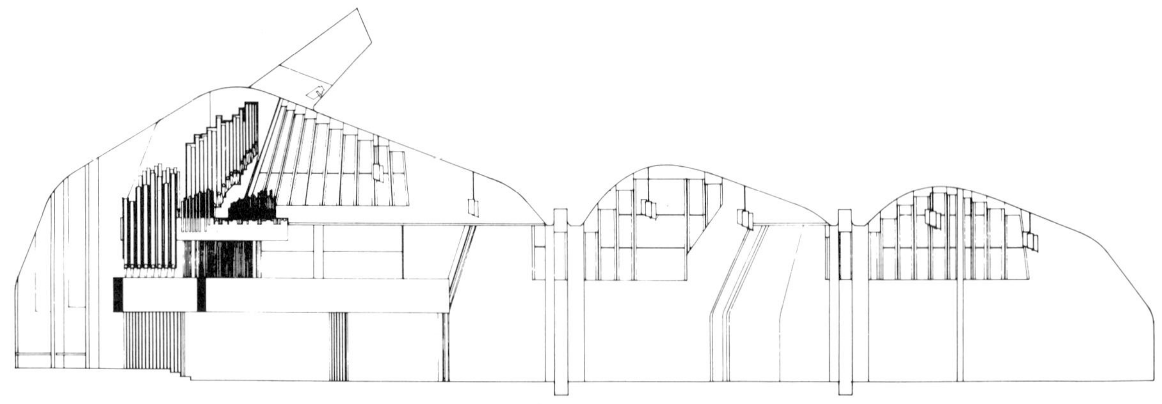

35

36

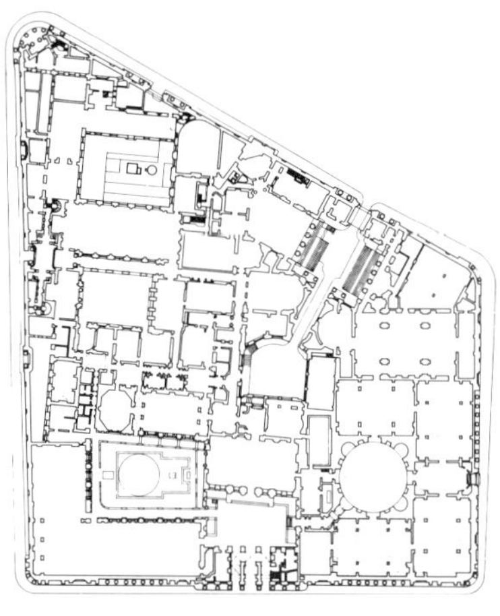

37

35 Imatra Church, Vuoksenniska; Section; Alvar Aalto, 1957-1959

36 Bank of England, London; The Consols Office; Sir John Soane, 1798-1795

37 Bank of England, London; Plan, 1732-1910

tion, the glass curtain wall, and so on. In addition, we suffer a certain impoverishment of choices brought on by the decline in craftsmanship and the failure of industrialization to serve the purposes of architecture, giving us rigidity rather than greater choice. This poverty of means, coupled with sub-conscious attitudes derived from the concept of the *Existenz Minimum,* can result in grimly uninteresting rooms. There is also the persistence of some ill-rationalized inhibitions, such as the imperative that the real structure be expressed, whether important to the central concept or not.

Despite all these negative factors, I maintain that with inventiveness, a good eye, and a little more careful thought about the composition of the wall, we have many resources that we can apply to the design of good walls and good rooms that would be within the strict canon of modern architecture, provided we can examine our inhibitions and modify those that do not stand up to critical scrutiny. ■

38

39

40

38 Lansdowne House, Berkley Square; Section through Library; George Dance
39 Lincoln's Inn Fields, London; Breakfast Room Plan and Section; Sir John Soane, 1812
40 Lincoln's Inn Fields, London; Breakfast Room

The Voluminous Wall

Spence R. Kass

This article is the result of an investigation of St. Peter's that was undertaken while the author was a Fellow at the American Academy in Rome during 1980-81.

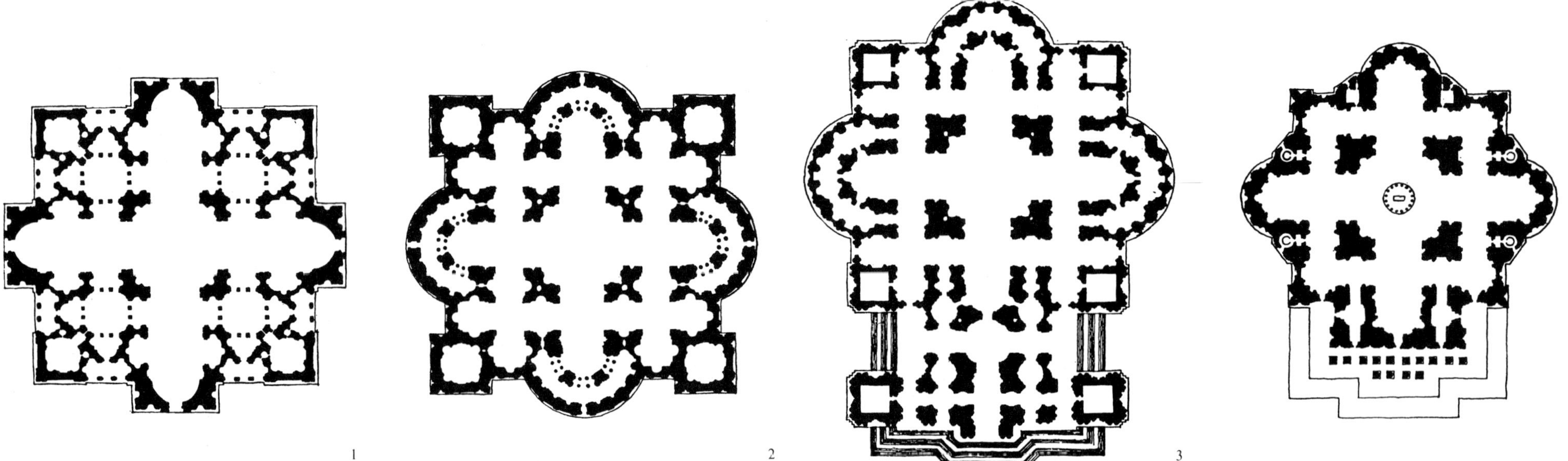

1 2 3 4

1 St. Peter's, Rome; Plan; Bramante, 1506
2 St. Peter's; Plan; Bramante-Raphael, 1515-1520
3 St. Peter's; Plan; Sangallo, 1539
4 St. Peter's; Plan; Michelangelo
5 St. Peter's; Aerial View

5

Discussions of architectural production inevitably center around the simplified conventions of plan, elevation, and section, each an abstract, two-dimensional fragment of spatial totality. Before the modern era, the load-bearing nature of masonry construction had provided some continuity between these representative realms. By necessity, walls emerged from plans and extended across the section to embrace interior volumes. With the innovations of frame construction, however, mass ceased to be a significant factor. Structural walls dissolved into independent skins while the complexity of the section was replaced by the liberties of the free plan, set between continuous floor slabs.[1] Without any structural imperative, perhaps for the first time, plan, section, and elevation could be classified as separable events. With the reduced obligation of the wall and section to modulate space, it is hardly fortuitous that the first generation of modern architects should display a prejudice towards the plan.

Not surprisingly, a renewed interest in the medium of the wall has been approached primarily through the study of plans. Michael Dennis, through an analogy with the organizations of the free plan, introduced the role of thick walls and habitable poché in resolving idealized figures within the irregular site configurations of the French hotel.[2] In "Space and Anti-Space," Steven Peterson acknowledged the role of the wall in configuring positive space, and examined the negative space of habitable poche found within the thickness of the wall between the surfaces of the building interior and the facade.[3]

If the recognition of poché has helped to reestablish a dialogue between the wall and the plan, it may be expedient to divert some attention to the effects of poché on the vertical surface as well, and initiate an argument for facades not as autonomous screens, but as integral with the wall matrix behind. Poché, then, is seen not merely as a condition of planar organization, but as a three-dimensional cement that merges throughout the building mass.

An emphasis on unity and totality is perhaps most evident in the free-standing object building where continuity between the interior and exterior seems to be greatest. St. Peter's is a prime example of this condition. With the mid-sixteenth century conversion of St. Peter's by Michelangelo, the expressive possibilities of the wall gained new definition. This change, marked not so much by new types of surface articulation, can be described as a more holistic conception of the wall as an organizer of the complete building matrix. In this way the wall is capable of integrating the complex articulations of the plan, elevation, and section.

The facade of St. Peter's elaborates on motifs found in Michelangelo's other architectural works. The alternation of major and minor bays can be traced to both the Medici Chapel and the facade projects for San Lorenzo, while the colossal order is used as a dominant feature at the Campidoglio. Previous works also exhibit the tensions and juxtapositions of large-scale tabernacles and niches inserted within a corset of strong verticals and horizontals. Each of these examples transform preexisting chaotic situations into highly ordered works of singular beauty and intensity. There are, however, some important differences that distinguish St. Peter's from these previous projects.

Although the Medici Chapel and the Campidoglio can be seen as complete in themselves, their designs, in fact, represent only an integral part of the complexes they occupy. The Medici Chapel is restricted to an interior space within San Lorenzo. Similarly, the Campidoglio can be interpreted as an outdoor room, the architecture contolling the facades that face the piazza. On the other hand, at St. Peter's, Michelangelo devised an entire building fabric around the incomplete portions of the church initiated by his predecessors. The internal facades of the former projects resemble buildings turned inside out, space framers that set the observer in the symbolic center of the composition. But the church, in recognition of a higher authority, is a space occupier, an object that consigns the viewer to its circumference. Michelangelo conceived of St. Peter's not as a series of discrete facades but as a building in the round.

Both the Medici Chapel and the Campidoglio make the distinction between frame and infill. The Medici Chapel frames white marble tabernacles with pilasters of grey *pietra serena*, while the Palazzo dei Conservatori at the Campadoglio differentiates structural bays of travertine from the infill of brickwork within. The wall of St. Peter's, however, is seemingly carved of one large block of stone, a continuous cloak of travertine whose taut skin is modeled aggressively by a series of bulges and indentations. The emphasis on mass rather than on surface, on the object instead of flat facades, on the whole as opposed to the sum of constructed parts, suggests an attitude more characteristic with Michelangelo's sculpture than any other of his architectural works.

The construction of St. Peter's must be seen as an evolving process. When Michelangelo, at age seventy-one, reluctantly became the architect of St. Peter's, he inherited nearly a half century of previous building activity and became embroiled in a struggle that would occupy the last seventeen years of his life. The complexity of the building, as well as the ongoing nature of its construction, suggested the need for a design that might set the tone for all subsequent phases of construction, even those beyond Michelangelo's lifetime. Michelangelo, by viewing the wall as a sculptural totality, expanded its conception beyond the mere resolution of the outer surface, extending it to synthesize with the internal organizations of the building.

One can begin to analyze this new type of wall by comparing it with the plans that preceded Michelangelo's tenure. Bramante's Plan of 1506 established a Greek cross for the plan of St. Peter's, the centralized theme finding its immediate precedent at Santa Maria della Consolazione in Todi, where the apsidal ends of the cross bulge out beyond a constraining square that buttresses the dome. Due in part to St. Peter's enormous size and program, Bramante's plan expands the square container to the point of almost consuming the apses and fills in the spaces between the arms with smaller Greek crosses and domes that echo the center. While Todi is unmistakably a single object, Bramante's St. Peter's is somewhat less so, being compartmentalized into distinct spatial units. It lacks the overall unity of Todi, although it retains its focus by reading as a

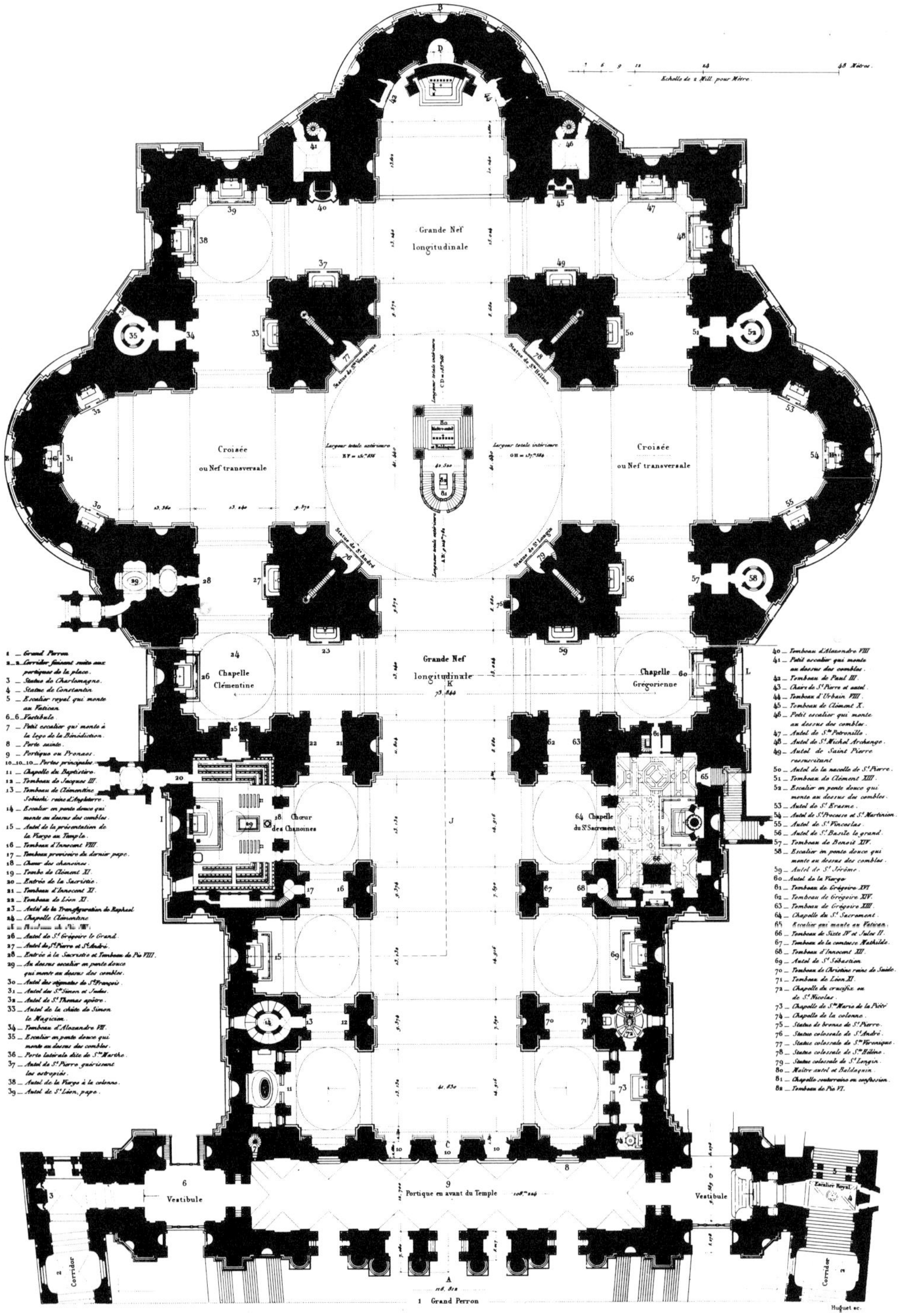

6

7

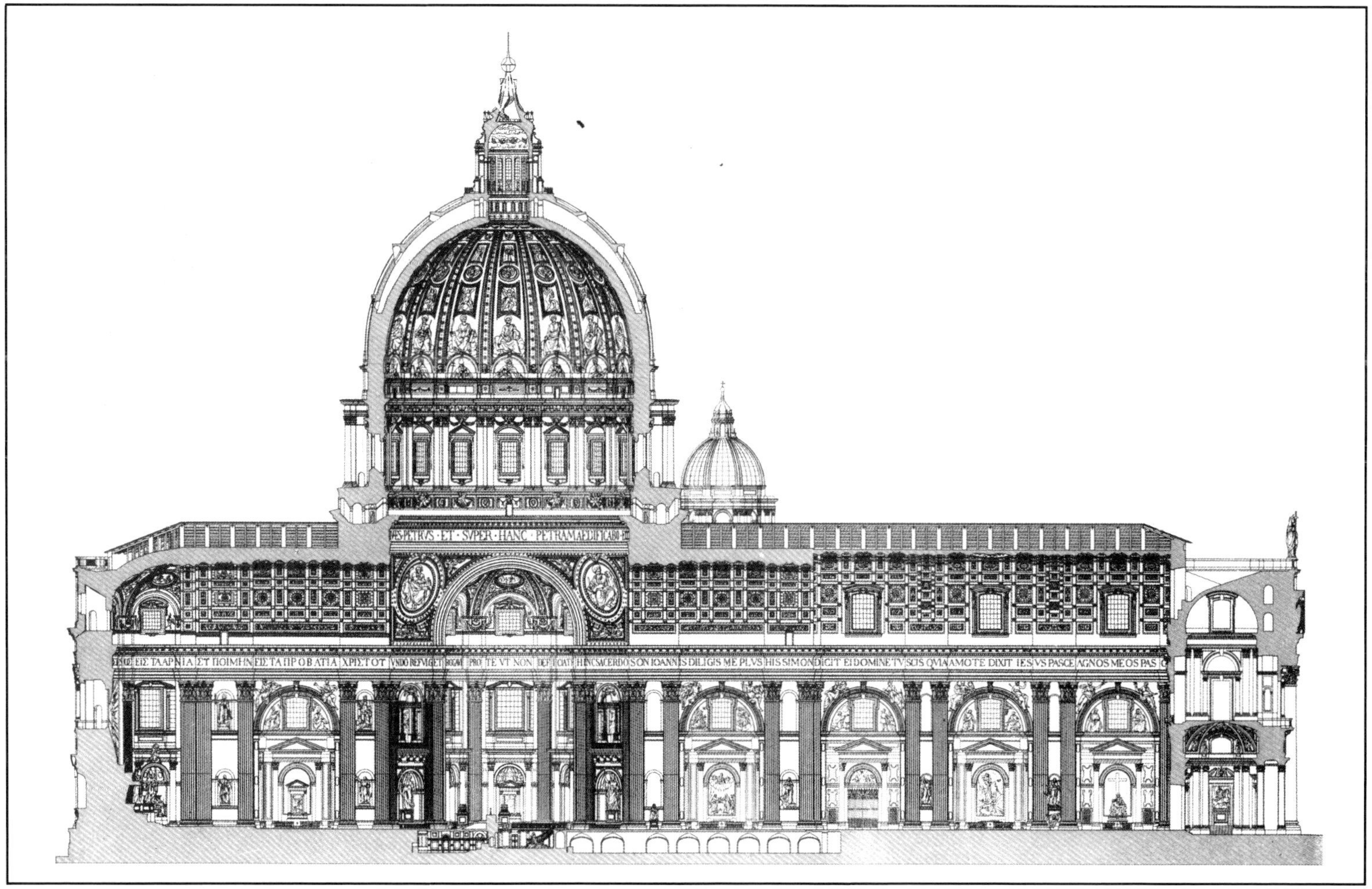

8

6 St. Peter's, Rome; Plan; Letarouilly, 1882
7 St. Peter's, Rome; Transverse Section
8 St. Peter's, Rome; Longitudinal Section
9 St. Peter's, Rome; Plan at Level of First Floor Windows
10 St. Peter's, Rome; Plan at Level of Octagonal Rooms and Entablature
11 St. Peter's, Rome; Plan at Level of Attic Story

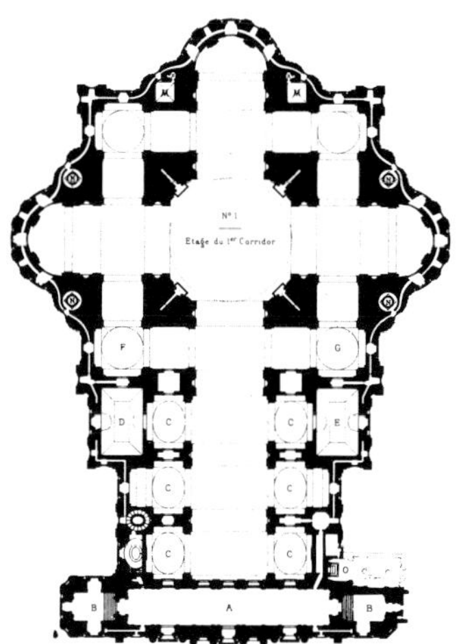

9

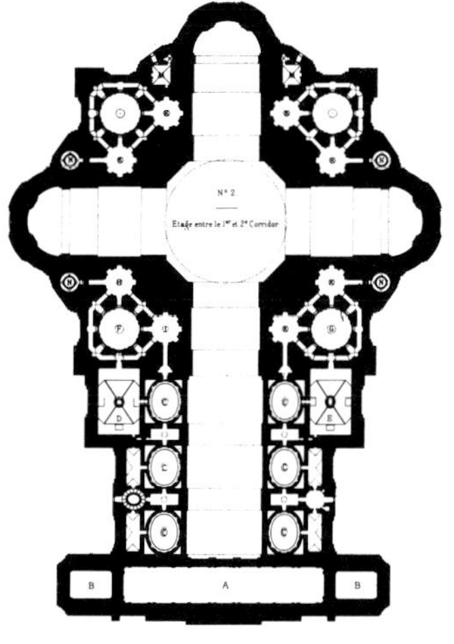

10

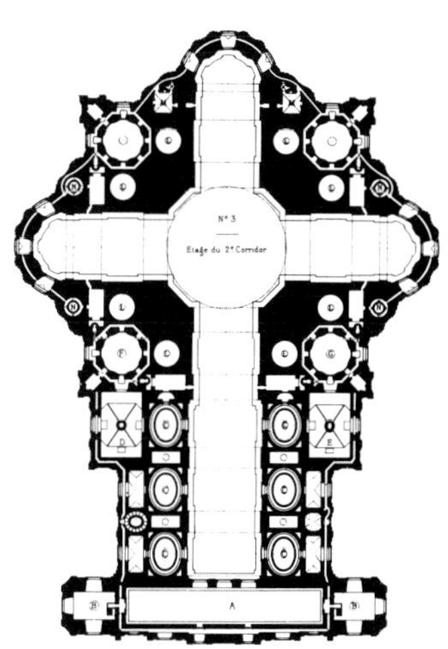

11

tight bundle of diminutive parts. The successive plan by Bramante and Raphael, 1515-20, provided secondary buttresses for the dome. In addition, colonnaded ambulatories were wrapped around the apses to accommodate processions around the church. Antonio da Sangallo's Latin cross scheme of 1539 isolated these ambulatories from the arms of the church. Access to them was provided by carving large passages into the secondary buttresses. The additive quality of Bramante's scheme here gives way to a huge arcaded wall that rises the full height of the cross arms. The proposed facade was triple-tiered, a continuous ribbon wrapping double-storied ambulatories and surmounted by a huge attic. Any desire by Sangallo to create a unified building is belied by the discovery that this wall scarcely engages in any sort of debate with the main interior. In fact, the wall remains detached from the crossarms throughout its entire circuit. The ensuing interior would have been progressively dark, cavernous, and labyrinthian.

Michelangelo assumed control over the design of the basilica in 1546 after the death of Sangallo, and immediately began to revert to the initial vision of Bramante. With the central areas of the church nearing completion, Michelangelo confined his work to the outer and upper portions of the design. He removed the outer ring of masonry around the ambulatories, thereby making the inner hemicycles into the outer walls of the building and merging the facade once again with the interior of the building. While this action compromised a more complex liturgical program for the church, it saved both time and expense in completing the edifice. Michelangelo also eliminated the four corner towers and reduced the chapels in between the arms to mere niches within the walls of the main interior. The resulting perimeter reaffirms the presence of both the Greek cross plan and the corset of vaulted spaces that surround it and merges them into one coherent whole.[4]

If the plans of Michelangelo's predecessors can be characterized as additive, repetitive, or fragmentary, this new plan was not simply reductive; rather, it carefully integrated and transformed previous construction. In the corners of each hemicycle can be seen the vestiges of the removed ambulatories. Since Sangallo had already hollowed these secondary piers, Michelangelo was able to insert spiraling ramps into these spaces with a minimum of demolition. In this way, formerly public spaces were absorbed into the matrix of the wall to become private service spaces, which aided in the movement of materials during the construction of the upper areas of the church. The outer facades enclosing these ramps became the connective tissue that merged the bulging convex apses with the corset created by the square of vaults. Functioning as secondary buttresses for the dome, these walls angle not at forty-five degrees, as might be expected. Instead, they extend further on the sides adjacent to the bulging apses as though deformed by the expansion of these internal forces. The angular surfaces, along with their newly incorporated internal spaces, reinforce the reading of the wall as a unified, carved block. Michelangelo's wall does not really eliminate the outer wall of Sangallo as much as collapse it forcibly inwards to create a sandwich that captures space within it.

Paul Marie Letarouilly's engravings, published in Paris in 1882, offer extensive documentation of Michelangelo's portion of the basilica, although they also include Maderno's seventeenth-century extensions of the nave. While the longitudinal section exhibits a simple reciprocity of interior and exterior, the cross section reveals a surprisingly intricate network of spaces that have been incorporated within the wall matrix. This hybrid wall becomes a composite of three diverse conditions. The interior surface of the wall houses an assemblage of separate chapels that provide the backdrop for the spectacle of the elaborate ecclesiastical program. Secondly, the interstitial zones conceal the private service portions of the building. Lastly, the outer facade coordinates the complex disposition of these spaces within the building without compromising its public monumentality. Letarouilly's cross section is actually two drawings in one. The left half is taken through Maderno's nave while the right half presents a section through Michelangelo's square of vaults that surround the main crossarms. Occupying the space above the barrel vaults is one of eight octagonal storage rooms that reduce the mass of the church.[5] Horizontal sections cut through the basilica show the extent to which interstitial spaces or habitable poche pervade the building. As the walls and piers rise, they join over the ancillary spaces adjacent to the primary cross to become one thick wall. In turn, this mass is aggressively carved and modeled, teeming with a network of passageways that connect windows, stairs, and service spaces.

Michelangelo's outer facade is composed of giant order pilasters surmounted by a bold cornice and attic story. Alternating between major and minor bays, the perimeter engages in a lively discourse with the internal portions of the church. The major bays correspond to the principal openings in the hemicycles and to the inside corners of the square surrounding the Greek cross. Here, large openings in the facade tie directly into the body of the church. On the other hand, the minor bays align with the array of service spaces within the wall itself. The wall can be likened to a quilt that wraps the basilica, oscillating between areas with padding and portions where the outer and inner surfaces have been sewn together, with some of the threads aggressively torn away to leave those enormous sockets where light streams through. Incorporated within the minor bays are a series of stacked openings, blank niches, and decorative panels that are easily punctured to light the interstitial spaces held within the wall. In the rear of the church, Michelangelo filled in the secondary buttresses, not with service ramps, but with a series of rooms known as the *fabbrica*, or archives, of the building. This becomes the equivalent of two five-story office buildings, each of which are served by a small spiral staircase. Each niche and decorative panel in the minor bays corresponding to the fabbrica is pierced with windows that permit natural light to enter all of the five levels as well as the adjacent service stairs.

The interstitial zones held within the tripartite wall act as diaphragms that regulate changes in scale between the exterior and interior as well as varying the amount of light entering the body of the building. Windows are not placed on the outer surface of the

12

12 Santa Maria della Consolazioni, Todi; Cola di Caprarola
13 St. Peter's, Rome; Longitudinal Section; Letarouilly; Antonio da Sangallo, 1539-1546
14 St. Peter's, Rome; View of model; Antonio da Sangallo
15 St. Peter's, Rome; Exterior View of Apse
16 St. Peter's, Rome; Section through Fabrica and Side Aisles

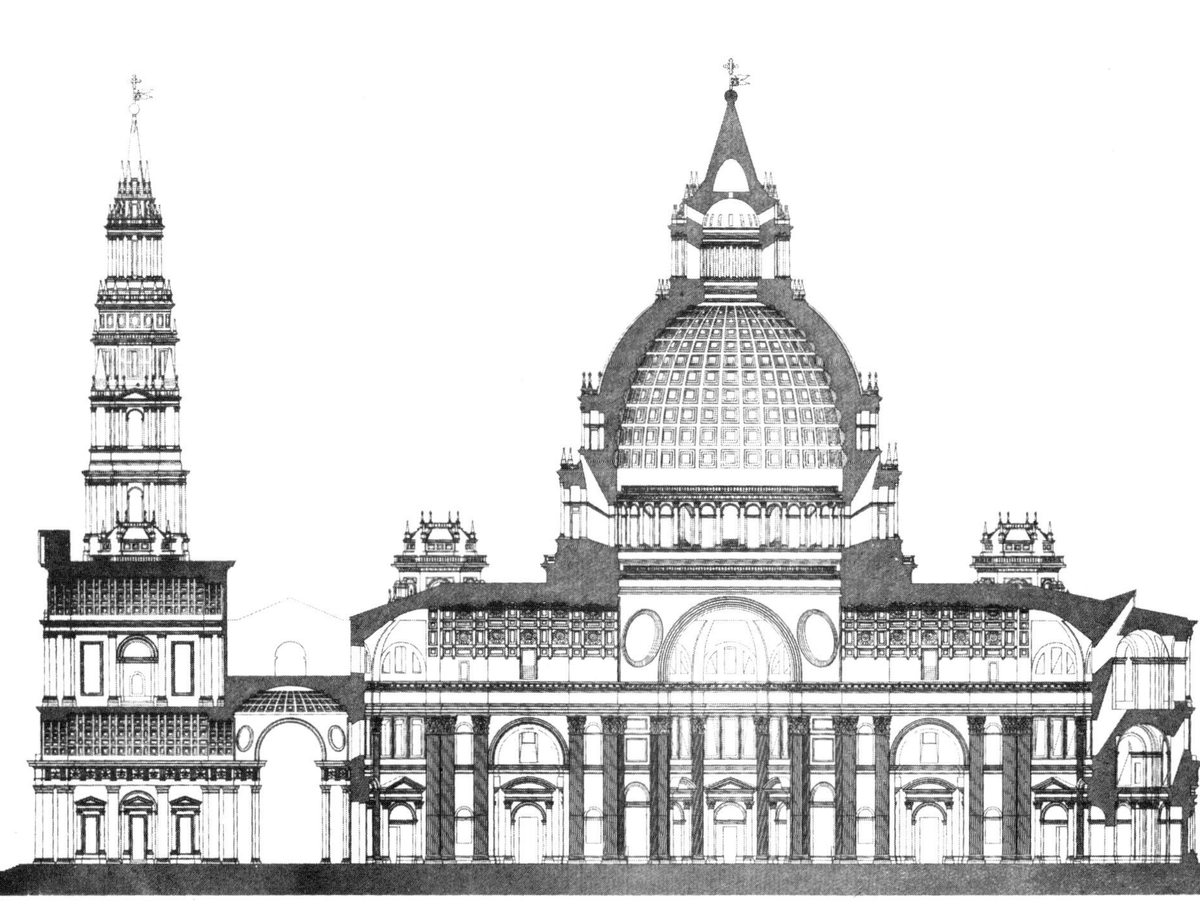

13

14

15

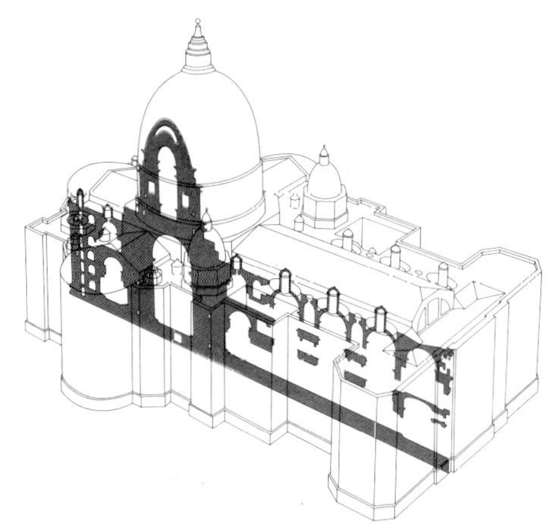

16

facade, but well back into the thickness of the wall. By locating the windows to the back of the service corridors, Michelangelo maintained a plastic freedom in the modeling of the huge sculptural openings on the facade, which the window frames might have compromised. This also allowed the actual glazed areas to be reduced to the smaller scale of the inner openings. The deep sockets that puncture the apses have splayed walls that permit the recentering of the principal openings on the separate rotund surfaces of the interior and exterior. Set within the depth of the wall and operable from the service corridors, the windows remain flat and change their size and shape in accordance with internal requirements. Because of drastic changes in the scale of the assorted chapels that line the sides of the church, the service passages and internal windows slide up and down within the wall without distracting from the overall unity of the facade. This slippage can be seen by comparing the internal areas of various sculpted wall sockets contained in the major bays.

While the rooms and passageways in the walls of St. Peter's are contained within a thick masonry corset, it is possible to achieve similar effects by implication. Sir John Soane's Museum at Lincoln's Inn Fields has complex layerings of thin walls that group bands of major and minor space together to orchestrate rich sequences of interwoven volumes. This sandwiching of space is emphasized by the front facade, which grafts an additional layer of space onto the face of the building as an extension of the internal layerings. At a larger scale, the loggia along the north side of the Governor's Court at Soane's Bank of England creates an outdoor passage similar to those in the walls of St. Peter's. Furthermore, the loggia is articulated as a punched window wall rather than a colonade. It is as though the inner facade had been sliced off from its glazing and pulled outwards to capture the space of the loggia between.

Although Soane's walls simulate thickness by layering, grafting, and, perhaps, telescopic means, they do not quite approximate the unified quality of the wall at St. Peter's. Soane's work delights in play and multiplicity. Each part of the composition is expressed in

17

18

19

20

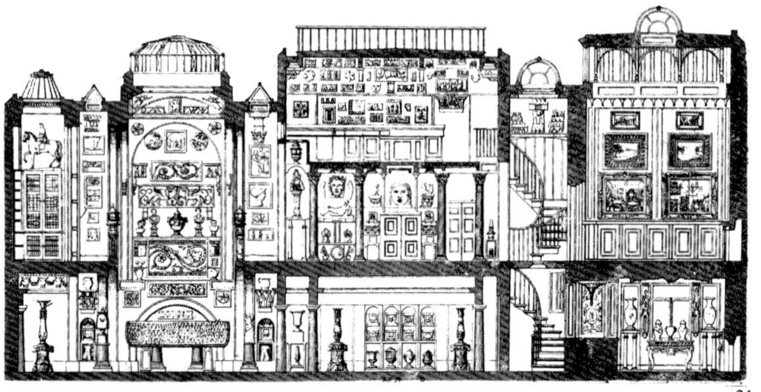

21

22

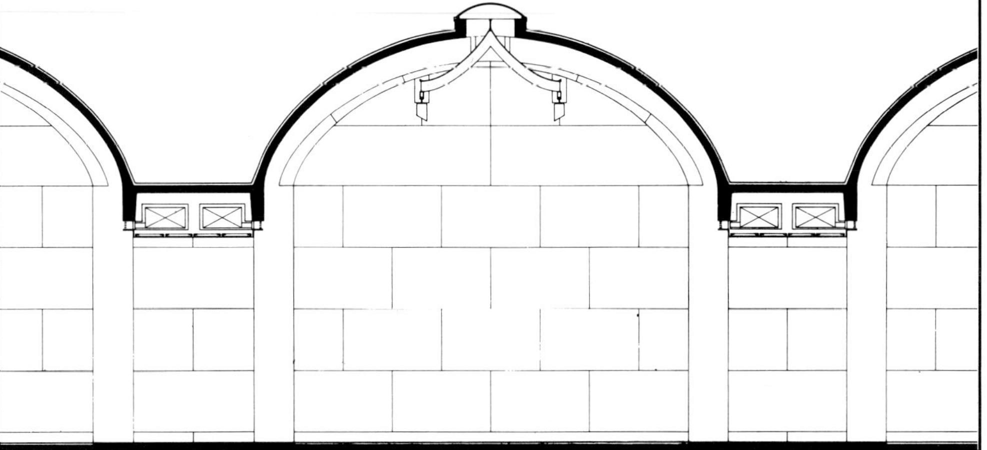

23

17 St. Peter's, Rome; Detail of Interior Window
18 St. Peter's, Rome; Detail of Exterior Window of Apse
19 Bank of England, London; View of Governor's Court Loggia; Sir John Soane, 1804-1805
20 Lincoln's Inn Fields, London; View of Facade; Sir John Soane, 1792-1825
21 Lincoln's Inn Fields, London; Longitudinal Section of Museum
22 Lincoln's Inn Fields, London; Section through Breakfast Room
23 Kimbell Art Museum, Ft. Worth; Section, Louis Kahn, 1967-1972
24 Kimbell Art Museum, Ft. Worth; Plan
25 Trenton Bath House; Plan; Louis Kahn, 1954-1959
26 Trenton Bath House; View

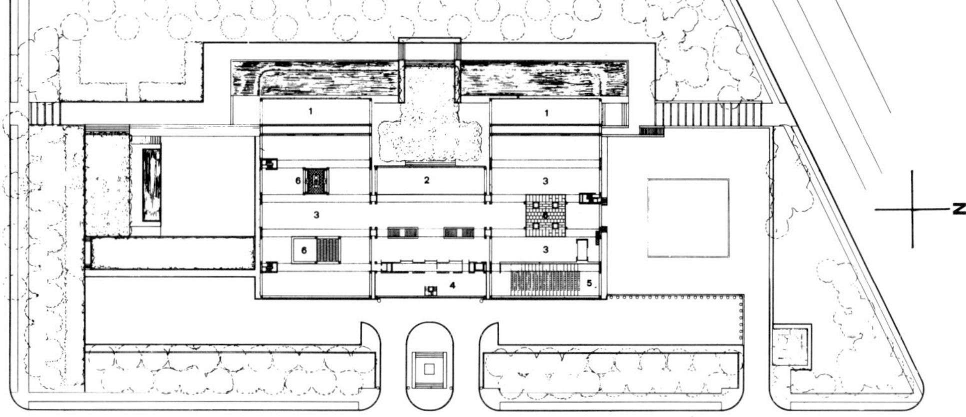

24

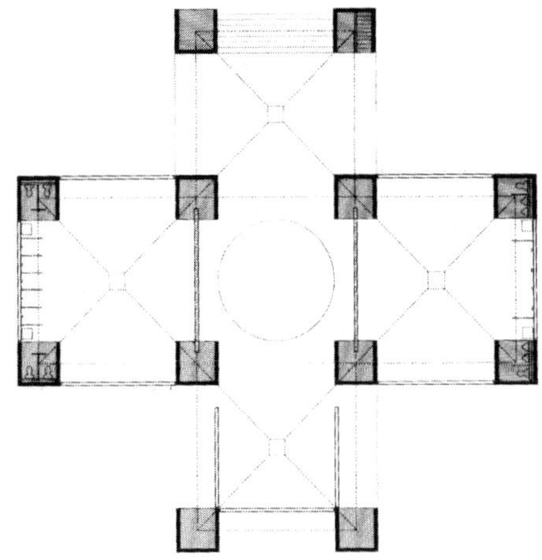

25

26

an extremely assertive way. In Michelangelo's wall this kind of diversity is subsumed within the overall packaging of the whole. The spaces in the wall hardly exert their presence. Instead, they are subordinate to the powerful order of the wall itself, fitting neatly into an overall framework. The wall, then, remains a singular element whose internal organizations are of a more calm and subtle nature.

The work of Louis Kahn also exhibits an interest in interstitial space as an elaboration of the notion of "served" and "servant" spaces. The Kimbell Art Museum, for instance, with its three adjoining units of layered major and minor space punctuated by courtyards and covered by extensive roof monitors, is like a restrained version of Soane's Museum. The vaulted rooms and adjacent low "servant" spaces are not dissimilar in section to Soane's Breakfast Room. However, whereas Soane detaches his dome from the walls along the interstitial zones to flood light around the edges of the room, Kahn infills the top of the interstitial space with an air plenum and opens instead the ends of his vaults with a glazed slot as an expression of the vault's structural independence from the end walls.

If Kimbell suggests a simplified parti of Soane's Museum, Kahn's earlier Trenton Bath House could be a diagram for St. Peter's. Although the marble revetment and fenestration of St. Peter's are not mirrored in the blank concrete block of the Bath House, the hollow piers are somewhat analogous to the minor bays at St. Peter's. These portions of the perimeter wall are not understood as thin facades but as three-dimensional structural forms that absorb service spaces and transition passageways. In turn, these "piers" frame larger areas of intervening wall that have a more direct relationship to the interior volumes. Consequently, both thick wall and thin become equally meshed in the definition of the exterior and interior.

In Kahn's Bryn Mawr Dorms the three main halls are wrapped by a thick wall comprised of student rooms. Like Sangallo's ambulatories the continuous outer circuit remains detached from the inner volumes, which receive light only through roof monitors. The composite wall of his Exeter Library is more consciously integrated and contains some of the characteristics of sectional scale shifting found in the wall at St. Peter's. Kahn thought of the library as a "sanctuary of books and ideas" and wrapped all of the functional requirements around a large central hall the full height of the building. The ring surrounding this space is a thick sandwich created by the engagement of two structural systems: an inner doughnut of concrete holding multiple tiers of book stacks and an outer ring of brick containing tall passageways lined by study carrels near the light.[6] The large circular holes in the concrete screen walls that define the scale of the central hall operate with the same freedom as the sculptural openings on the facade of St. Peter's. Detached from the four balconies behind, they not only unify the inner facade but also imply the surface of a thick wall that organizes the multiple scales and varying requirements contained within its depth.

If the analysis of the extensive sectional carving in St. Peter's suggests a Gothic sensibility, quite the opposite is really the case. Gothic construction turns the wall inside out, pulling the structure to the outside of the building in the form of external buttressing. Both St. Peter's and the Exeter Library not only contain the structure within the body of the building, but capture space within its interstices. The outer brick wall at Exeter, for example, is internally buttressed, the space between providing the passageways lined by study carrels. And while a Gothic church gives up interest in continuous facade articulation for the infill of vast areas of glass, the basilica not only elaborates the wall surface, but with the addition of domes and lanterns extends fenestration over the roof. The dome's circular drum contains a variation on the major and minor bay system with coupled columns surrounding an outer arcade with large windows set between. Above, the dome and lantern become the natural conclusion of an object building's vertical axis. Furthermore, the numerous minor domes and lanterns on the roof are fascinating supplements to equivalent openings in the wall surface.

Unlike the usual profile of a basilica, with its high nave and lower side aisles, the outer

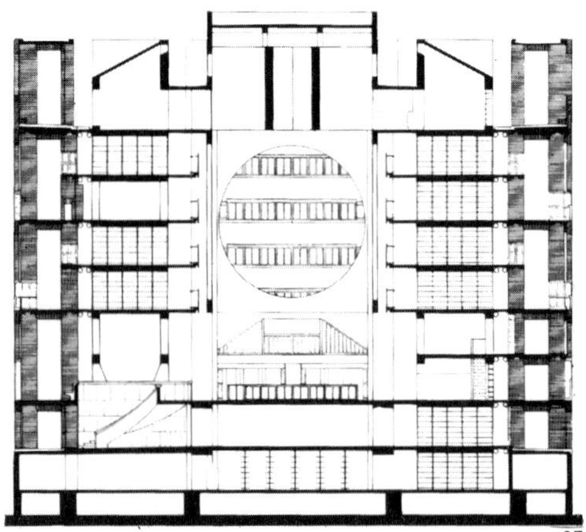
27

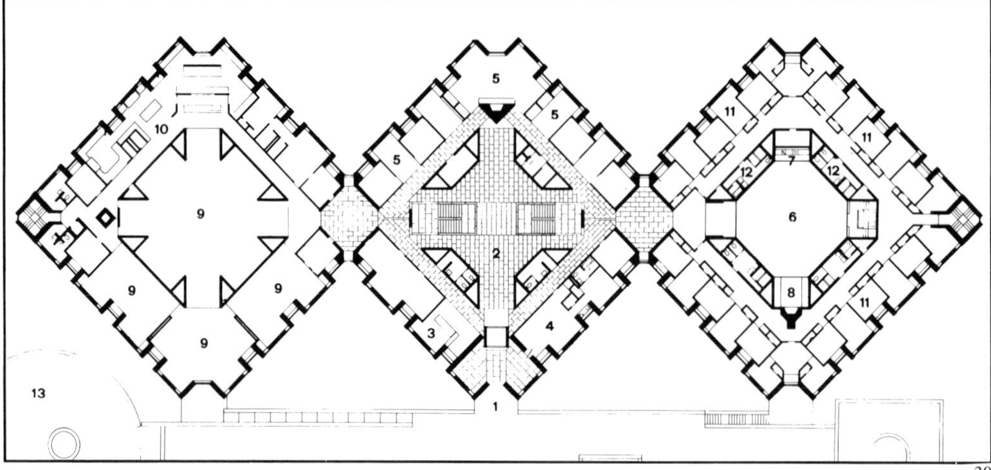
30

28

29

31

27 Exeter Library; Section; Louis Kahn, 1967-1972
28 Exeter Library; Central Hall
29 Exeter Library; Reading Areas along periphery
30 Bryn Mawr dormitories; Plan; Louis Kahn, 1960-1965
31 St. Peter's, Rome; View of Roof; Letarouilly
32 St. Peter's, Rome; Section through Corner Domes and Capella del Coro
33 St. Peter's, Rome; Cross Section of Chapels Along Maderno's Nave
34 St. Peter's, Rome; Interior of Basilica; Giovanni Paolo Pannini, 1691-1765

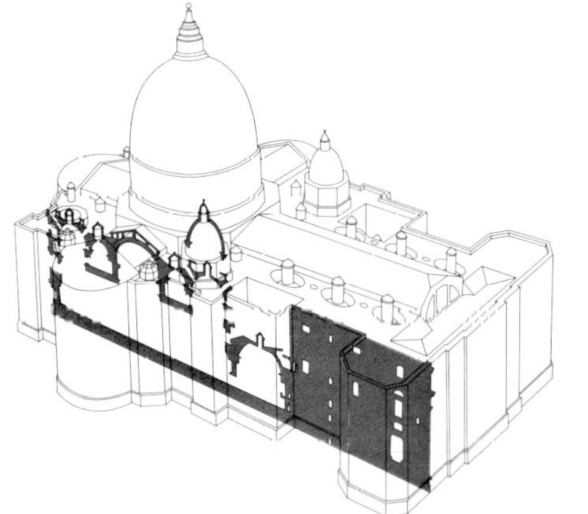

32

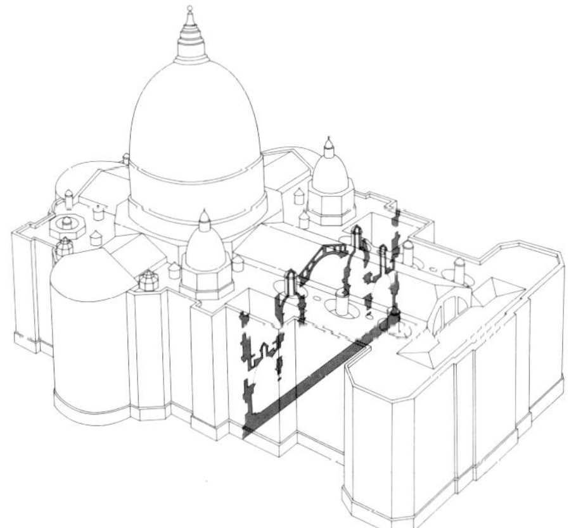

33

34

walls of St. Peter's wrap the basilica at the height of the nave without any indication of the side aisles and the many small chapels that line its central core. This extension in the height of the wall complicates the ability of the interior to receive multiple sources of light. Consequently the roof has been carved and manipulated in such a way as to resemble the walls of the church turned sideways. Roof openings alternately light major spaces the height of the church and the network of interstitial rooms held above smaller scaled elements. The four corners of Michelangelo's plan are capped by domes that are consumed within the body of the church. Light provided by small central lanterns is supplemented by a series of rondels carved into the vaulted surfaces of each dome. The drums to these captive domes have windows that borrow additional light from the adjacent octagonal rooms that occupy space above the barrel vaults. The purely decorative domes provided by Giacomo della Porta hover over two of these assemblages.

At the juncture of Maderno's addition are two depressions that facilitate the illumination of two chapels set deep within the church, and reveal more of the openings that would have been along Michelangelo's outer circuit. Since these chapels sit along the perimeter of the building, the facades that travel by these carved out areas become mere screens. As it is on the south side of the church, the Capella del Coro's dome receives some sunlight through the opening in this screen wall. The Santissmo Sacramento, however, resorts to other means. It has a taller lantern extension to compensate for its northern position, and the southern edge of this deep pit has been carved back to allow more light to penetrate. The complex carving that encircles Maderno's nave displays many instances of sectional reciprocity that allow light into a number of spaces at once. For example, the outer surfaces of the sunken domes over the side aisles are complemented by the locations of windows puncturing the sides of the nave, while a sloped roof drain over the vault of the Benedictine Loggia permits vast quantities of light to flood the body of the nave. The extent of these shapings can be appreciated in Pannini's paintings of the interior which display the continuous spatial readings once permitted by openings in the interstitial spaces above the aisles.[7]

A general disregard for the thick wall stems from the misguided belief that thickness necessarily decreases the relation of the interior and exterior while inevitably increasing the material cost of a structure. Yet what distinguishes the wall at St. Peter's is not its physical thickness but the capacity of the thick wall to act as an organizational device, weaving a complex program into one coherent structure whose spatial connections are both generous and dramatic. With regards to cost, the voluminous wall, by containing space within its interstices, need not have actual material thickness. As at Exeter, the wall is perceived mostly as open volume, not solid mass. Even the hollow space within the wall does not need to be hidden or filled up with unseen storage closets and forgotten space, but can be more openly exploited. The hollow walls at Alvar Aalto's Imatra Church modulate both light and acoustics while incorporating structural columns and the sliding panels that can divide the church into three separate rooms. Because the internal glazing is more expansive than that of the exterior, the sliding panels remain visible even while being stored, acknowledging them as an integral element in understanding the tripartite form of the building.

Le Corbusier's diagram of the "Four Compositions" could be modified to provide another description of the voluminous wall, while comparing it with other types of building organization. In the first diagram the whole is understood in terms of the parts. Each part is a separate episode; each exhibits a specialized shape and section. The composition remains a series of combined fragments, a collage. It is analogous to a book of short stories, each interesting in itself, but perhaps not adding up to a complete novel. The second diagram could be seen as representing complexity and contradiction, a building that presents one thing on the outside only to contrast it with another in favor of the difficult whole.[8] Consequently, the relation of the interior to the exterior or to the space in between may be of little or no consequence. The undu-

35

36

37

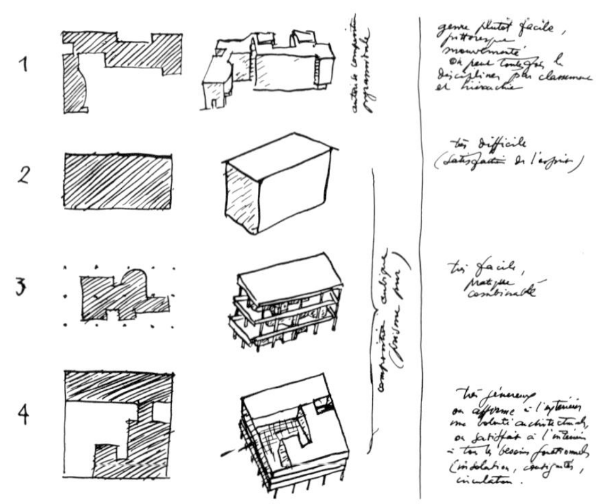

38

35 St. Peter's, Rome; Detail of Cross Section of Elliptical Chapel; Letarouilly
36 St. Peter's, Rome; Model; Spencer Kass
37 Imatra Church, Vuoksenniska; Interior View; Alvar Aalto, 1957-1959
38 Four Compositions; Le Corbusier, 1935
39 St. Peter's, Rome; Model
40 St. Peter's, Rome; Partial Section, Martino Ferrabasco, 1634

39

40

lating ceiling of the lecture hall in Aalto's Vipuri Library, for instance, stands in marked contrast to the building's box-like exterior and to the repetitive window fenestration along the room's edge.[9] It is comparable to a mystery novel whose surprise ending may not follow from the given clues. The third diagram indicates the dissolution of both facade and section in favor of the liberties of the free plan. The wall is diminished to a dotted line of columns; the cantilevered slab exhibits the only vestiges of wall poche. It remains more an outline than a complete story. Yet, it is the fourth diagram, that of the Villa Savoye, that approximates the characteristics of the voluminous wall found at St. Peter's. At Savoye we are no longer presented with a series of discrete components wrapped by an external skin, but with a matrix of space that occurs between the circulation ramp, which rises the full height of the structure, and the outer facade. The screen walled terraces on the first floor result when portions of this matrix are selectively removed. This allows the living room and main ramp to be extensively glazed without any disruption to the continuity of the facade. Additionally, the surface of the terrace is dotted with skylights that illuminate spaces below.[10] Like the many domes atop St. Peter's, the rounded forms of the rooftop solarium enhance the vertical axis and activate the building more completely as an object in the round. The formal synthesis of Savoye resembles the dense novel whose plot and characters unfold page by page, chapter by chapter, into an orchestrated network of interwoven ideas.

The voluminous wall, then, like the novel, cannot be judged solely by its cover. Its facade is more than skin deep. It fuses plan, section, and elevation, permitting the classification of internal complexity without external distortion. Assembling a series of sections cut through St. Peter's reveals a record of the voluminous wall; a simultaneous reading of interior and exterior that exposes the interstitial space as a three-dimensional connective matrix. Its significance extends beyond consummate packaging by supplementing the art of the plan with a virtuosity of section which, in turn, enhances the integration of the facade with the fabric of the building. ■

Viennese Facades Between 1890 and 1910

Werner Goehner

The facades following this article are the work of the 1982 Cornell Summer Studio in Vienna, Austria.

1 Köstlergasse 3, 1898-1899
2 Looshaus, 1910
3 Haus Portois & Fix, 1899
4 Schottenring 23, 1877
5 Zacherlhaus, 1903-1905
6 Häuser Wienzeile, 1898-1899
7 Ankerhaus, 1895
8 Palais Wagner, 1889-1890
9 Majolika Haus, 1898-1899
10 Artaria Haus, 1910

" 'Artis sola domina necessitas.' No less a person than Gottfried Semper has directed our attention to this truth."

Otto Wagner
Die Baukunst unserer Zeit

"The work of art is the result of a determined and conscious artistic will, which after a hard struggle overpowers both the sensuous material and the technique."

Alois Riegl
Stilfragen

"We possess the art that has eliminated the ornament."

Adolf Loos
Ornament und Verbrechen

Around the turn of the century, over a span of about twenty years, a fundamental change in the perception and articulation of the vertical building surface occurred in Vienna: a change from round to flat, from eclectic to the 'Expression of our Times,' from High Renaissance to *Neue Sachlichkeit.*

The ten facades discussed here, developed between 1889 and 1910, reflect the revolution of ideas then taking place in the cultural life of Vienna. Although similar phenomena can be observed in other European capitals, the clash between the high bourgeois culture and the newly evolving avant-garde was particularly fierce in Vienna. Only in the "Capital of Decoration," as Hermann Broch dubbed Vienna, would ornament become a crime.

A critical attitude toward ornament is evident as early as the eighteenth century. G. Boffrand, for example, was sharply critical of Rococo designers for their abuse of ornament, especially for placing interior types of ornamentation on building exteriors. Laugier did not reject all ornamentation, but recommended that ornament correspond to building use. He was explicit about the use of orders. Establishing the primitive hut as a model for architecture, Laugier recommended that both the orders and all elements of architecture be used simply and rationally according to their original purpose. He condemned coupled columns, pilasters, and broken, curved, or superimposed pediments.

In the early eighteenth century the Italians Algarotti and Memmo wrote about Carlo Lodoli's ideas for a new and rejuvenated architecture. Lodoli wanted to create a new and better architecture by eliminating from structures everything that did not have a definite function or derive from the strictest necessity. Useless ornament should be forbidden. Anything contradicting these principles, which he regarded as the cornerstones of architecture, was condemned. There should be no architecture that does not conform to the very nature of the material. Not until architecture had attained these objectives would it be honest and reasonable. The influence of those ideas in Vienna can be observed in the work of Joseph Kornhausel (1782–1860). The facades of his buildings in the Seitenstettengasse and of the Schottenhof clearly show a flattening and reduction of architectural and decorative elements.

The writings of these eighteenth century theoreticians illustrate a general attitude toward articulation of the facade. They do not, however, give us the key to understanding the transformation from Otto Wagner's facade of the Apartmenthouse Schottenring 23 (1877) to Adolf Loos' building for Goldman and Salatsch on the Michaelerplatz (1910). That understanding must be sought in Vienna itself.

Two protagonists of the late nineteenth century must be mentioned: Gottfried Semper, a German historian and architect, and Alois Riegl, an Austrian art historian. In his book, *Der Stil in den technischen und tektonischen Künsten oder Praktische Aesthetik,* Semper laid the foundation for a school of thought that maintained that the origin of all human artistic creation lies in making a virtue of necessity and is conditioned by the materials used in its fabrication and the process by which it is made. He also believed that clothing was the primary stimulus for all figuration. Semper understood clothing *(Bekleidung)* not only as protection, but also as adornment for the human body (and he considered tattooing as one of the root phenomena of art[1]).

The materialistic view of the origins of all artistic creation was strongly opposed by Riegl. In his view, the artist could not be thought of as conditioned by the materials and techniques of manufacture, but only by his intellectual horizon and artistic impulse. In his book, *Stilfragen*, Riegl writes, "There is something in man which makes him feel pleasure in the beauty of form, something which neither we nor the follower of the theory of the technical material origin of art are able to define." Later he continues, "I am the first—as far as I know—to have proposed an hypothesis according to which the work of art is the result of a determined and conscious artistic will, which after a hard struggle, overpowers both the sensuousness of material and technique." This concept of the artistic impulse was further developed by Riegl into the concept of *Kunstwollen*, or will to form, a formal imperative transcending the individual artist.

Let us now return to Wagner and Loos, whose works exemplify the changes in articulation of the vertical surface in Vienna between 1890 and 1910. Wagner is obviously still rooted in Semper's concepts, for he says that "something unpractical cannot be beautiful" and, "The composition always has to yield to the material and to technology and not vice versa. The composition must clearly consider the building material and the building technology."[2]

In 1895, when his book, *Moderne Architektur*, was published, Otto Wagner was a successful architect who had received commissions for many buildings in connection with the development of the Ringstrasse. His personal interpretation of historical styles is clearly evident in the two residential buildings at Schottenring 23 (1877) and Rennweg 3 (1889). In the first building he still uses the classical division of the facade: a two-story base, a two-story main facade, and an unusual one-story cornice. The center is accentuated not only by the sizes of the windows, but also by the use of color: red terracotta lines the windows and red triangular wall patterns. The pylons on the sides document the individuality of the building. Emphasizing the horizontal, the overall articulation is sculptural yet restrained when compared with the buildings on either side.

In the four-story *palais* on Rennweg, Wagner provides us with another example of the endless variations on the classical tripartite division of the facade. The main floor, which sits on a one-story base, is articulated by two deep loggias on the sides as well as by single and double pilasters that support an architrave. In contrast to this classical language for the base and *piano nobile*, with its skeletal appearance, the two upper floors appear as a flat wall with Baroque and late Rococo motifs: round windows and stucco garlands and trophies. The surprising characteristic of this facade is the clash of classical and Baroque motifs. The Baroque had just begun to be rehabilitated by Wickhoff and Riegl.

In the facade for the Graben 10 Ankerhaus (1895), Wagner followed two principles that he had articulated that year in *Moderne Architektur*: the primacy of utility and the use of modern materials in terms of their inherent properties. A strong band of glass and iron placed in front of the load-bearing structure delineates the first two floors as commercial space. This principle of the separation of the load-bearing element from the enclosing element is considered to be the beginning of the 'curtain wall.'[3] The attic is used as a photography studio and is composed of pyramidal and spherical structures made of iron and glass. Despite the introduction of modern materials for the base, the facade for the office space above still shows the old, eclectic diction; it is heavily articulated and sculptured as appropriate for an insurance company. In addition to the principle of structural honesty, that of functional honesty dictated that the residential and commercial functions could no longer be hidden behind a Neo-Renaissance facade, as Wagner had done in his earlier houses, such as on the Stadiongasse.

The real break in the treatment of the vertical surface came with Wagner's two apartment houses on the Linke Wienzeile (1898–99), helped by the advent of the Secession (1897) with its strong anti-historical attitude ("to the era its proper art, to art its proper freedom"). Above the two stories that house commercial functions, which are articulated in a way similar to the Ankerhaus iron and glass structure, the residential area is represented by a flat wall rather than by one that is heavily articulated and indented. Ornament recedes into and is absorbed by the wall. The wall emphasizes its primary function as a wall. Its additional function as carrier of meaning is dealt with by graphics. Clarification of the tectonic has been abandoned with plastic elements restricted to the surface. Where one would usually find *chiaroscuro* one finds flat, colored, ornamental designs. In the case of the Linke Wienzeile 40 apartment house, the majolica tile surface, from the third level upwards, depicts a rose tree. The traditional repertoire of vertical surface treatments was enlarged by shifting the formal values from plastic to chromatic, from *chiaroscuro* to color, from the three-dimensional to the flat, or as Riegl would say, from the tactile to the optical.

In his later facades—the station on the Karlsplatz, the Schützenhaus (1906-07), and the Postsparkasse (1904–10)—Wagner transcends the decorative, naturalistic, and symbolic ornamentation of the Secession and arrives at an aesthetic in his facades that originates in the process of building rather than from history. In the station on the Karlsplatz the walls are paneled with large thin marble panels, reducing the structure to lines. In the other buildings the walls are clothed with thick marble plates attached with round aluminum bolts.

Despite his technical innovations and his use of modern materials Otto Wagner was still rooted in Semper's insistence on the conceptual separation of structure and material from the "clothing of the wall." The artistic element is thus confined to the decorative and ornamental.[4]

Another aspect that characterizes Wagner's facades is that they are conceived of in relation to a viewer placed in urban space. The facades are consciously seen as determining and qualifying urban space and even the silhouette of the city. The plasticity of the profiles and ornaments is, in his view, directly influenced by the surrounding urban space. In his book, *Moderne Architektur*, Wagner writes:

> The composing architect has to pay attention to the perspective effect; that is, he has to organize silhouette, mass distribution, the projection of the cornice, interpenetrations, the

11

12

13

14

11 Schottenhof; Josef Kornhausel, 1827
12 Schottenring 23; Otto Wagner, 1877
13 Stadiongasse; View of Facade; Otto Wagner
14 Palais Wagner; Otto Wagner, 1889-1890
15 Ankerhaus; Perspective View; Otto Wagner, 1895

15

plasticity of the profiles and ornaments, etc. in such a way that they appear in the right accentuation from one viewpoint. This point will naturally be always the one point from which the work can be seen most often, most easily, and naturally. Almost every monument shows the importance which their creators have given to this phenomenon; there are examples (Chiesa di San Pietro in Montorio by Bramante) in which the architect created limited viewing distances in order to force the viewer to perceive their work in a particular way. Buildings on narrow streets have to be profiled totally differently, with more shallow ornamentation and more delicate structure than those on wide streets and squares or than those buildings which serve as a distant visual accentuation.[5]

In his apartment house on the corner of Linke Wienzeile and Köstlergasse, Wagner responds to the increased viewing distance on the Wienzeile by differentiating the first two commercial floors of a glass-iron structure from the upper two residential floors, with their flat medallion and gold-leaf ornamentation. On the Köstlergasse, Wagner responds to the decreased viewing distance of the narrow, quiet residential floors, which lack the gold-leaf ornamentation of the Wienzeile side. The whole facade of the Köstlergasse is quieter and more traditionally unified. Similar differentiation in the treatment of vertical surfaces due to their viewing distances can be observed in the Ankerhaus on am Graben and Spiegelgasse and the Postal Savings Bank, with the main entry facing a little square off the Ringstrasse.

Interesting variations and further developments in reducing the wall to a flat surface, or clothing the wall, can be found in buildings done by students of Wagner. Josef Plečnik's independent interpretation of clothing the wall can be studied in his Zacherlhaus (1903). Using polished granite as cladding material, the wall takes on an almost metallic appearance. Within a strong tripartite division of the facade, the uppermost residential floor and the attic floor are unified by the expressionistic language of the sculptural elements. Max Fabiani's facade for the house for Portois and Fix (1903), Ungargasse 59, is a further development of Wagner's Majolikahaus facade. Here again the ornamentation is absorbed by the wall surface—small pyrogranite tiles—yet the theme of the ornamentation is not naturalistic but abstract and geometric. Certain details of the sculptural element of the cornice as well as the bronze curtains in the upper part of the windows allude to the importance of textile arts in Semper's aesthetic theories and to the influence these theories had on Viennese architects. In the facade of the Kohlmarkt Artaria House (1900) Fabiani goes one step further and completely strips the wall of any ornamentation. Even though Fabiani's roots in the traditional technique of ornamentation are seen in the treatment of all other elements of the house (such as the bay window, cantilevered cornices, and so on) his unadorned wall, free of any additional layer of meaning, could be seen as a precursor of the wall of the Looshaus on the Michaelerplatz ten years later.

In his 1898 article, "Die Potemkinsche Stadt," published in the Session's journal, *Ver Secrum,* Loos fought the Potemkin spirit, which he thought was haunting nineteenth century Vienna: "Whenever I stroll along the Ring, I always feel as if a modern Potemkin had wanted to make somebody believe he had been transported into a city of aristocrats."[6] Going beyond the modern style propogated by the Secession and Wagner, he wanted to remove all style, ornament, and clothing from walls. In his most famous article, "Ornament and Crime," Loos characterizes the formal imperative of his time: "See, the grandeur of our time is that it is incapable of producing a new ornament. We have overcome the ornament....Soon, the streets of the cities will shine like white walls."[7] In another place he denounces the practice of the Secession: "The architect has caused architecture to sink to a graphic art,"[8] clearly alluding to Wagner's residential blocks on the Linke Wienzeile and Max Fabiani's building for Portois and Fix. By excluding architecture from the realm of art, Loos overcame the conceptual split between the technical and artistic, which in the past had reduced artistic phenomena to "applied art" on the facade.

The subsequent translation of his writings into building can be observed in his 1910 house on the Michaelerplatz for Goldman and Salatsch, opposite the Hofburg. Not only did the emperor take offense at the facade—"house without eyebrows" — but it was attacked by the city planning officials and even Loos' colleagues. With his Ankerhaus and the residential blocks on the Linke Wienzeile, Otto Wagner seemed to have found the classical solution for a building with mixed residential and commercial use in the inner city of Vienna. The glass-steel articulation of the commercial base highlights the splendor of the upper residential floors. This is not so in Loos' case; the facade of the upper residential floors is without any representational elements. It is a simple white, flat, stuccoed wall with openings cut out, devoid of any molded ornamentation or abstract geometrical pattern. He considers Vienna a city traditionally made of stuccoed walls and therefore uses stucco for what it is—a skin—and not as a material to imitate stone.

In contrast to the flatness and matter-of-factness of the upper residential floors, the facade of the commercial base is very tactile and plastic, uniting precious material (Cipolino marble) with classical and vernacular architectural elements (Tuscan columns and bay windows). In allusion to the portico of the Michaeler Church, Loos uses four Tuscan columns in the facade on the Michaelerplatz, creating a two-story loggia-like entry hall to the shop. The mezzanine gallery above is articulated through brass bay windows between pillars.

The scale changes from the facade on the square to the side facades on the streets. The motif of the columns of the main portal reappears on the side facade, but this time the columns begin on the mezzanine floor rather than on the ground floor, thus uniting the upper two of the three commercial floors. The articulation of the side facades, which is instrumental to the perspective from Herrengasse and Kohlmarkt to the Michaelerplatz, is as follows: wall-pillar, column, bay window,

16

17

18

19

20

16 Häuser Wienzeile; View of Corner; Otto Wagner, 1898-1899
17 Zacherlhaus; Josef Plecnik, 1903-1905
18 Zacherlhaus; View down Wildpretmarkt
19 Artaria Haus; Detail; Max Fabiani, 1910
20 Portois & Fix; View of the Facade; Max Fabiani, 1899
21 Artaria Haus; View down Kohlmarkt
22 Portois & Fix; View towards the Facade

21

22

column, wall-pillar, and so on. This corresponds to the articulation of the facade of the Michaeler Church, as well as the Hofburg, though on a smaller scale. The effect of this articulation is not derived from any style, but from the column itself. Loos uses the column not within a classical order, but independent of it. He rethinks the formal relationships of column-entablature, column-pillar, column-base, and column-wall. For example, on the side facade, the load-bearing pillars next to the smaller columns and bay window are not separated from the above architrave by a capital, as the classical order requires. In another example, he reverses the expected sequence of pedestal, column, architrave to column, architrave, pedestal, as can be seen in the loggia-like entry hall on the main facade. The architrave is so thin that it is associated with a stretched girder rather than an architecturally classical order.

One has to bear in mind that the smaller columns on the side facade, as well as the four two-story columns on the main facade, are nonstructural, and in fact, these four were the last to be put in place. The true bearing system is a frame, which would have allowed horizontal strip windows on all floors. Loos, however, does not want to show the frame. He fills in the strip windows so that the windows appear as discreet openings in a load-bearing wall. The wall appears, then, to be supported by four large columns that actually do not support anything but themselves. The axes of the pillars of the upper residential floors are not aligned with the axes of the columns of the commercial base, which clearly demonstrates the contradiction between the apparent and actual structural system and violates the "utility" principle of Semper and Wagner. Loos is not interested in structural honesty but rather in playing with the associative structural values of single architectural elements, in this case the column. His concept of honesty or crime is based not on construction but on cultural factors. The discontinuity of the axes from the upper part to the lower part of the facade reveals another contradiction: the additive principle of the rental apartments above contradicts the wholistic compositional principle of the columnated entry hall below. The columnation of the loggia cannot be deduced from the grid of windows of the upper apartments or vice versa.

In Otto Wagner's facades this contradiction never surfaced, for in his book, *Moderne Architektur*, he explains that after adding up all the elements and needs of a program one should manipulate the spaces and their forms so that the result is a clear, axial, and simple solution—an academic plan, or building type as he calls it. In other words, the rental apartments should have been integrated into a compositional whole.

Having freed himself from historicism, replacing it with a strong emphasis on principles of utility and a fervor for new material and technology, in his late work Otto Wagner also arrived at the flat surface. He came to the flat surface through a slow reduction and abstraction of ornament and not by obliterating it completely. Still bound to the tenets of Gottfried Semper, he could never overcome the split between the technical and artistic in which the artistic phenomenon wasted away as applied art on surfaces under the predominance of utility, material, and technology as the major form determinants. Only the new paradigm, formulated by Alois Riegl, that a work of art is the technique and the sensuousness of material, could overcome that split.

Loos' enthusiasm for the new paradigm enabled him to withstand the hostility and criticism leveled against his building on the Michaelerplatz: the contradiction between structure and appearance (structural dishonesty), two-story columns that are not load-bearing (violation of the utility principle), the discontinuity of axes from the residential facade to the commercial facade (additive sum vs. classical whole), and stripping the wall of all meaning. All of this criticism naturally came from those adhering to the old paradigm. On the other hand, the house at the Michaelerplatz has often been interpreted as a precursor of the *Neue Sachlichkeit* and the Modern Movement. To fully agree with that assessment would deny the Looshaus a richness it possesses because of its contradictions and ambiguities that most of the buildings of the *Neue Sachlichkeit* and the modern movement did not achieve.

The Looshaus may be viewed as a built article by Loos. In his pamphlet and *feuilleton*-like diction, Loos' discourse might go like this:

> Look, my dear fellow Viennese and architect colleagues, the centerpiece of architectural discussion in 1910 should no longer be ornament. Architecture will be reduced to a graphic art if this goes on much longer. Should we not try to rejuvenate architecture by concentrating our architectural discourse on the more essential elements of architecture, such as walls, windows, columns, entries, and unembellished material? True, the program, the function, the material, and technology are important, but let's not kid ourselves—we should not be a slave to these aspects. We have a mind, a will to form (ask Alois Riegl), and with it we can use these aspects and make them serve our artistic will. Material that is not bound to an artistic will or concept renders itself independent and becomes superfluous ornament.
>
> The classical language in architecture? This is much too important not to be questioned from time to time. Let's experiment with it and see if we can formulate a new sentence. Since my generation of architects has not been part of the historic movement of the last forty years, we can displace that classical language. Otto Wagner cannot do that because until too recently that was the only language spoken. ■

23

24

25

26

27

23 Looshaus; Detail; Adolf Loos, 1910
24 Looshaus; View as seen from the Hofburg
25 Looshaus; Detail compared to the Hofburg
26 Looshaus; Detail compared to St. Michael
27 Looshaus; View from Michaelerplatz

Vienna, Austria; 1910

1 Köstlergasse 3, 1898-1899
2 Looshaus, 1910
3 Haus Portois & Fix, 1899
4 Schottenring 23, 1877
5 Zacherlhaus, 1903-1905
6 Häuser Wienzeile, 1898-1899
7 Ankerhaus, 1895
8 Palais Wagner, 1889-1890
9 Majolika Haus, 1898-1899
10 Artaria Haus, 1910

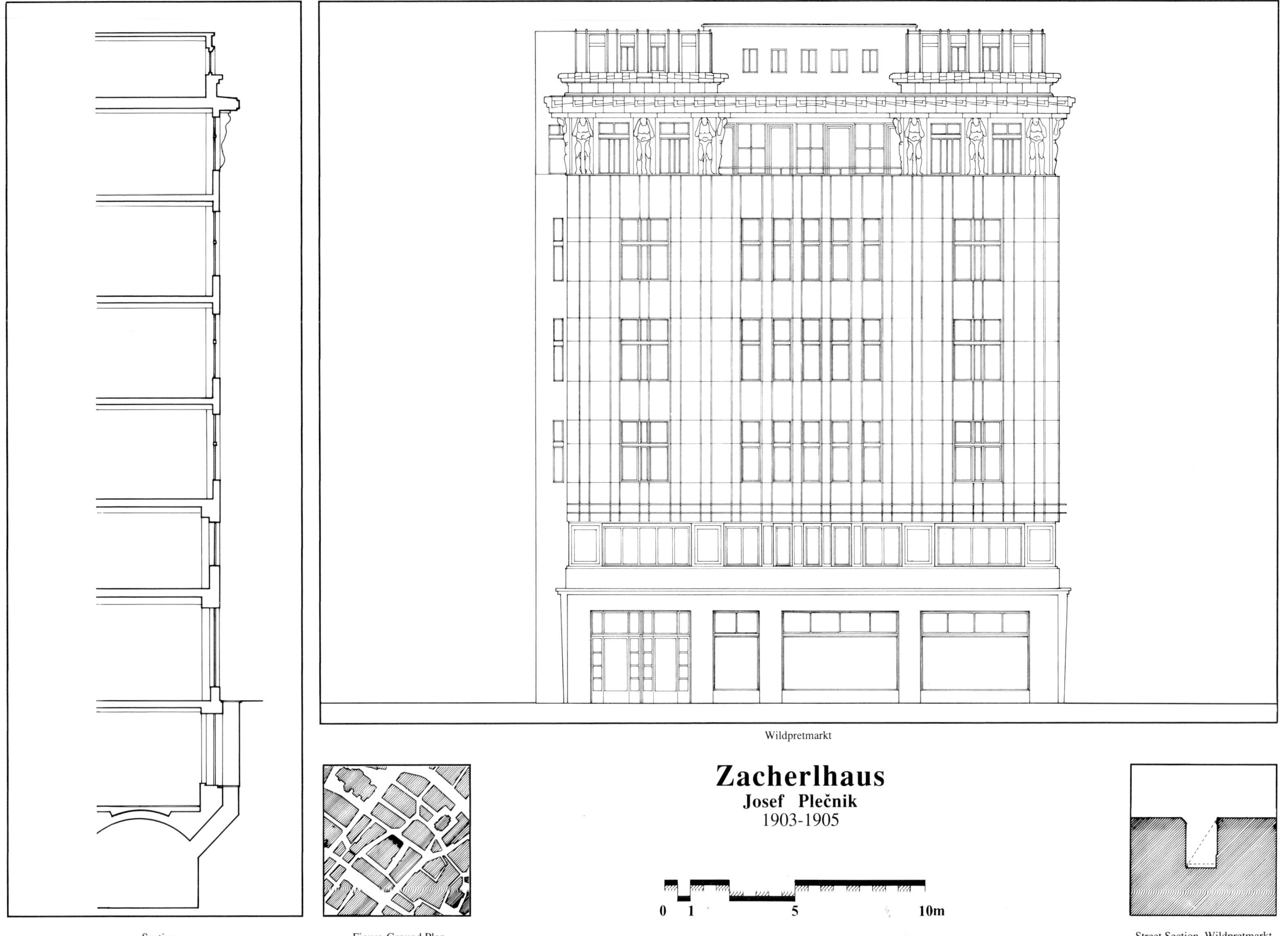

Section

Figure-Ground Plan

Street Section, Wildpretmarkt

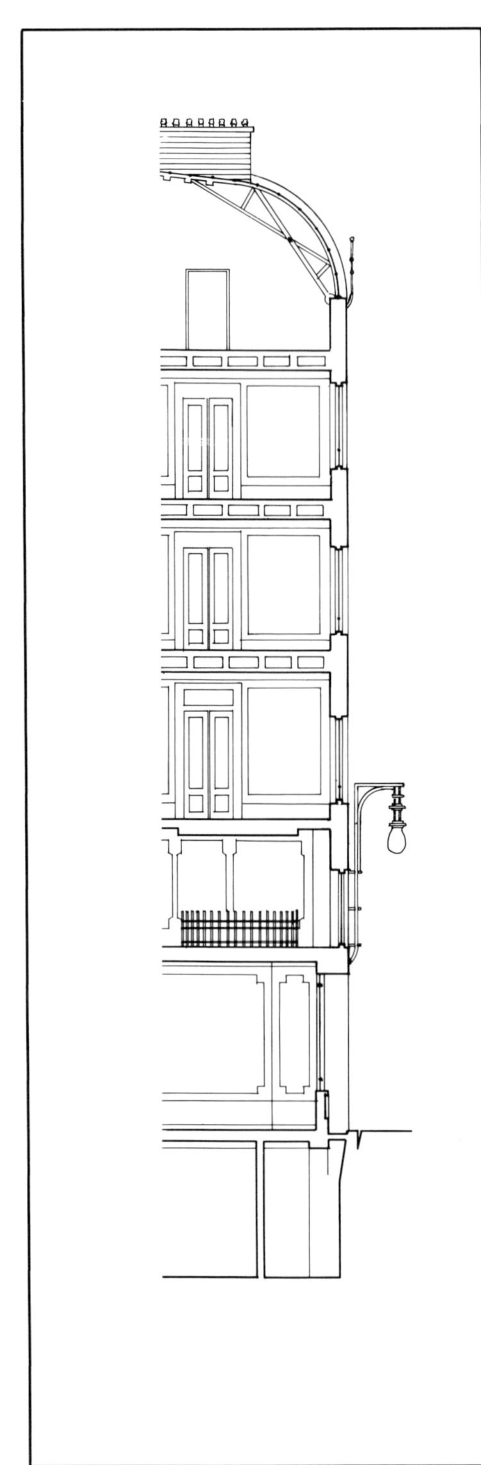

Section

Ungargasse

Haus Portois & Fix

Max Fabiani

1899

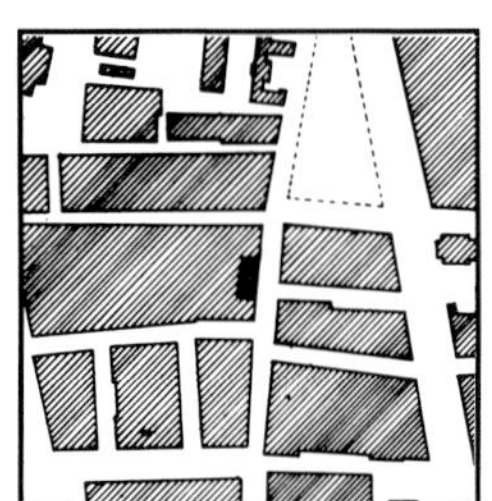

Figure-Ground Plan

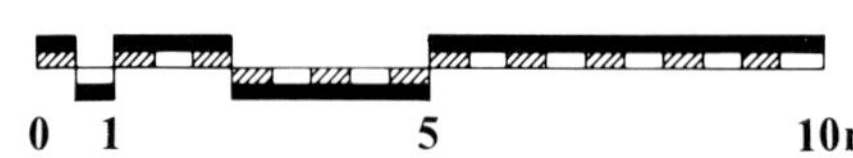

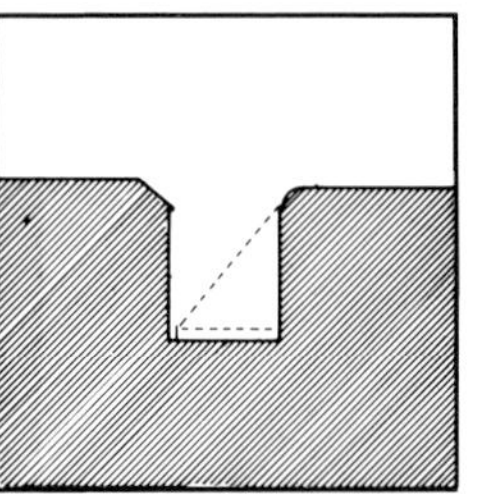

Street Section, Ungargasse

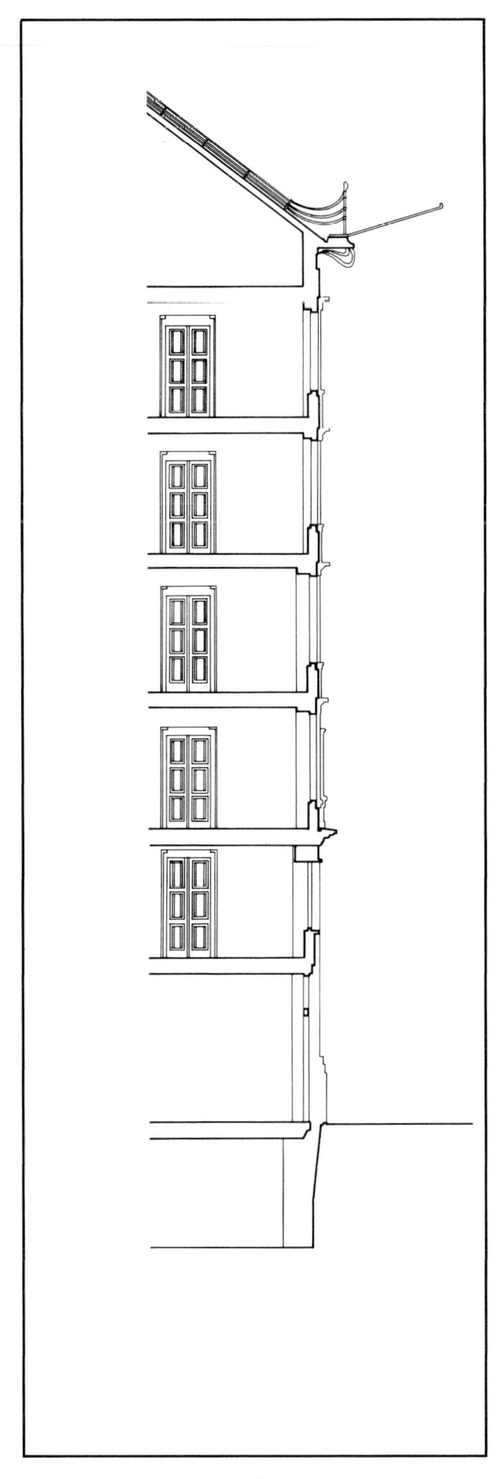

Section

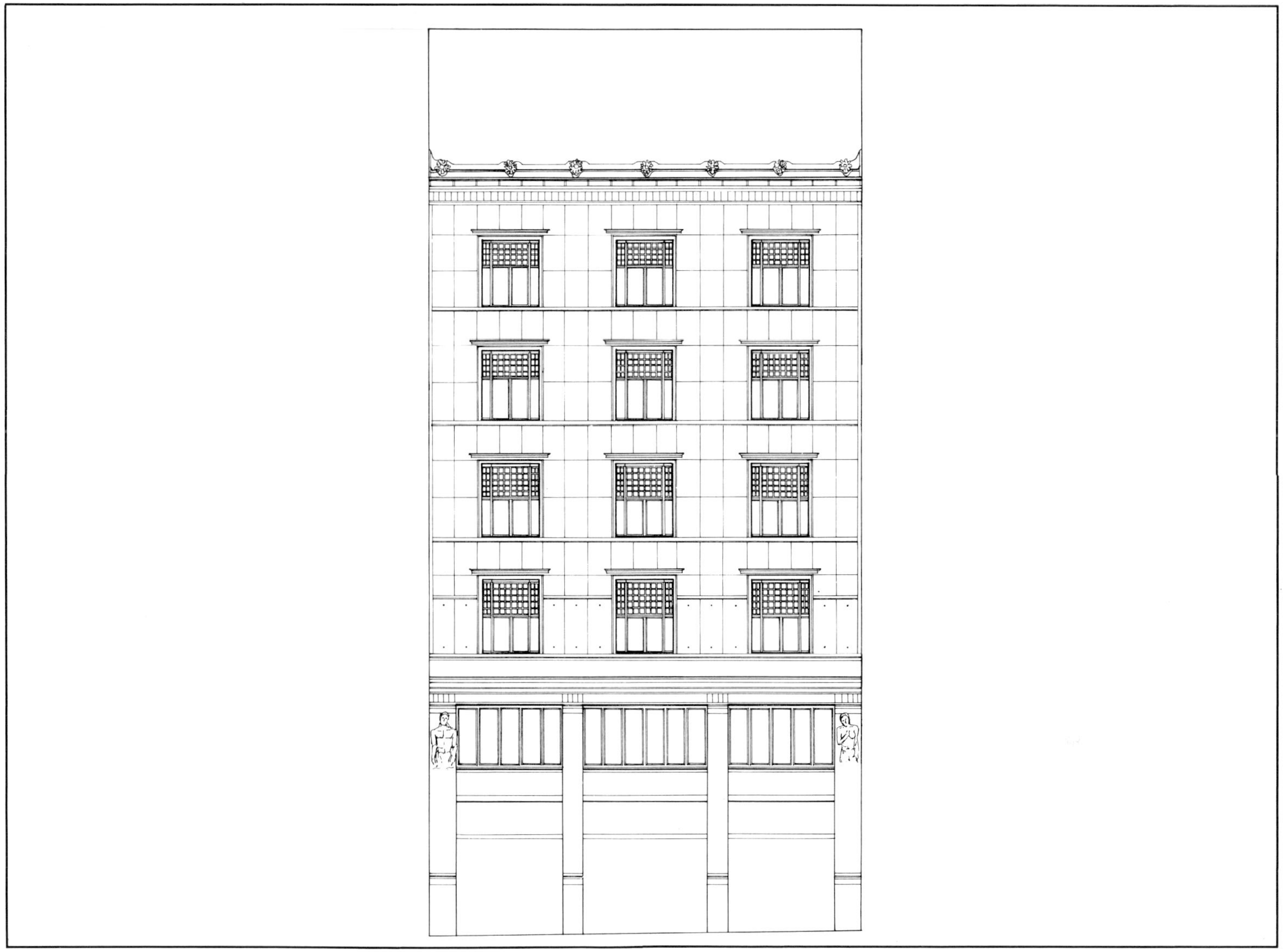

Kohlmarkt 9

Artaria Haus

Max Fabiani

1910

Figure-Ground Plan

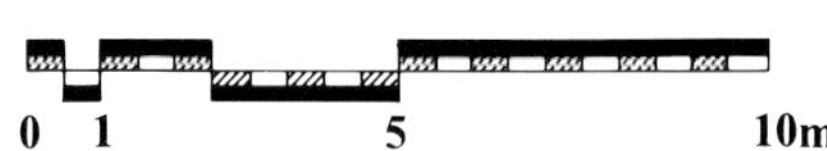

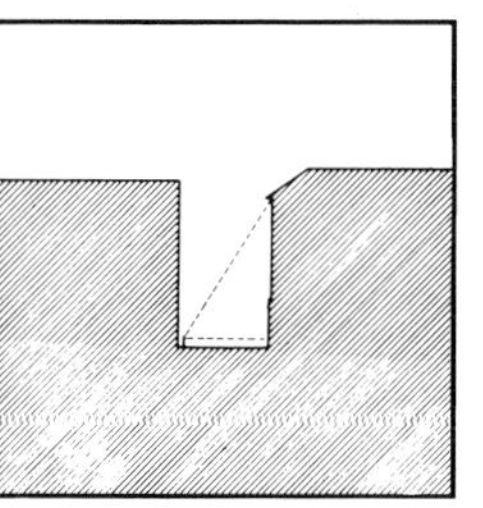

Street Section, Kohlmarkt

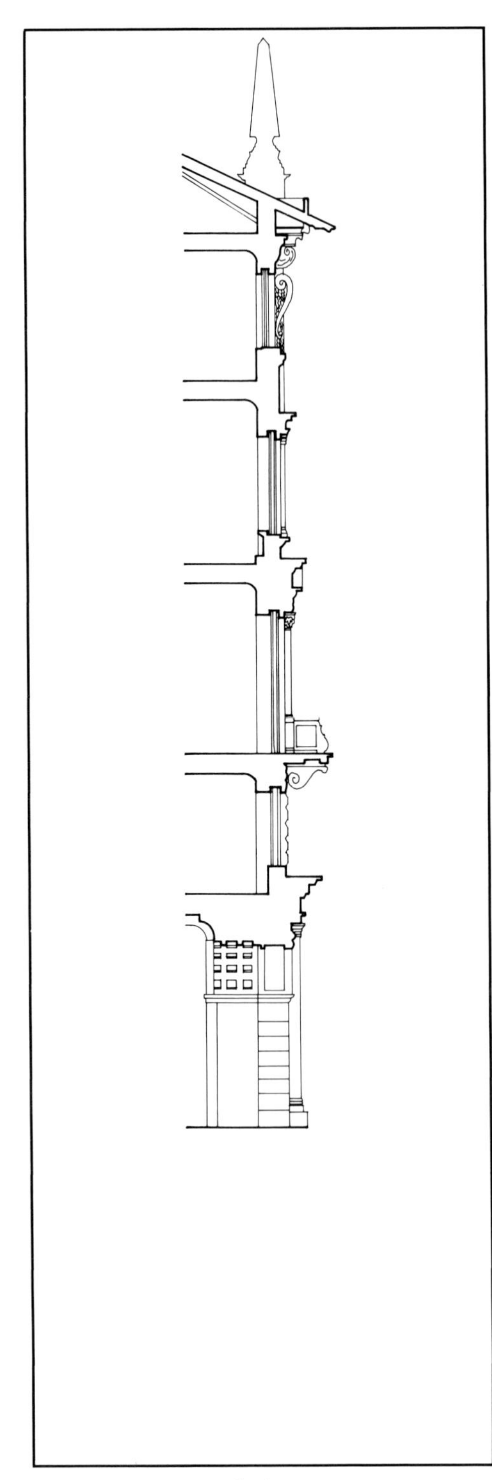

Section

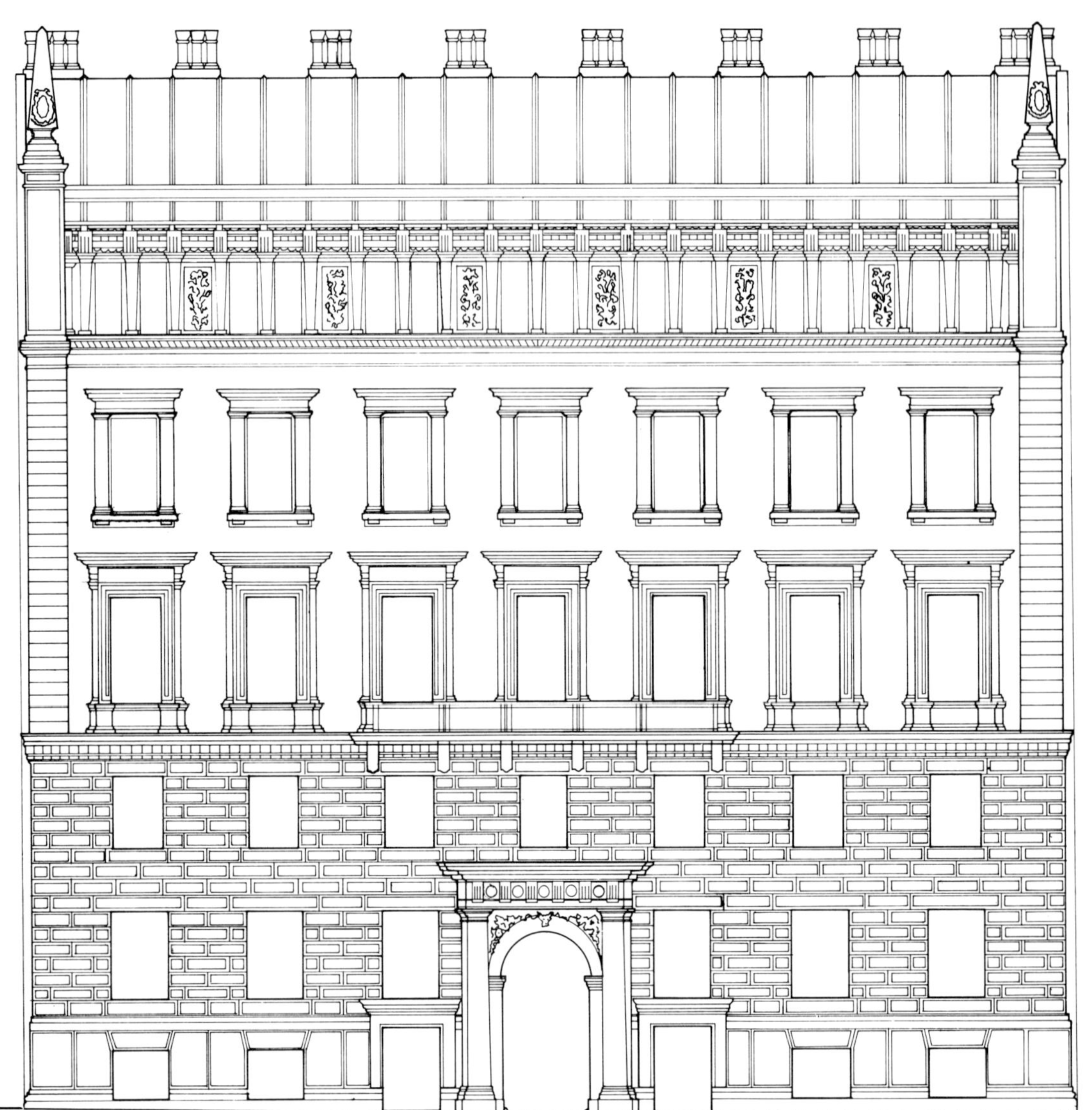

Schottenring 23

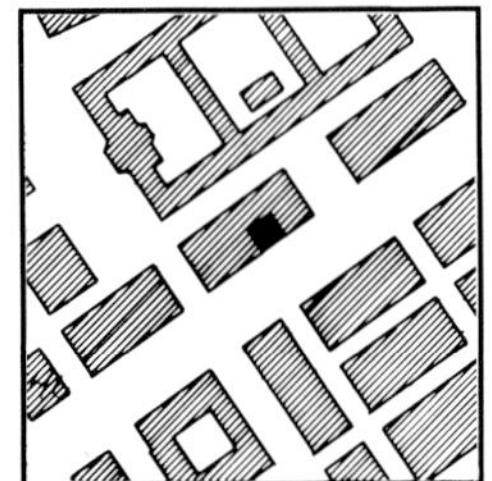

Figure-Ground Plan

Schottenring 23

Otto Wagner

1877

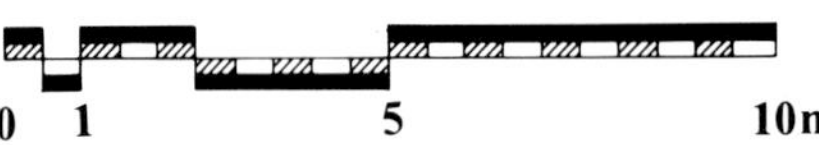

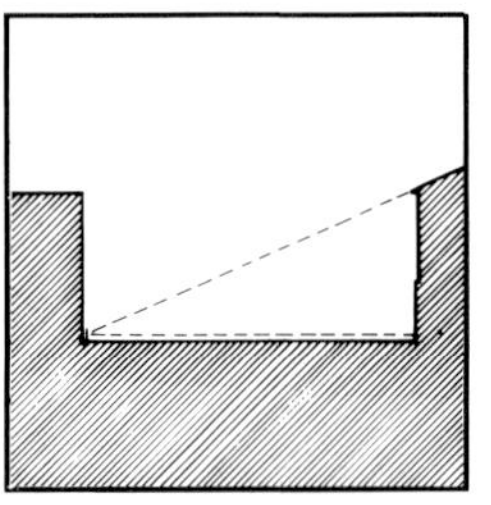

Street Section, Schottenring

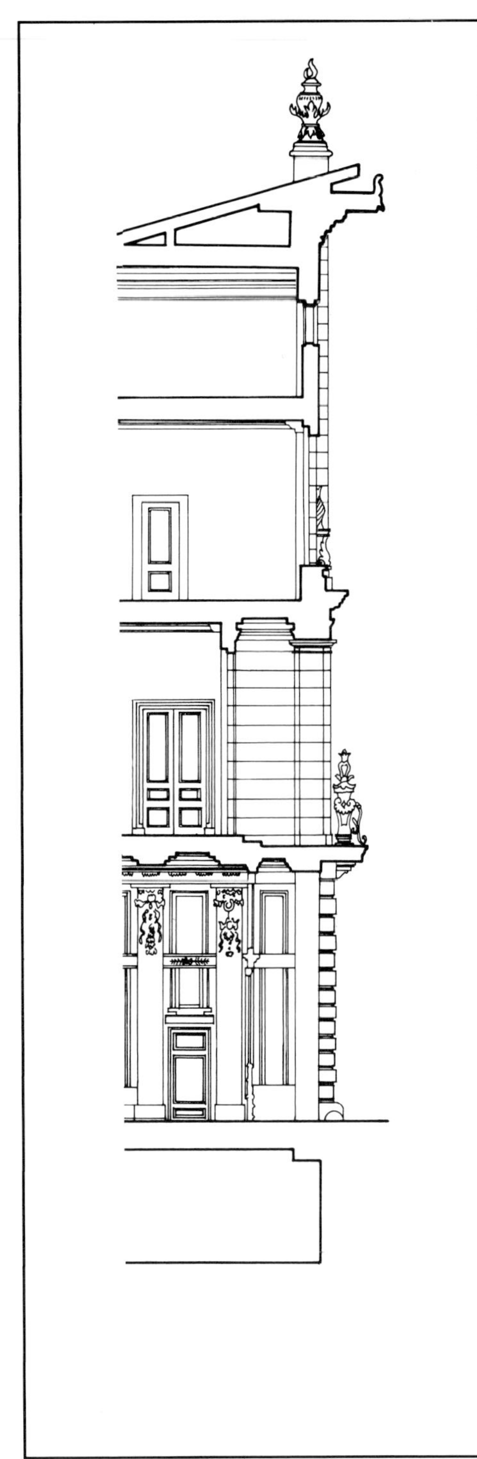

Section

Rennweg 3

Figure-Ground Plan

Palais Wagner

Otto Wagner

1889-1890

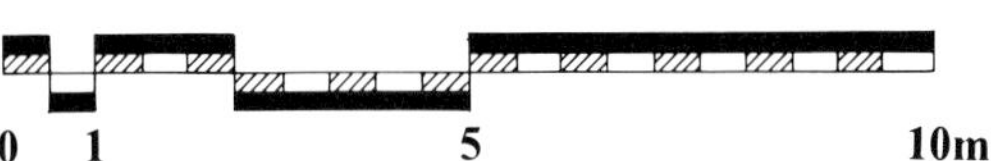

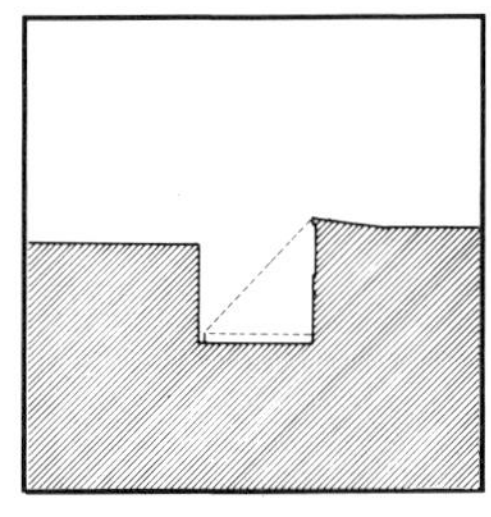

Street Section, Rennweg

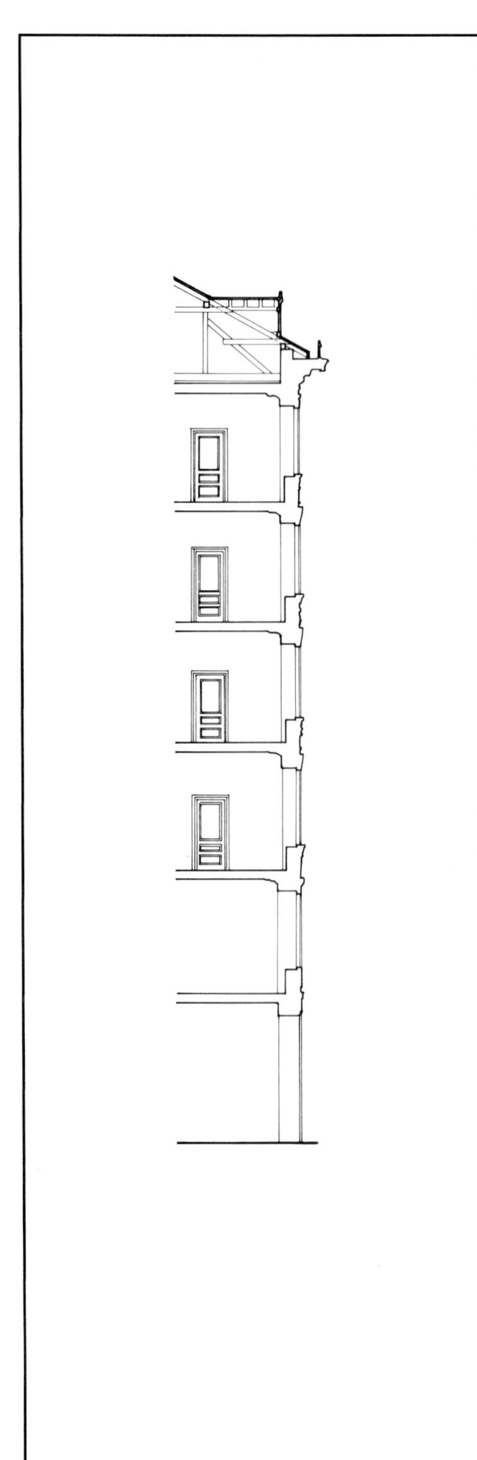

Section

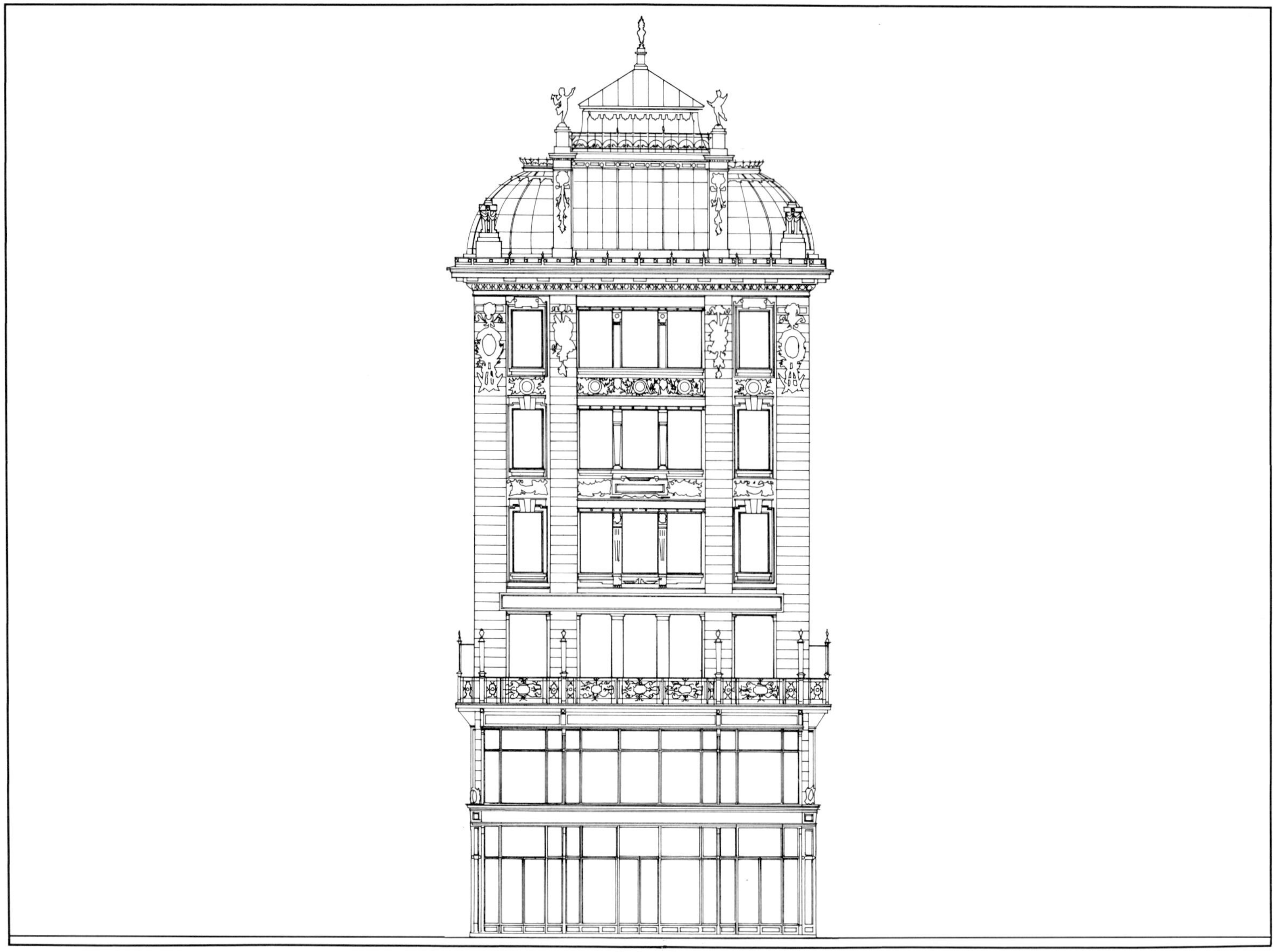

am Graben 10

Ankerhaus

Otto Wagner

1895

Figure-Ground Plan

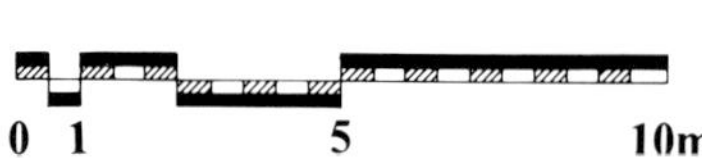

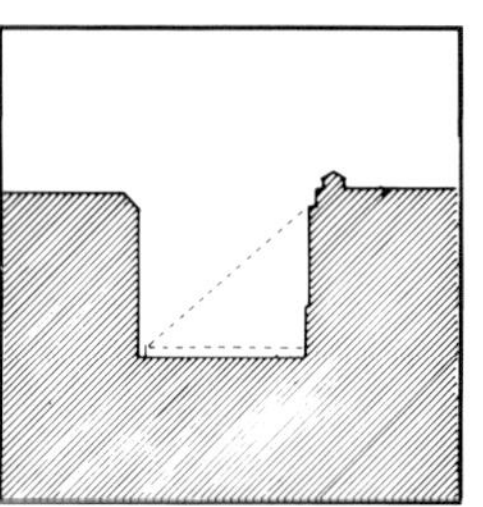

Street Section

Spiegelgasse 3

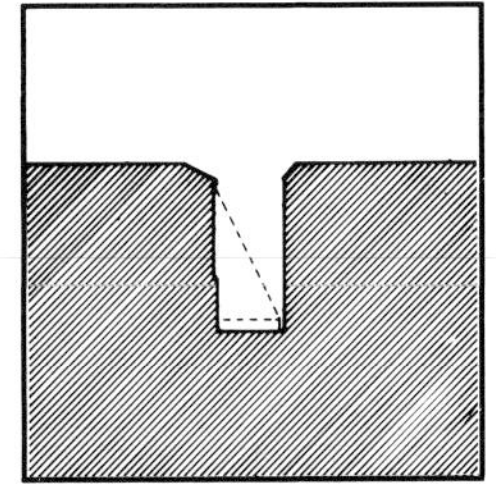

Street Section, Spiegelgasse

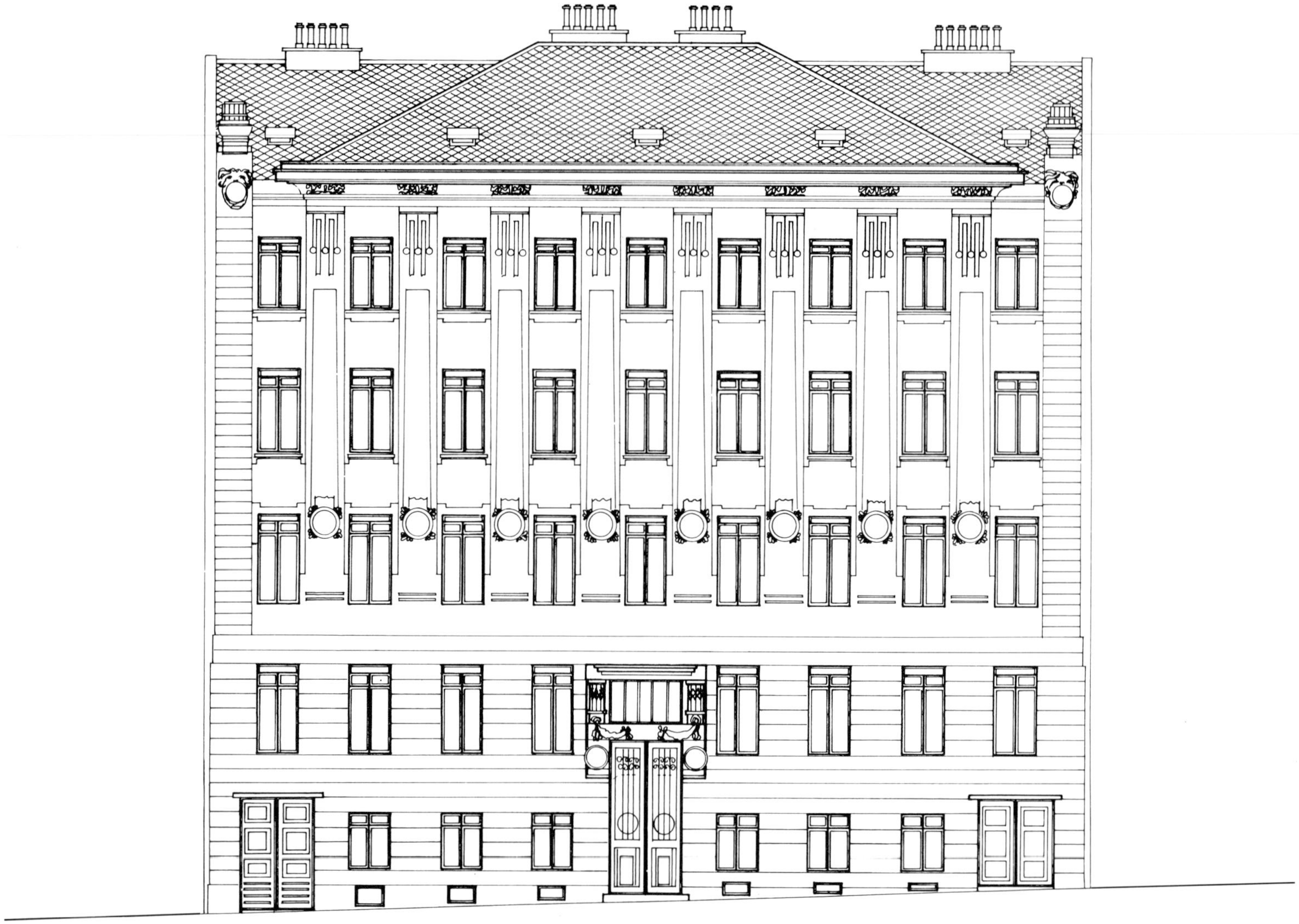

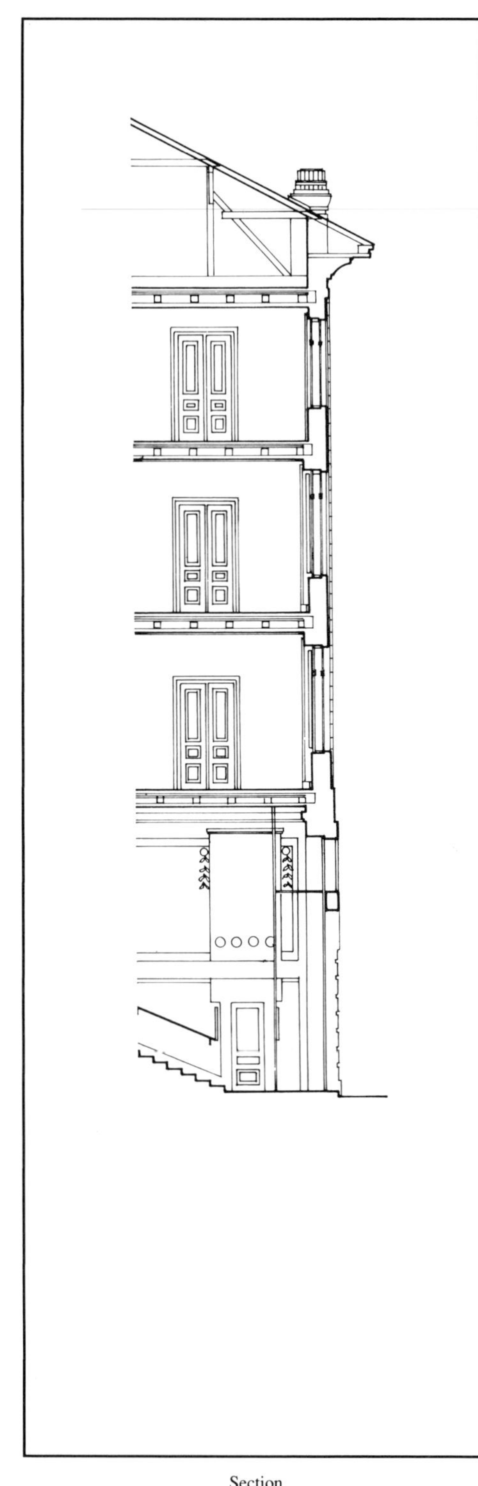

Section

Köstlergasse 3

Köstlergasse 3

Otto Wagner

1898-1899

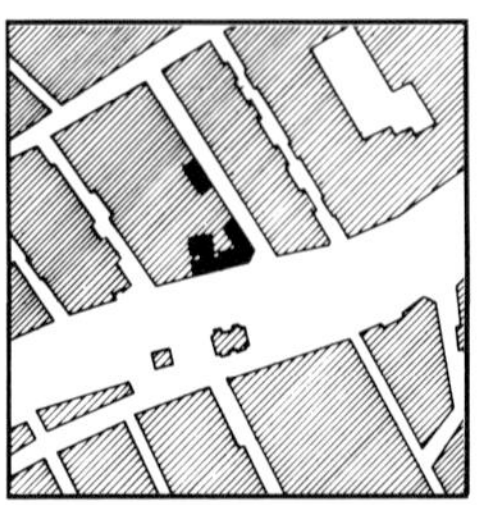

Figure-Ground Plan

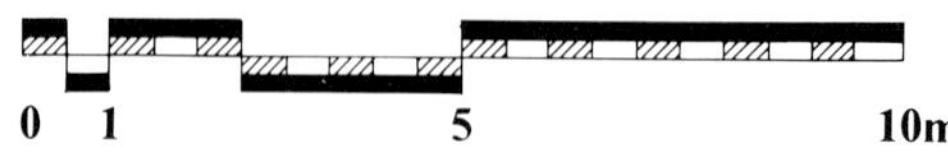

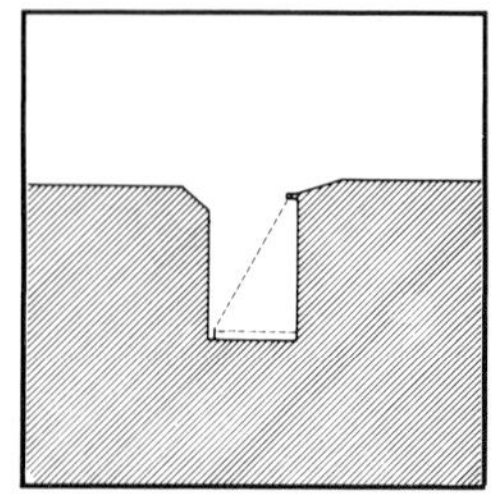

Street Section, Köstlergasse

Linke Wienzeile 40

Majolika Haus

Otto Wagner

1898-1899

Section

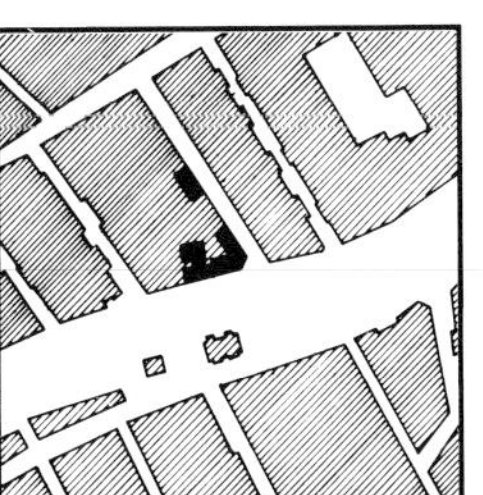

Figure-Ground Plan

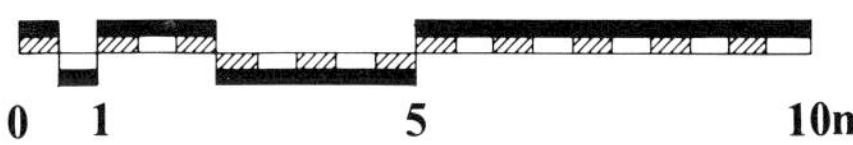

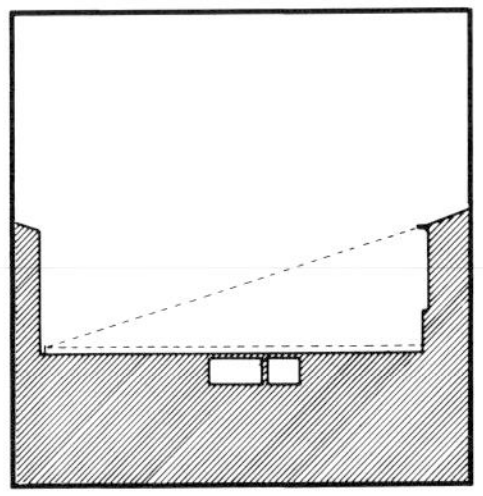

Street Section, Linke Wienzeile

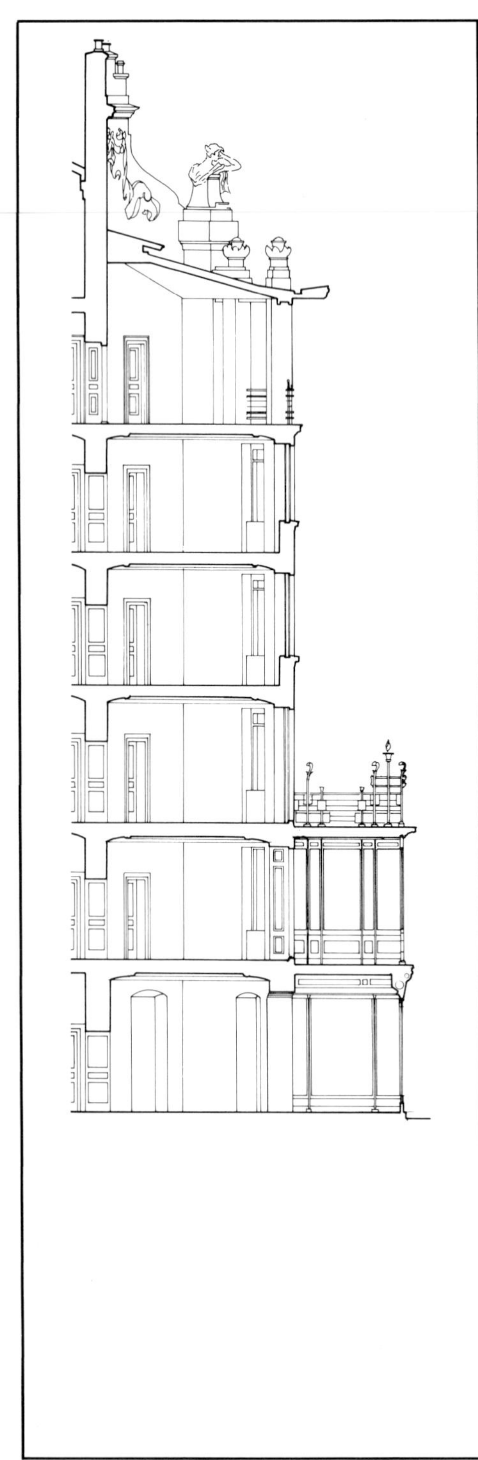

Section

Linke Wienzeile 38

Häuser Wienzeile

Otto Wagner

1898-1899

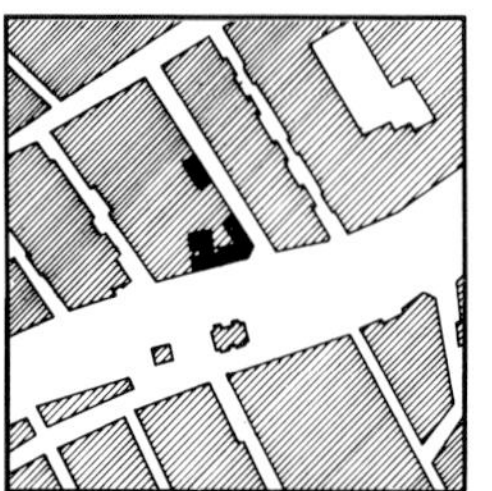

Figure-Ground Plan

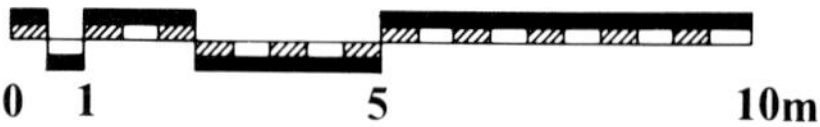

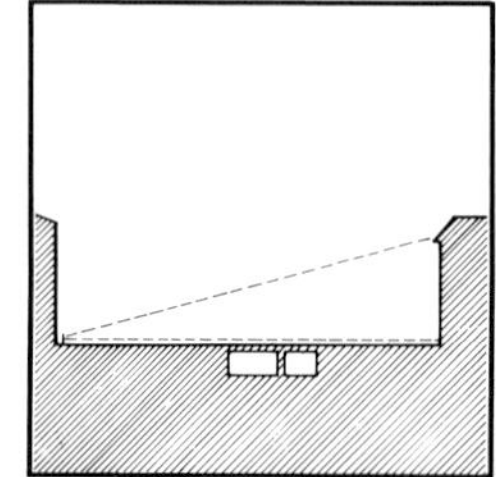

Street Section, Linke Wienzeile

Köstlergasse 1

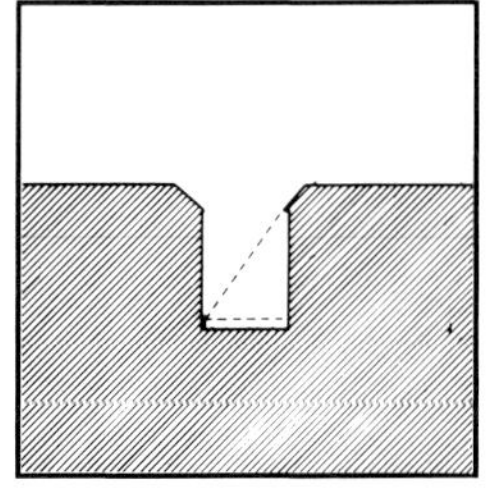

Street Section, Köstlergasse

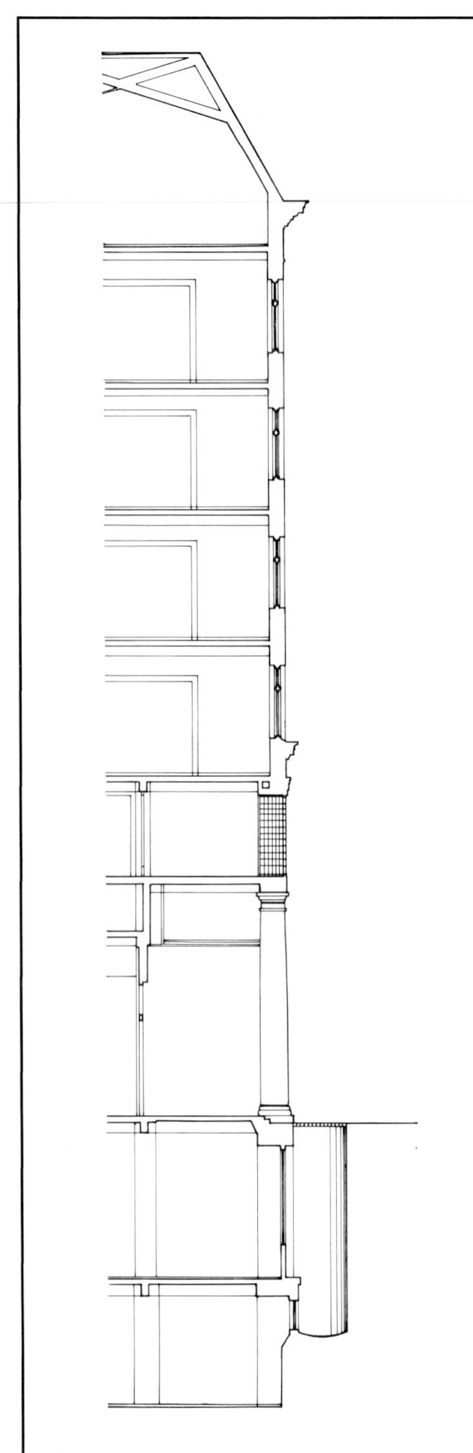

Section

Michaelerplatz 3

Figure-Ground Plan

Looshaus

Adolf Loos

1910

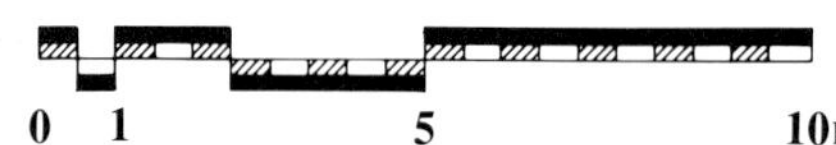

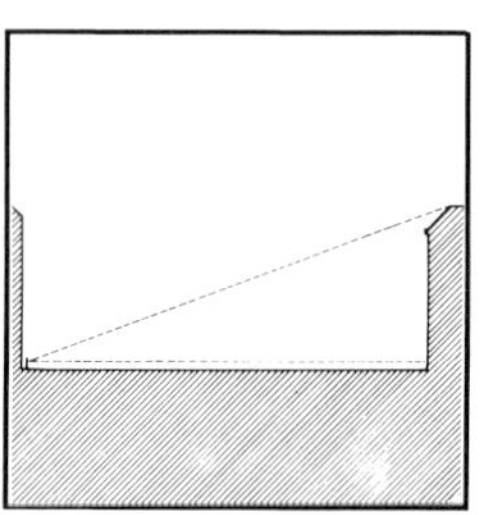

Street Section, Michaelerplatz

Herrengasse

Kohlmarkt

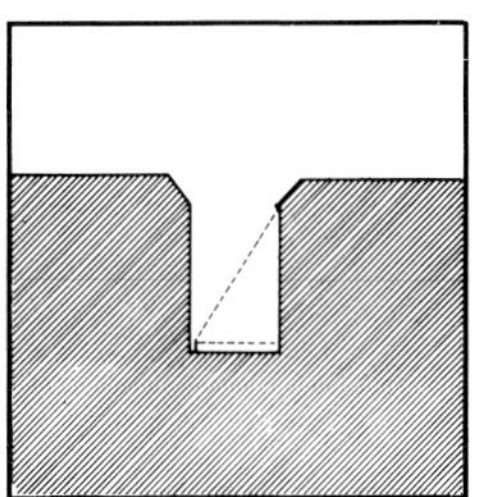

Street Section, Herrengasse

The Plight of the Object

Val K. Warke

I placed a jar in Tennessee,
And round it was, upon a hill.
It made the slovenly wilderness
Surround that hill.
Wallace Stevens

Among twenty snowy mountains,
the only moving thing
was the eye of the blackbird.
Wallace Stevens

1

1 *Woman in a Blue Dress;* Picasso, 1941

I: THE STATE OF THINGS

Over-zealous, yet well-intentioned, attempts at reversing the figure/ground plans of this century's architecture have caused the object building to be cast as 'villain', guilty of anti-urbanism and all manners of monumental hedonism. This has, in some circles, been accompanied by a newly re-discovered infatuation with the facade—hero of the city, defender of space—causing what might best be described as an antipathy toward the outside corner and a dereliction of the art of the elevation.

Furthermore, there is currently, and surprisingly, a schism of techniques used in the design of facades for those buildings impacted in urban contexts and the techniques used for those buildings caught free-standing in the city or loitering in the garden. For while it is an assumption of most current theories and practices that the acts of designing both objects and facades will not be disastrously hindered by looking at history (indeed there is more than just a little benefit to be extracted), there have been abundant distinctions made between the ways in which an object building and a facade should refer to the past.

For some reason, the descendants of the semiologically-based approach toward a theory of architectural forms, prevalent in the seventies and early eighties, while promoting a considerable enthusiasm for what may be all the proper, or at least long-neglected concerns, has had their practical syntheses dominated by the production of object buildings: singular monuments, an occasional tower or two, and, in the case of complex programs, compounds of aggregated objects.

Ironically, while the city is generally the sourcebook for their morphological menus, most of these earnest architects find that the re-application of their morphologies to urban situations tend to result in building ensembles more closely resembling dense urban campus plans than normative urban texture, even, at times, to the point of reverting to nineteen-sixtyish megastructures, the only difference being that these megastructures now run parallel to the streets and are crafted with gray stone veneers and an endless number of four-lite windows instead of being engineered with lots of red trusses and endless curtain walls.

The contemporary interests have resulted—through no fault of their own—in only two prevailing interpretations for the free-standing building: as the repository for typological concerns and as the recipient of tropistic operations; the latter attitude rooted in the eighteenth century, the former fostered in the nineteenth. With the first sort of emphasis, one often finds unpolluted, untransformed object buildings leaning toward typological purism. Concern with cross-cultural legibility tends to result in a reductivism of a given type to what approaches a neutered status and, ultimately, a level of interpretation potentially limited to identity and deprived of all the assets of multiple interpretation (e.g., Building is a Loggia, Building is a Circus, Building is a Temple).

Given a larger scale or more room, today's object building *a la mode* will express its obligation for more than a schematic development by becoming more elaborated, and this additional play will often cause the introduction of the architectural equivalents of more advanced linguistic constructs such as the three tropes (e.g., Metaphor: Building as a Gate; Metonym: Building as a Duck or as a Grandfather Clock; or Synecdoche: Building is an Acropolis, a Column, a Stack of Gazebos, a Pile of Loggias). The architectural projects of Ledoux, Boullée, Lequeu, *et al.*, popular in many circles, clearly conform to an analysis by means of formal tropisms: the school as a bridge (metaphor), the tomb as a sarcophagus (metonym), the turret lantern as a temple (synecdoche). Yet in those buildings actually constructed by these eighteenth century architects, the rawness of the ideal projects was smoothed into piquant subtleties; the conceptual strength of the ideal projects remained, but the prosaic modes of expression were subdued into more poetic modes of architectural discourse with the capacity for multiple interpretations and constructive hypotheses greatly amplified. In going from a shout to a whisper—from polemical project to practical implementation—the *architecture parlante* encourages a keener sense of hearing.

Meanwhile, today's rediscoveries of phenomena such as English grand terrace housing (where a certain degree of manginess is encouraged in the back as long as it is clearly disavowed in the front) and the more widespread urban mansion (tightly, almost awkwardly impacted in its fabric, from whence its spatial figure can be counted on to emerge like a phoenix, while the prim and proper street face provides little information on the building's internal turbulence) has caused a reconciliation with the art of the facade.

It would be disingenuous to claim that current attempts at facade design do not reveal interests in typological concerns. Occasionally, a vague bi- or tri-partite palazzo or arcade type may appear insofar as it can be used as the frame for the application of facade material: doors, windows, and moldings. Still, the principal mode of developing a facade design takes a considerably different turn once a general strategy is adopted. Rather than using the generalist notions of dealing with the past inferred by a typological approach, a facade design will often proceed elementally, by identifying more precise precedents, by utilizing a form of historicism—neither more nor less 'correct'—based on models rather than on types.

But this situation is reconcilable. Indeed, it is probably what is to be expected in the nascent, wobbly- legged stage which naturally follows the onslaught of architecture's self-contemplation as it has occurred over the past dozen years. Recent developments in architectural theory and criticism have provided an abundance of tools to be used in analyzing the city and the building. The synthesis of these investigations into architectural design is, as always, open to speculation.

As mentioned above, there has in the recent past been too much of a separation between the relationships of the object to the history of objects and of the facade to the history of facades. A combination of levels of concern, that is of levels of iconological and iconographical representation—from building as icon to window as icon, united by the intrinsic characteristic of an object to posit a shifty perception of center and edge, face and corner—should form the basis of an enriched architecture capable of inviting multiple levels of interpretation.

By investing the corner with the same amount of consideration as the front door, it should be possible to revive the potency of the object.

And there have been attempts.

In the 1960's, investigations into a formal rhetoric for the object focused on issues of frontality and rotation, often calling upon Mondrian and van Doesburg in an attempt to incorporate inadequately-explored spatial phenomena of the early twentieth century (one of the most influential of these studies was John Hejduk's *Three Projects*). This also served the purpose of extending modernism at a time when architects saw little else in which to place one's faith (excepting, of course, those directions which looked to the social sciences for their validation—a subplot not important to these present discussions). But, when applied to architecture, the lessons tended to result in an excruciatingly literal interpretation of Giedionesque simultaneity: the rotation of grids in plan sponsored simply a one- versus two-point perspectivism. When done well, one could perceive the changeling characteristics of the wall—at one moment the liner of a space, at the next the skin of a volume. When done badly, the building tended to fracture—as diamonds are wont to do—into innumerable shard-like voids, with any sense of unity dependent upon the regularity of color and of the container *cum* frame.

Derivative attempts, also traceable to the Cooper Union School of Art and Architecture, have focused upon the mechanical architectural drawing. By isolating the drawing as the central artifact in the process of producing architecture, and then performing a number of mechanical operations on the drawing (operations generally derived from techniques of drawing and photocopying, such as projection, enlargement, displacement, etc.), the work of architecture, the presence of which is only hinted at throughout the process, is assumed to undergo logical, parallel operations which would ultimately refer back to the graphic manipulations. What happens, however, is that since the process is so self-consciously performed and carefully pre-determined, it becomes both form and content, with any object produced in the process becoming only a record of the process itself, never achieving the status of product capable of independent interpretation, only of by-product reiterative of the inky chiropractics which generated it.

Today, designed urban space is seen as a predominantly planimetric phenomenon. Even when represented in the third dimension, it tends toward plan extrusion, while the object, urban or not, tends to be a predominantly axonometric phenomenon. The object building has far from disappeared. In fact, it is primarily free-standing buildings that architects are hired to produce. The same distastes for the cities of modern architecture which caused a re-evaluation of form-making have also guaranteed that, at least in the Western world, a single architect or group of architects will not be asked to produce a city for quite some time. A corollary enthusiasm for preservation makes the opportunities for intervention in dense urban contexts very rare.

However, while the object building has not disappeared, self-inflicted guilt has handicapped efforts at developing an enriched formal rhetoric for its evolution.

There has even occurred that insidious, albeit fascinating, phenomenon common to the spread of all fashions, whereby an element of the language of criticism, slipped into common usage, has displaced another concept: the increase in the use of the word 'facade,' though often a sloppy usage, has all but eliminated the use of the word, 'elevation,' even in the most unprogressive architectural journals. This is similar to the way 'static' and 'dynamic' displaced 'stable' and 'unstable' in common architectural lingo earlier this century, subverting the original meanings while enforcing implicit values. (Ironically, or naturally, depending on one's acceptance of fashion as a structure for determining form in architecture, 'stable' and 'unstable' are returning to the scene to see 'static' and 'dynamic' out the door.) While there are certainly *many* advantages to be found in the reintroduction of facade as an issue within the profession, the uncritical displacement of 'elevation' by 'facade' results in a tendency to see facade as an inevitable aspect of a building's volume—a shortchanging of the potential of the more precise notion of facade and its intrinsic relationship to the exigencies of a perpendicularly-oriented cone of vision. As well as implying to the uninitiated that *every* free-standing, four-sided structure has four facades—a ludicrous proposition—the absence of 'elevation' as a separate concept allows the architect to more easily ignore the fact that the same four-sided structure has a virtually limitless number of elevations.

Also unhelpful has been the absence of any formal rhetoric which has a specific function in shaping the object building. More and more methods for enhancing the spatial figures of a plan are being revived as an aspect of the growing enthusiasm for the rediscovery of old-time space: design tools such as one-point perspective, graphic devices such as the combination in plan of elaborated floor patterns with dashed ceiling shapes, cross-hatching as opposed to the inherently less spatial blackening of walls, puffier walls, fatter columns, and a growing awareness of plan-collage techniques following more frequent sojourns to the library.

What is necessary is a reinvestigation of the tools used in designing object buildings, since the architectural piece is always the result of the method used in producing it and of the theories of perception prevalent in the times in which it is produced. Because, although the development of methods for representing the third dimension two-dimensionally had initiated several hundred years of a fascinating coexistence between flatness and three-dimensionality, in this century (and one could trace the beginnings of the phenomenon into the eighteenth) the object and the surface have been generally kept isolated. While there are numerous discoveries advancing concepts of spatial representation, and while these discoveries were often recognized with great flourish, particularly in texts on architectural history and theory around the middle of this century—thank you, deStijl; thank you, Cubism—the architectural applications are considerably fewer than one has been led to believe. Few architects actually believed in the new modes of alluding to space, and even fewer understood them. And, while one might until recently have cringed at the phrase, "I guess I gotta project me some elevations," it has really only been supplanted by "I guess I gotta work on my facade." Architects have gone from sounding like pseudo-engineers to sounding like ersatz debutantes.

The net effect has been detrimental: by not recognizing the

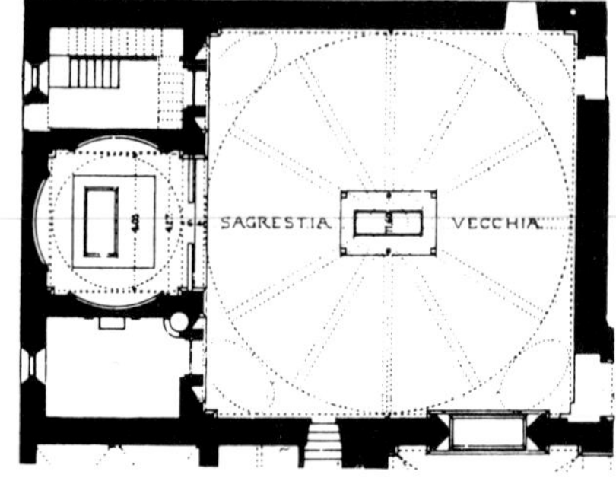

2

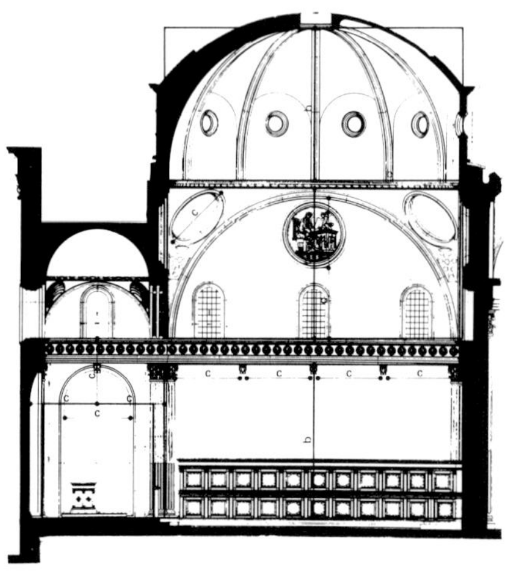

3

2 Old Sacristy at San Lorenzo, Florence; Plan; Filippo Brunelleschi, 1422-28

3 Old Sacristy at San Lorenzo, Florence; Section

4 Old Sacristy at San Lorenzo, Florence; View into Corner from Entry

4

increasingly more sophisticated methods of describing the third dimension developed in the earlier part of this century, architecture has retreated into an isolation of its three-dimensional from its two-dimensional aspects. This has been manifested most clearly in the autonomy of a building's mass from the design of its surfaces.

For our subject, the poor object building, its troubles always are greatest in those times when its formal potentials are being explored with rare intensity. Filippo Brunelleschi initiated the promise and demise of the object when he stood in the doorway of the Florence Cathedral performing one of his several major experiments with linear perspective, which he indelibly named the *construzione legittima*.

To prove the legitimacy of his perspective constructions, Brunelleschi at one time painted his perspective in a mirror and, at another time, cut the board on which it was painted so as to conform to the silhouettes of the buildings being depicted. In these ways, he could, by holding the construction in the right positions, 'prove' their compliance with reality *in situ* and with the real sky as sky (an interesting acknowledgment of the capacity of his construction for representing artifice, though not for representing nature). What is important to note in this method is that, while derived from the geometries of plan and section, Brunelleschi's perspectives depicting the octagonal Baptistery of Florence and the irregular Piazza della Signoria was conceived in terms of the *profiles* of surface and the *silhouettes* of buildings in an urban space as they meet the sky.

Brunelleschi's experiments were important not merely for having been among the first; or for having been among the first (if not *the* first) to utilize plan in the construction of a perspective, but for having been proposed by an architect. It is the synthesis of this knowledge through his work which most interests us here. Because it is in his architectural work that Brunelleschi reveals the relation between studies in the two-dimensional depiction of planes located in space and the formulation of locating planes in three-dimensional space as they are intended to be perceived by a viewer.

For instance, in his (Old) Sacristy of San Lorenzo (probably started around 1422 and finished six years later), Brunelleschi begins with what is essentially a cube of space—square in plan and only the width of the entablature taller than a square in orthogonal section—surmounted by a ribbed hemispherical dome with twelve vertical arched facets which recall the room's four principal walls. It is in designing the joint between the dome and the cube that Brunelleschi demonstrates the implications of perspective for the architect. Using pendentives to effect the transition between cube and dome, he chooses to use a series of eight roundels to encircle the ring at the dome's base: four on the vertical surfaces of the room and four on the pendentives.

Upon entering the room on the diagonal when coming from the basilica, the most immediate frontality presented to the viewer is established by the roundel on the pendentive to the right of the altar. This element colludes with its companions in distorting the perceived form of the room: rather than being a simple cube, the space begins to round out its edges implying at least an octagonal if not a round plan. The four round medallions which are truly vertical begin to warp their accompanying planes, implying that the dome actually begins lower than it does. This effect is strengthened by the persistent entablature ringing the room's perimeter (and penetrating into the altar space) which serves to disassociate the arched surface of the walls with their coplanar rectilinear lower components; by the fact that the pendentives actually connect with each other just below the ring of the dome's base, forming, in fact, a very subtle segmented dome; and by the vertical arched facets of the dome itself which are positioned so as to deny reinforcement of the four side walls (ribs are centered there instead) while centering themselves on the roundels in the pendentives.

A view into the altar of the Sacristy demonstrates a more literal application of the principles of linear perspective: the arch surrounding the altar apse is drawn back in real depth by the entablature to the rear plan of the altar; into this plane is set another plane, only slightly recessed, which seems to continue the space in illusory depth.

A similar phenomenon occurs in the Pazzi Chapel, begun by Brunelleschi around 1429. There the square of the entire plan minus the altar begins out on the portico to be completed and reiterated on the interior. The rushing perspective of the loggia on the left as one approaches the building tends to emphasize the penetrability of the chapel's facade. This facade inverts the loggia's solid/void surface relations while presenting a gridded and emphatically flat screen.

Inside, the chapel continues with its inversion of the forecourt. Here the plan expands laterally. This expansion is further emphasized by the concentric arches on each of the chapel's two sides: as in the altar at the old Sacristy, two arches in real depth frame a third in illusory depth. Here the illusion is aided by the elevated bench at the base which breaks the elements' contact with the gridded floor plane. But here the illusion is also subverted by the one undersized bracket which is centered beneath the entablature in this final arch. The unequivocally blank, singularly light surface of the framed piece of wall tends toward a phenomenal elasticity as it attempts to recede into an undifferentiated illusory depth. The tiny bracket always tends to snap it back into place, reasserting the wall's mass.

Yet, here again, a look at the corners of this room posits some amazing formal reading pertaining to an interpretation of the space as object. Here, too, the roundels in the pendentives initiate a series of apparent spatial distortions which are not easily resolved. For example, while viewing the roundel, the vertical arched surface surrounding the altar and the coffered vaulted arch leaping across the room are pulled into the same roles: alternately, both appear to be vaults and both appear to be vertical surfaces. The third arch on the side wall further obfuscates attempts at interpretation. These three surfaces of disparate dimensionality are further associated by the three vertical panels which accompany them below. These virtually identical elements are bound together by identical pilasters which appear to refuse to develop distinctions even when faced with the exigencies of the corner. Indeed, the interior corner resolution here differs significantly from that within the altar area: whereas the altar corner presents a fragment of a square column, a part of the room's three-dimensional spatial grid, nosing into the space and thereby emphasizing the immutability of the column

5

6

5 Old Sacristy at San Lorenzo, Florence; View into Altar
6 Old Sacristy at San Lorenzo, Florence; View into Dome
7 Pazzi Chapel, Florence; View to Side ; Filippo Brunelleschi, 1429
8 Pazzi Chapel, Florence; Approach from Forecourt
9 Pazzi Chapel, Florence; Oblique View
10 Pazzi Chapel, Florence; Oblique Elevation
11 Pazzi Chapel, Florence; Plan

7

8

9

10

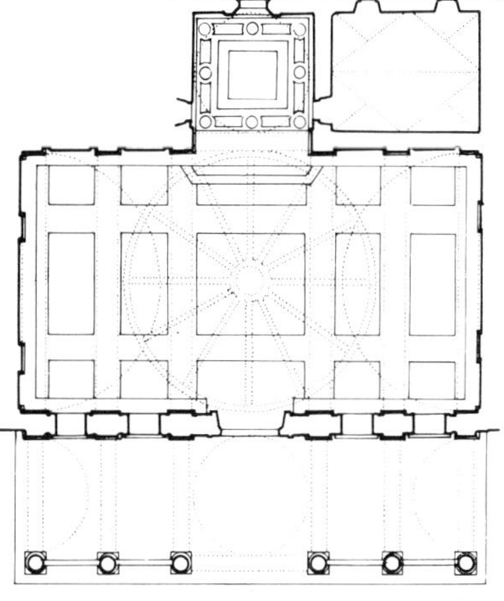
11

pilaster as an object and the wall as an infill plane, the corner of the chapel displays the column/pilaster as itself a planar element capable of being bent around the surface of an inside corner, determined by the confluence of the white walls, which, as the determinate elements, appear to *cause* the pilaster to distort. Following, then, the saga of the pilaster from the inside corner of the altar to the inside corner of the chapel's principal space, one is treated to four distinct interpretations of a single architectural element, interpretations which alternately reinforce the column as three-dimensional object and the column as two-dimensional surface.

A next important reference in developing the phenomenology of the object would of necessity involve Alberti, but not as much the Alberti of *de Re Aedificatoria* as the Alberti of *della Pittura*. While *de Re Aedificatoria* is bound to certain expectations regarding its textual format, specifically those aspects of its organizational strategies which are derived from Vitruvius' *de Architectura*, the substance of Alberti's message is best discerned from the deviations from Vitruvius and, particularly as we are here concerned, from the earlier text *della Pittura*. While much of the *fact* of Alberti's proposed architecture is presented in *de Re Aedificatoria*, much of the *substance* of his architecture can be gleaned from *della Pittura*.

Alberti does not let the reader of *de Re Aedificatoria* forget that the architect is an artist, saying, for example, that "we shall call the design a firm and graceful pre-ordering of the Lines and Angles, conceived in the Mind, and contrived by an ingenious Artist" (Book I, Chapter 1, Leoni translation). And, concomitant to that assumption, that the architect would be a master of elements of mathematics and painting, that "Painting and Mathematics are what he can no more be without, than a Poet can be without the Knowledge of Feet and Syllables" (Book IX, Chapter 10, Leoni Translation). In achieving this proficiency, "It may serve his [i.e., the Architect's] Purpose if he is a thorough Master of those Elements of Painting which I have wrote" (*ibid.*). In other words, Alberti assumes (or desires) that the readers of *de Re Aedificatoria* possess at least a working knowledge of the dicta of *della Pittura*.

These arguments are reinforced in *della Pittura*, when Alberti says, "Who can doubt that painting is the master art or at least not a small ornament of things? The architect, if I am not mistaken, takes from the painter Architraves, columns, facades, and similar things" (Book II, Spencer translation, p. 64). While this appears merely to allow that the architect might borrow elements of an iconographic nature from paintings, the (only slightly) later lessons posit a greater substance to our topic; specifically when Alberti says that, "First, in seeing a thing, we say it occupies a place" (*ibid.*, p. 68). From there he goes on to say that "painting is composed of circumspection [the drawing of barely visible outlines of the object], composition [the placement of the planes of a thing in their proper places], and reception of light [the determination of the colors and various 'qualities' of the planes]" *(ibid.)* Later, he proposes a remarkable concept, that a "body"—a term often used interchangeably with "thing"—be composed by producing it from the bones to the muscles to the flesh. (One could argue that the above passages go considerably farther in explaining the Palazzo Rucellai or

12

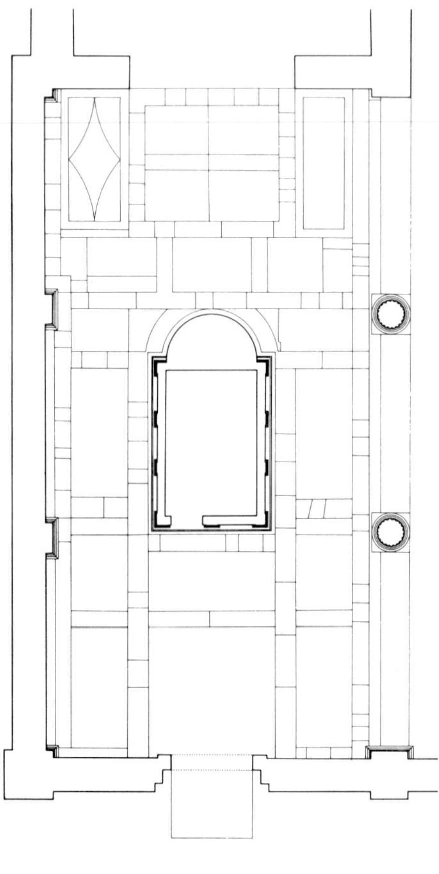

13

12 Shrine of the Holy Sepulchre in the Rucellai Chapel, Florence; View; Alberti, 1467
13 Shrine of the Holy Sepulchre, Florence; Plan
14 Tempietto of San Pietro, Montorio; Plan with Projected Enclosure; Donato Bramante, 1502-10
15 Project for St. Peter's, Rome; Plan; Bramante, 1506
16 St. Peter's, Rome; Plan; Michelangelo
17 St. Peter's, Rome; Aerial View; Michelangelo
18 Choir of Santa Maria presso San Satiro, Milan; View; Bramante
19 San Biagio, Montepulciano; View; Antonio da Sangallo the Elder, 1519

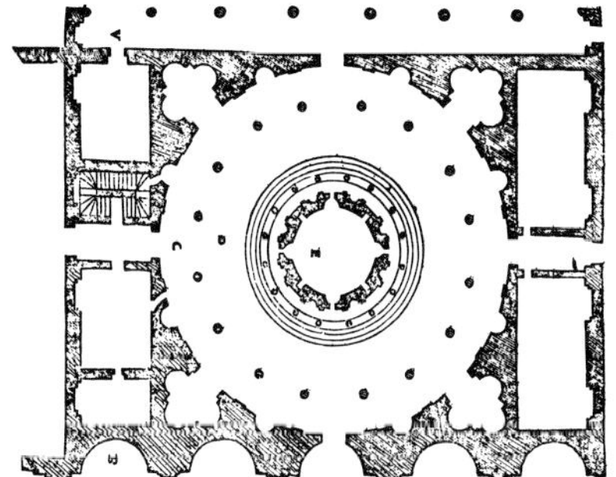

14

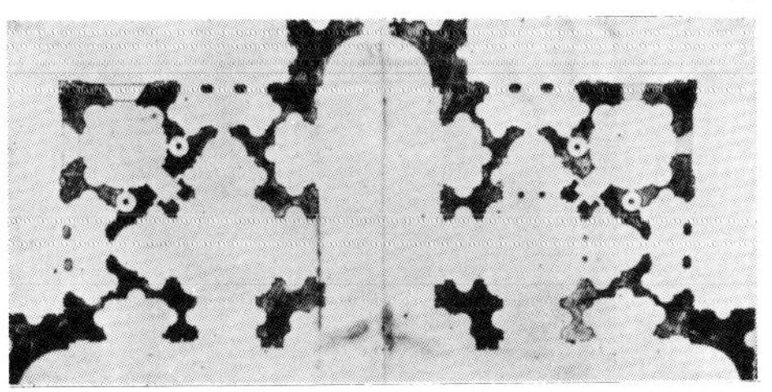

15

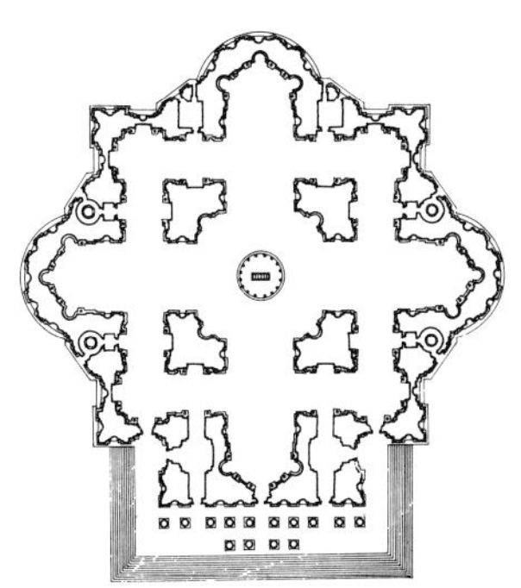

16

17

18

19

the later S. Andrea than the entirety of *de Re Aedificatoria*).

Alberti's Shrine of the Holy Sepulchre in the Rucellai Chapel exists as his single, most fundamental example of this idealized "thing" occupying a "place" and positioned inexorably in its volume. The object and the space which encapsulates it are bound together by the relationships posited by their surfaces: proportional, iconographic, typological. The Shrine appears as a miniaturized model of its enclosure at the same time it appears to generate its surroundings by projecting itself outward against the relatively blank surfaces of the Chapel, as if it were an exercise in perspective caught in the midst of an act of construction. The pilasters of the Shrine propose the pilasters of the Chapel (or is it *vice versa*?); the patterned surfaces of the Shrine seem to have been assembled from the patterns on the floor (or is it *vice versa*?); and the plan of the Shrine seems to have shaped the section of the Chapel and of the arched opening to the altar bays (or is it *vice versa*?).

One could go on. As architects learned new ways of seeing three-dimensional objects two-dimensionally, they found ever new modes of building three-dimensionally. I would propose the undertaking of a study of the vicissitudes of objects and walls, starting sometime around 1421, somewhere in Florence. After mentioning much of the above, one could later focus on the literal perspective illusionism of Bramante's choir at Santa Maria presso San Satiro in Milan; or study his design for the Tempietto of San Pietro in Montorio as being really just the petrified hole in a large spatial donut, an eloquent extension of the reciprocal object/enclosure phenomenon of the Rucellai Chapel, but here even the space between has substance. Or one could make a *big* point about the relationship which exists between the shaping of tower and terrace in Bramante's design for St. Peter's, a simultaneous molding of object and space which provoked an erudite conclusion in Michelangelo's proposal for the same job, where every instance of potential frontality is belied by the centrally asserted projection of apse or corner. In Michelangelo's St. Peter's, the object is given fronts, while fronts are resolute to return to objects. One would then probably go on to mention Antonio da Sangallo's design for San Biagio at Montepulciano, making points about the physical autonomy yet surface dependence of the towers, clearly articulated objects comprising a facade. Then, one would have to move on to Santa Maria della Consolazione at Todi, which, although very well known, could still contribute to the arguments here, especially when noting that the four corners of the base cube are actually obtuse angles; in one of the most emphatically objectified buildings in Western architectural history, the corners are actually flattening into surfaces. One might then be tempted to note in passing the manner in which Peruzzi's Palazzo Massimo alle Colonne goes from being a taut, subtly trabeated surface on the edge of a slowly curving block (when viewed obliquely) to a cylindrical object when viewed from the original alleyway opposite (looking at Portoghesi's reconstruction). From the surface which becomes object, one would be obliged to consider the opposite, in order: Cortona's S. Maria della Pace, Bernini's Project for the Louvre, and Guarini's Palazzo Carignano, as three seventeenth century examples of the object which is gradually being consumed into the wall.

All the while, one would be looking at the concurrent developments of pictorial space, often as practiced by the architects themselves. What one would discover is that, at least until sometime in the eighteenth century, as the disciplines of painting and drawing — intrinsically two-dimensional — aspired toward the third dimension with increasing levels of sophistication, architecture — intrinsically three-dimensional — aspired toward the second dimension. The development of more proficient means of representing space two-dimensionally did *not* result in the making of deeper buildings (buildings had already been very deep by the fourteenth century); it facilitated a proclivity toward shallowness.

This tendency began to reverse in the eighteenth century as the so-called Age of Reason resulted in new emphases on objectification in all the arts. Romanticism and various academic revivals re-established content over form as the primary focus for the arts. With the shift from depiction to depicted came a shift in the role of the object — both as painted icon and as built form — from being the malleable agent of a formal polemic to being the formally stabilized recipient of attributed meanings. The round temple, for example, which had undergone considerable formal transformations during the fifteenth through early eighteenth centuries, underwent a petrification of form in the eighteenth and nineteenth centuries, while accumulating significations. It is in this petrified state that the round temple is being revived today.

Whether out of reaction or evolution, this century has already seen an unprecedented proliferation of 'styles', most of which have had allied architectural applications. And while there is very little which might be generalized, I think that it might be fair to say that in the two-dimensional arts there has been an almost universal abandonment of the search for optical exactitude — the development of photography relieved the visual arts from any obligation to reliably replicate real things, permitting an examination of more reflexive content (with several obvious exceptions, each dependent on a painting's ability to use the starkness of realism to seduce viewers into a subverted, amplified, or otherwise transfigured understanding of the real). While the visual arts have certainly always contemplated themselves, the self-contemplation was facilitated, even demanded by this century's liberation from pictorialism. Consequently, concern for the more literal representation of objects began to dissolve as concerns for the various constituent elements of art itself became the new subjects of the discipline. When objects were recognizable at all, their recognition was often reduced to several suggestive characteristics, so that the artist could use what the viewer knows of the inferred object to initiate a cognizance of the artist's manipulation of that object, that is, to initiate a cognizance of art.

The architecture which has been associated with these various 'styles' of the twentieth century has, not surprisingly, also adopted a tendency to sublimate its more representational nature in favor of aggrandizing the abstracted forms of a polemic. It is a mistake, however, to dismiss the forms contrived by the early modern architects simply because they exhibit this characteristic. Condemning forms of modern architecture for the lack of literal representation of canonical forms (from Vitruvius to vernacular) is equivalent to dismissing Picasso's *Woman in a Blue Dress* because nostrils don't look like that.

20

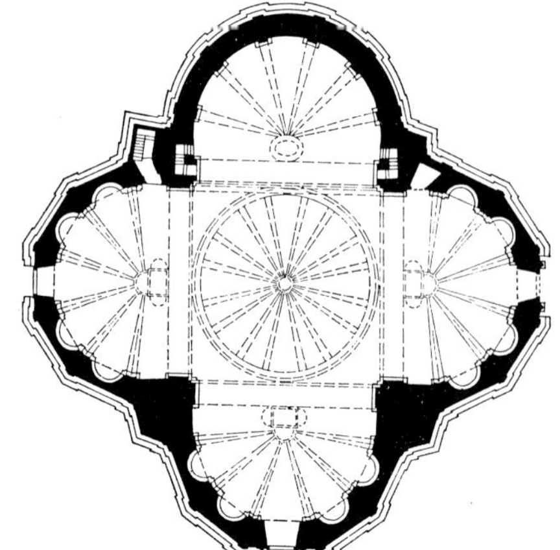

21

22

23

20 Santa Maria della Consolazione, Todi; View; Cola di Caprarola
21 Santa Maria della Consolazione, Todi; Plan
22 Palazzo Massimo della Colonne, Rome; Reconstruction; Paolo Portoghesi
23 Palazzo Massimo della Colonne, Rome; Oblique View; Baldassare Peruzzi, 1525
24 Palazzo Carignano, Turin; View; Guarino Guarini
25 Schroeder House, Utrecht; View; Gerrit Rietveld, 1924
26 Villa Stein, Garches; Entry Facade; Le Corbusier, 1927
27 Santa Maria della Pace, Rome; View; Pietro Cortona
28 First Project for the Louvre Addition; Paris; Gianlorenzo Bernini

24

25

26

27

28

Modern architecture also depended upon assumptions that the viewer was always relating what was being seen to what was known. Often, the juxtaposition was immediate and forceful: Rietveld's Schroeder House, the crowning jewel of deStijl architecture, depends upon the house to which it is attached for supplying the basis of its discourse, it challenges as it decomposes and recombines notions of chimney, wall, railing, and window, as they are professed by its neighbor. Similarly, Le Corbusier's Villa Stein, using the inferences supplied by its neighboring suburban Parisian villas, is found to be 'rusticated' by a garage door and a large hall window, and displaces its main entry from the center so that the proportion and dimension of a door, combined with the characteristics of a canopy (too large for the traditional entry portico, too small to be a *porte cochère),* begin to engage the visitor in a subtle and sophisticated investigation of how architecture conveys meaning.

Whether out of reaction or evolution, there has recently been a massive move to return to an architecture which is more literally representational of canonical forms, as stated as the beginning of this essay. And, also as mentioned above, this representation of forms has tended to be highly mimetic. If there are any art styles serving as precedents for today's architecture, they would probably be the various forms of twentieth century realism and surrealism, both of which utilize the faithful replication of known things for the purpose of either elevating the status of the object while emphasizing the technique of representation (as in realism), or for the purpose of displacing the accepted meanings of known forms in order to question, subvert, or revoke these meanings (as in surrealism). In any case, both of these stylistic attitudes tend to emphasize the *subject* of the work in occasional combination with the *craft* with which it is produced. In this close identification of the subject of a work with its object, the artist is able to facilitate the viewer's interpretation of the work. If ideas are to be challenged by these recent works of art and architecture, if awarenesses are to be heightened, they are not usually going to be reflexive in nature; that is, they are not going to be about the art itself or, more specifically, about depiction. For this reason, realism, in its various guises, commands an apparent ease of accessibility to the public.

But, certainly, this is not always the goal of art: to facilitate direct perceptions, to emphasize the What over the How, to tell rather than to show, and to reduce opportunities for ambiguous interpretations. And, certainly, the current brands of realism in this Age of Reasonability —the present time seems less evocative of a search for Reason than suggestive of a willingness to be Reasonable — need not be as stodgily unprepossessing in their reactions against the exuberance of the beginning of this century, though, granted, some of that exuberance has proven to have been misdirected. It should be possible to have an architecture which poses a representational legibility while utilizing more abstract notions of the perception of form. It should be possible to accompany the new-found prosaics of architecture with a resumption of the art's poetics.

'Plight' is an interesting word. It can mean the state (usually bad) of something, or it can mean the promise (usually good) of something. I said above that with the architectural object, its troubled status generally occurred at those times of its greatest potential: for over three centuries, those same inventions which assisted in depicting the object inevitably led to its physical dissolution. Now the problem is different. Perhaps somewhere in the current destitution of the object building can be found its revivification. Perhaps the object, lapsing into a new rigidity, can be benevolently compromised and freed from its formal archaism through the reconsideration of modes of two-dimensional depiction.

II: ASPLUND'S VILLA SNELLMAN: AN APPRECIATION

Situated somewhere between Paul Cézanne and the Villa Savoye, in the second decade of this century, is Erik Gunnar Asplund's Villa Snellman. The building was designed and constructed between 1917 and 1918 for a banker, and is located in Djursholm, a suburb of Stockholm.

At first glance, the villa is singularly unremarkable, even somewhat homely. The type of windows as well as the proportion of aperture to surface, the massing of the house, even its position relative to the road, are all fairly normative for rural Swedish houses, particularly in Djursholm. The traditional basis of the house even penetrates to its basic plan configuration: the two room wide house had been a staple of vernacular Swedish houses for over three hundred years.

However, even slight investigation reveals that this house can hardly be considered typical: it is a *tour-de-force* of articulate subtleties. (Though its first major publication was in the National Association of Swedish Architects' *Gunnar Asplund Architect 1885–1940* [Stellan Ståls Tryckerier ab Stockholm] with its introductory essay by Hakon Ahlberg, the contemporary importance of the villa was established in the U. S. by Michael Graves in his article, "The Swedish Connection" in *The Journal of Architectural Education.* It has been further analyzed by Stuart Wrede in his *The Architecture of Erik Gunnar Asplund* [M. I. T. Press]. The author acknowledges his debt to these three introductions to the building.)

The original site plan shows the site divided into four quadrants. One first views the house from a distance, on the main road, and across the garden quadrant. The house, parallel to the road and viewed frontally through a row of trees (an effect now made difficult by the subsequent subdivision of the site and the construction of another villa suburbana where the tennis court would be) would appear to have two parallel rows of windows surmounted by an attic row, evenly disposed on a large, monolithic surface (original designs show it to be yellow; it is currently blue-gray).

Upon closer inspection, the two rows of windows are misaligned vertically, becoming increasingly more so as they proceed to the right. Wrede's interpretation of this phenomenon is quite perceptive: it is a manifestation on the garden elevation of the rotation of the service wing behind, as though the windows were being pulled out of alignment in reaction to the cranking of the single story wing to the right. This initiates a means of interpreting the house which will prove to be especially helpful: the surfaces and volumes possess a plasticity and a dynamism which utilize inherently non-architectonic phenomena to convey a multitude of messages about the building's status, phenomena which are more typically to be found in the disciplines of painting and physics.

One can go further in analyzing this elevation. The misalignment of windows (not, incidently, as Ahlberg asserts, generated by internal concerns; the plan bears this out) is further emphasized by the sloped ground plane, itself emphasized by the ubiquitous base of the villa. The elevation is anchored by the arch and window to the cellar, and the extended 'foot' to the right containing an accessway to the cellar. This arch is further balanced compositionally by the only chimney on this slope of the roof.

The two aberrant windows on this elevation also convey specific information: behind the fanlight attic window is a roundish room; behind the subdivided second story window is (was) a subdivided room.

Also notable is the unusual use of swags on this elevation. They appear to float on the surface between windows and, oddly, cause the bays at the left and right of the elevation to be interpreted as minor bays.

This is resolved upon moving around the corner, up the secondary street. When viewed obliquely from the direction of the tennis court, the errant left swag is again situated between two openings, and the second story windows form a band of apparently equally-spaced openings. This band effectively causes the corner to disappear, with the entire new elevation having its phenomenal center at the fanlight. Furthermore, the three arched elements on the new elevation tend to contradict real issues of near and far by actually increasing in size from left to right, beginning to imply perspectively a rotation of the elevation directly opposite that of the building's actual orientation.

Upon entering the site at the driveway (the projected gate pavilion was never built), one eventually glimpses, between a large oak and a planted knoll, the corner of the main block of the house. Here something fascinating occurs: at the moment the receding perspective of the roof aligns with the slope of the end elevation up to the peak of the gable, the ground plane and the carefully articulated base of the house form a straight counter-slope from the front steps to the door accessing the crawl space. Here, when the viewer is close to the building, perspective lines are used to eradicate the corner in what could be seen as an adroitly improvised application of Alberti's principles of circumspection, composition, and reception of light, as put forward in his *della Pittura.* The various components of the elevation reinforce these readings. The line of swags, now located between the second story and attic windows on the court face, places one last swag in the upper position as if it were immune to the vagaries of perspective. And as the base starts dropping away, it not only drags down the (later) cellar fanlight, it also pulls down with it the small window on the right (actually in a study niche below the stair landing), thereby disorienting the effects of floor plane. As the oblique elevation of the court further illustrates, the row of four- lite windows on the service wing continues onto the main body of the house, all contributing to the villa's tendency to dissolve its corners, thereby positing a consistently oblique frontality.

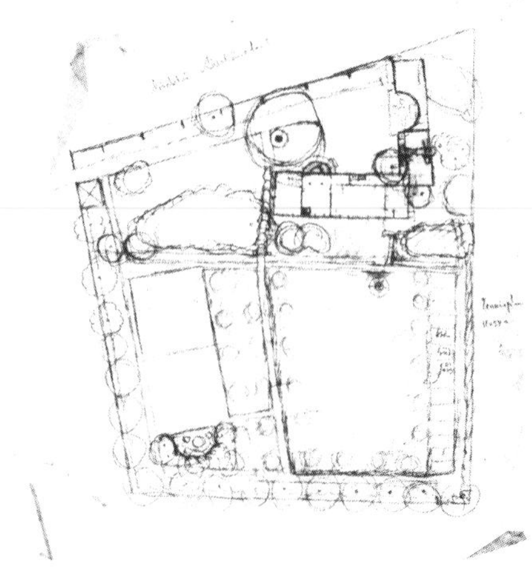

29

30

31

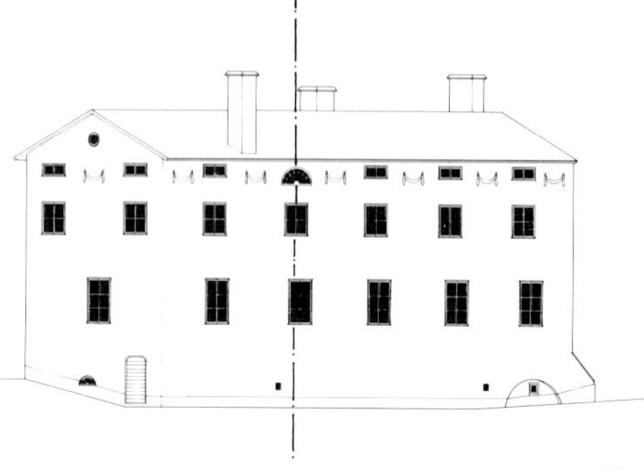

32

33

34

29 Villa Snellman, Djursholm; Site Plan, Early Version; Erik Gunnar Asplund, 1917-1918
30 Villa Snellman, Djursholm; View from Main Road
31 Villa Snellman, Djursholm; Court/Side Oblique View
32 Villa Snellman, Djursholm; Garden/Side Oblique Elevation with Center Line
33 Villa Snellman, Djursholm; Garden Elevation
34 Villa Snellman, Djursholm; Garden/Side Oblique Elevation

On this oblique elevation, it is the large central window on the gabled face which resolves the imbalanced ground floor of the court face, continuing the spacing of the apertures and resulting in an apparent center on the French doors, which are surmounted by a small relief.

Here, too, on this oblique view, elements conspire against perspectival clues through scale manipulation. The nearby crawl space door is surprisingly diminutive when compared to the main door to the house, and the single six-lite window on this elevation begins to loom in the same plane as the French doors to the hall.

Even when frontal to a surface of the building, rotation seems to be implicit. While this rotation is extra- referential on the garden elevation (i.e., referring to the service wing then out of view), it is self-referential on the service wing itself. On this single story wing, the windows are spaced increasingly farther apart as they move away from the block of the building, depicting while exaggerating the fact that the left side of the wing is pulled toward us as we move down the driveway. The window spacing seems to be registering a perspectival rotation. Incidentally, the early site plan shows a niche carved in the service wing, terminating the approach axis while implying a dynamism for the form: it appears to have been literally derived from the cylindrical entry stair on the main house; the wing and house seem almost in danger of snapping closed.

Another mode of eliciting this phenomenon of rotational movement is presented by the gabled end elevation of the main block. The elevation is comprised primarily of components present elsewhere on the building. However, once seen fully after having been seen peeking between the bushes upon approach, the elements have here been so disposed as to offer an explicit case of anthropomorphism. But still, with the gable and circle establishing a vertical axis on this elevation (these elements are again recombined on the opposite elevation) there is an unmistakable misalignment of the elements: the 'nose' is clearly to the right of center, the 'mouth' clearly to the left.

This compositional problem is partially understood by looking at Cézanne's *Man with Arms Folded* (reproduced here in reverse for purposes of example). While the man's torso, the opening in his jacket, and the position of his outer arm tend to reinforce axes of symmetry and of frontality, numerous other cues tend to emphasize a rotational posture, such as : the lower arm in relation to its improbably extended hand, the shifted misalignment of the wainscoting in the background from one side of the painting to the other, the slight droop of one shoulder, and, most notably, the distortion of the facial features as if they were depicted on a flat plane which was itself rotated into the canvas. The direction of the man's gaze is clearly marked by the location of his nose to one side of center and of his mouth to the other.

An understanding of these and other spatial paradoxes found in Cézanne's work can certainly assist in understanding Asplund's work. If, in its flatness, the anthropomorphic end elevation can be said to be simultaneously rotated in space, its rotation can be understood to be 'glancing' in a direction perpendicular to the service wing behind. This phenomenal rotation is countered by the shift in ground plane. Asplund's emphatic baseline emphasis serves as an underscoring of the

35

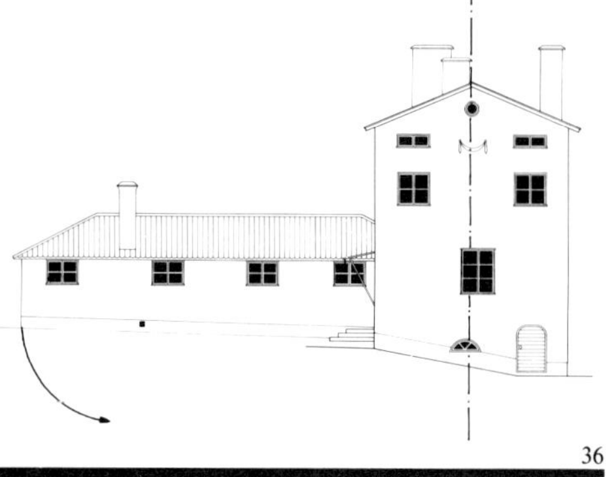

36

37

38

35 *Man with Arms Folded*; Reversed Reproduction, Paul Cezanne
36 Villa Snellman, Djursholm; Side Elevation (Street) with Center Line
37 Villa Snellman, Djursholm; Court/Side Oblique Elevation
38 Villa Snellman, Djursholm; Side Elevation (Street)

intentional qualities of his manipulation of the ground plane, just as the double-lined wainscoting of Cézanne's portrait leaves no doubt as to the level of intention, and absence of the arbitrary, in his work.

Continuing the spiral procession to the villa, one enters the court, moving around the — quite literally — pivotal large oak on the site. Facing the entry elevation, the four sets of apertures are again imbalanced to the right, ending with a too small piece of wall which is resolved by the window around the corner, as mentioned above. Yet, if one were to look only at the ground floor, and not at the entire surface, the elevation *is* apparently resolved, though it is centered on the preponderant blankness of the wall's surface which is in turn relieved only by the small square window which straddles the baseline as it coyly nudges to the left and toward the main door of the house. In fact, each of the three main pieces of blank surface on this elevation has a corresponding base window which serves to qualify its respective surface, much as a dot below a vertical line qualifies an exclamation point. One should also note how the new location of the line of swags emphasizes the vertical alignment of elements (even a chimney assists in indicating the entry bay) while augmenting the dominance of the blank surface. On the garden elevation, the swags' placements emphasized the horizontal series of openings reducing any potential of seeing the blank surfaces as figural.

However, one should note that this elevation does not subscribe to completely neat alignments either: both sets of doors, the solid canopied doors to the vestibule and the glazed French doors to the main hall, are slightly shifted off the axes of their accompanying windows. That they are both shifted *away* from the center serves to further tighten the surface between them as well as to sponsor another perception of the house's dimensionality. There are only two locations where one can see clear through the house: through the French doors and out through the main hall, and through the second story window above the French doors and through the ovoid room. In order to look through the building at the hall, one must become aligned with the elevation not frontally, but at an angle which parallels the rotation of the service wing. In other words, one is encouraged to look at the surface of the building on a slight oblique, at an angle which is more or less proposed by the wing to one's left. When looking from the court through the second floor hall window, there is another angle, less steep, which penetrates the center of the window, the center of the ovoid room's doorway, and the center of the fanlight (which, because of the angle, is made to appear as if it were resting on the window sill). This angle duplicates the angle of the partition in the corner bedroom. In this instance, looking at the surface on the oblique is not tempered by an element of the foreground, but is actually reiterative of an element buried in the background, a partition which in turn refers to the inflected service wing (although, admittedly, one should be careful not to make too much of these types of arcane references in a house consisting of a multitude of overtly perceived events, the absence of gratuitously-located elements inspires such interpretations).

One should note here that the ceiling in the hallway occurs just above the second story window. The ceiling of the ovoid room and of

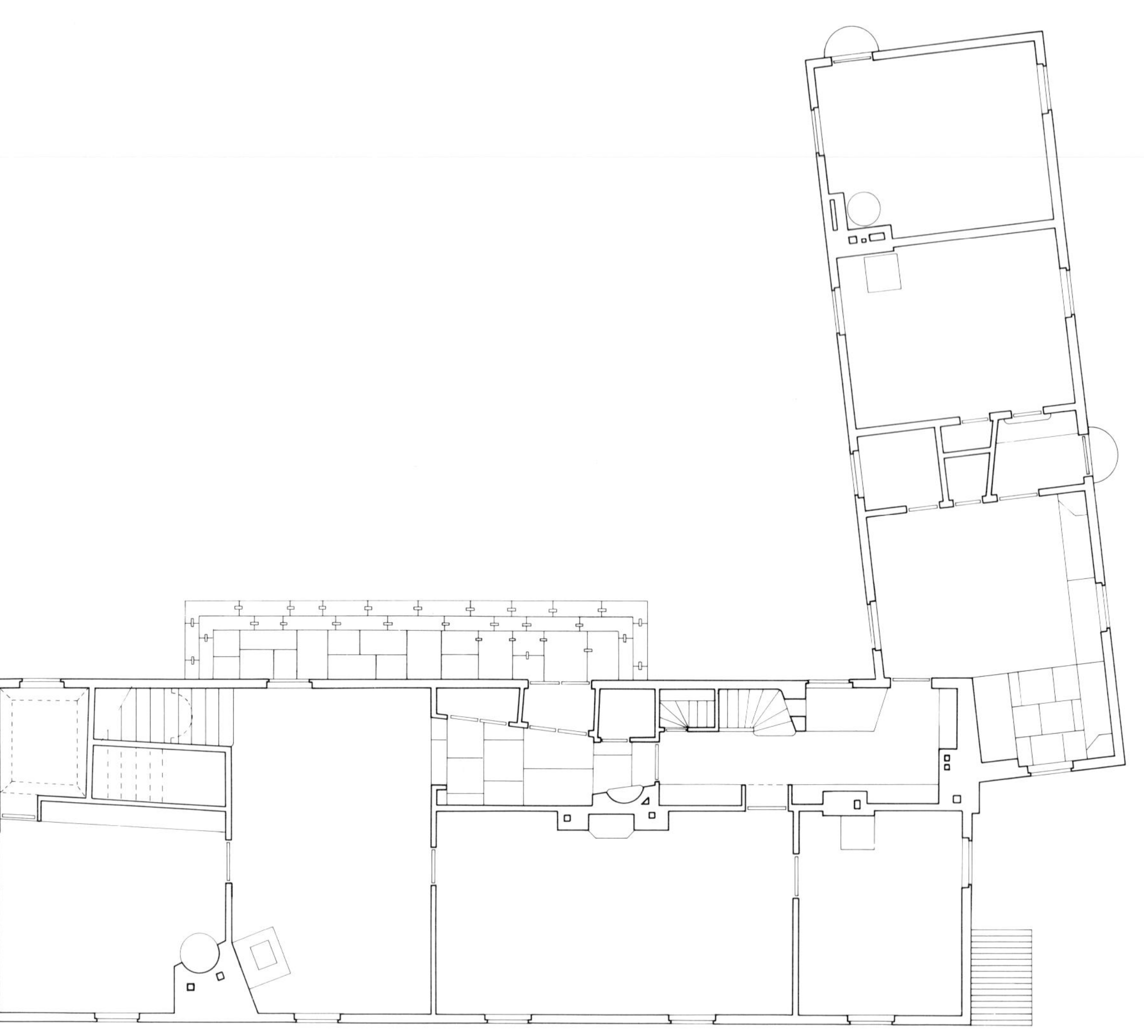

39

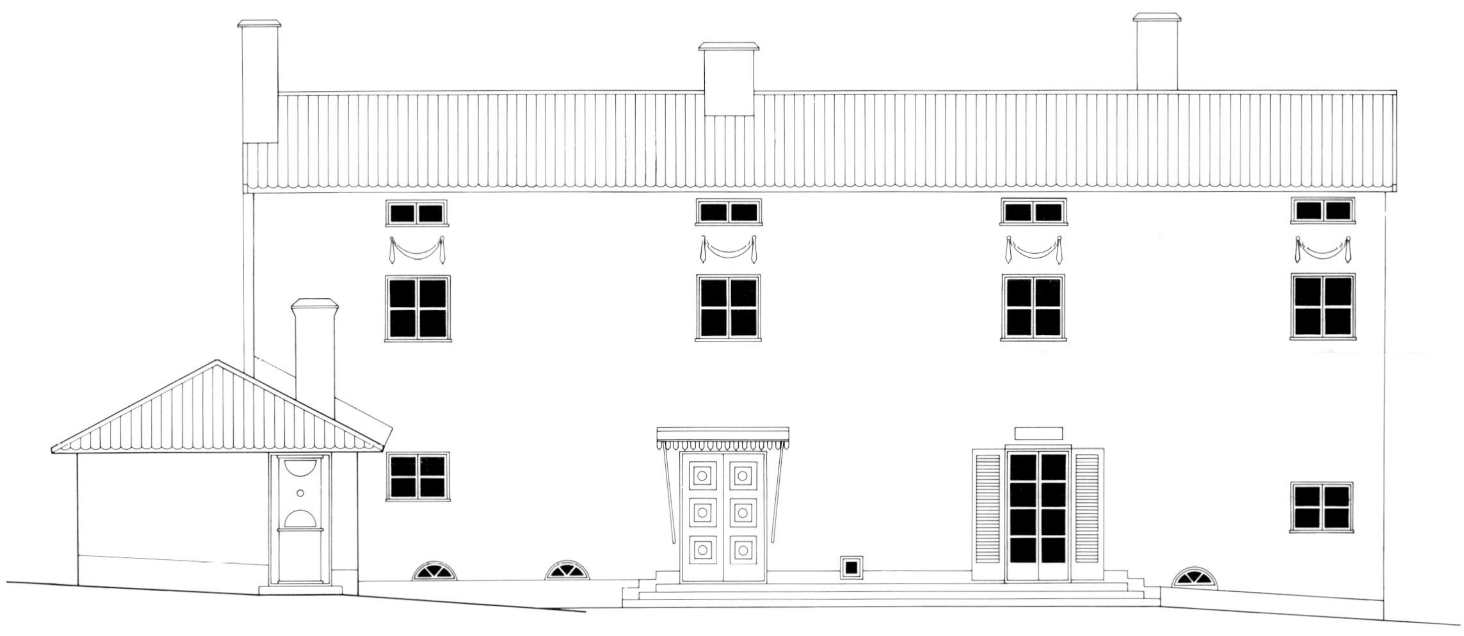

40

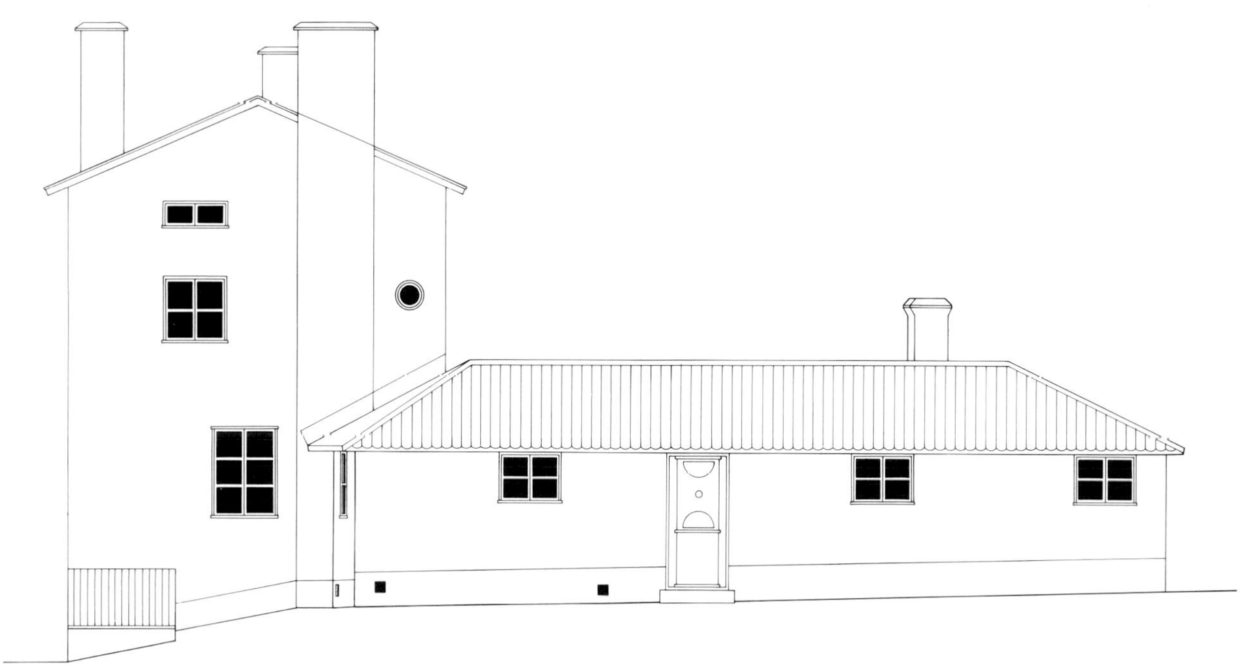

41

39 Villa Snellman, Djursholm; Plan, First Floor
40 Villa Snellman, Djursholm; Court Elevation
41 Villa Snellman, Djursholm; Side Elevation (Boundary)

the other rooms along the garden side of the second floor occurs above the 'attic' level of windows. Therefore, the swags on the two elevations are truly complex in their meanings, as they also refer to the levels of the ceilings.

The spiral of approach as well as the elements of perceiving the building's vertical surfaces, proceeds into the house itself, with the entry sequence more or less terminating in the main hall. Even in here, one can stand in the doorway and see the room's corner dissolve before one's eyes, as the door to the study and window to the garden are centered by the stove which is at a slight angle, defying clear visual placement.

And throughout the villa, surfaces accede and recede in simultaneous reinforcement and denial of frontality and obliqueness, of foreground and background. The ovoid hall on the second floor seems to be caught in a perpetual instability: when approaching from the direction of the stair, the walls appear relatively flat; but once inside, the room begins to become rounder and more enclosing. Even the plan of this space is reminiscent of a moment frozen in a photographic sequence immediately after a ball (the room) has been hit by a bat (the hallway), and starts wobbling away through a series of deformations.

And it is in the building's constructed deformations, as it was in Cézanne's painted deformations, that Asplund is able to articulate a poetic for the object. The Villa Snellman is Asplund's portrait of a peasant; but it is a work of architecture where the content of the work does not terminate at the level of the subject matter. While an intrinsic knowledge of the Swedish vernacular house (some might call it a collective memory) is helpful, it is not because Asplund's villa aims at a nostalgic remembrance or a polemical reiteration; it is because the remembered house establishes the prosaic basis for Asplund's poetic statement. ■

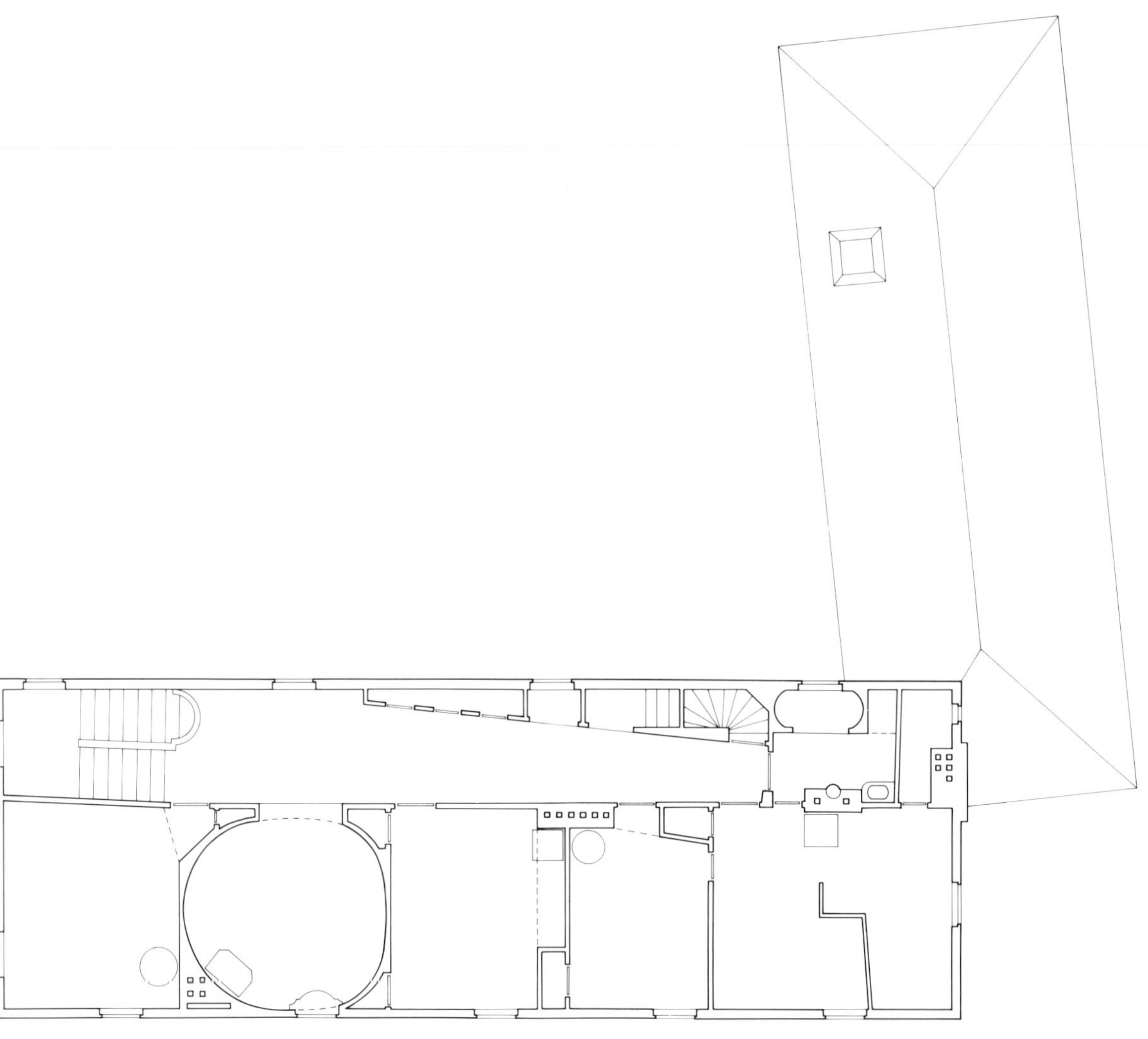

42

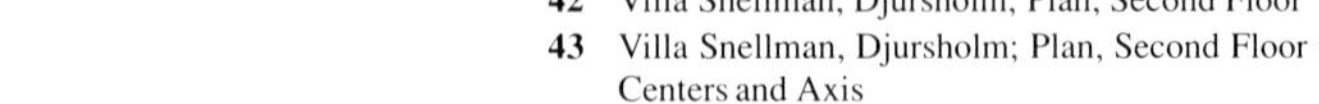

42 Villa Snellman, Djursholm; Plan, Second Floor
43 Villa Snellman, Djursholm; Plan, Second Floor with Centers and Axis
44 Villa Snellman, Djursholm; Section
45 Villa Snellman, Djursholm; Oblique Elevation, Main Hall
46 Villa Snellman, Djursholm; View through Second Story Window

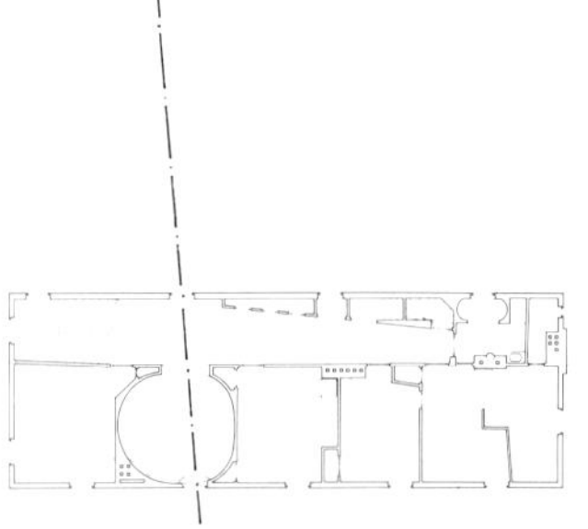

43

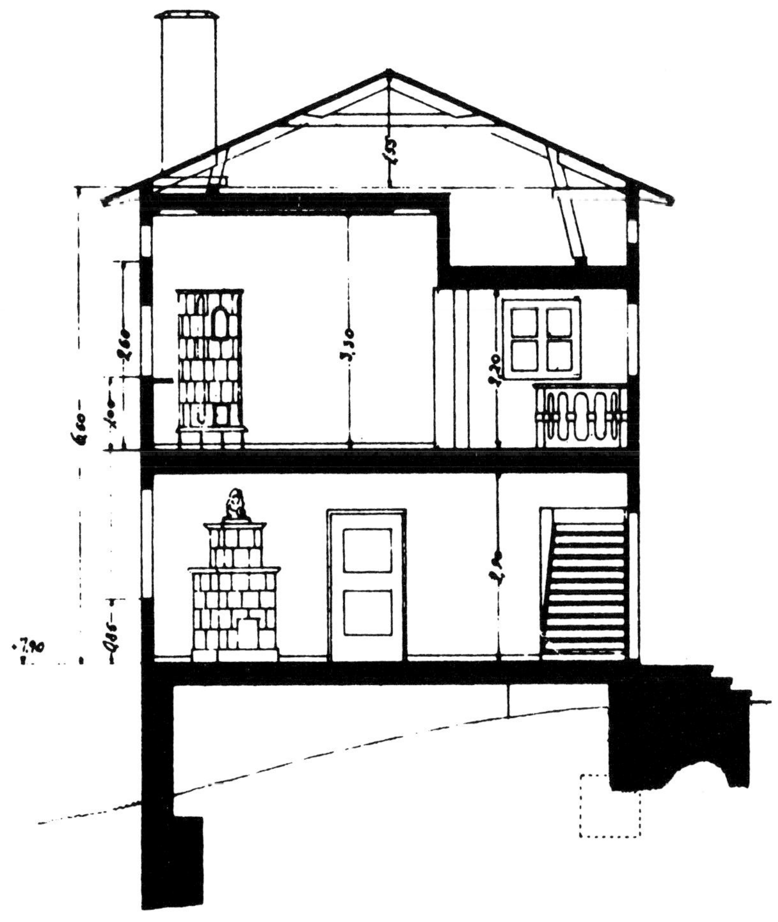

44

46

45

Elementary Investigations In The Third Dimension

The Fortuitous Emergence of Vertical Surface or ..., Handsome Faces in Unexpected Places

Vincent Mulcahy and John Zissovici

The projects herein illustrated were produced as part of the First Year Design curriculum at Cornell during the Spring of 1986. They resulted from a series of allied exercises primarily intended to focus attention on the vertical dimension of an architectural conception, .. that which might be called, after the graphic abstraction which is conventionally employed to explore and portray it, 'The Section'.

These exercises formed the final stages of a design curriculum which, while precise in its objectives, tended to be highly speculative—one might say even opportunistic—in its pedagogical methods. This curriculum began as a loosely directed collaborative experiment and evolved as a format for experimentation and exploration. It was never intended to reveal a precise definition of what might constitute an appropriate beginning to an architectural education, nor was it meant to produce axioms or formulae which might be applied and reapplied to this matter of a beginning. Still, from a curriculum which would neither willingly adopt nor overtly discover an approach for itself, something of an approach and certain near axioms could be argued to have emerged.

Central among these axioms was the notion that an introductory design experience and, perhaps by implication any design experience, ought to encourage and sustain the instinct and the devices necessary to explore within the medium of architecture, that, in the absence of this instinct and these means, principles of composition become dogma, the culture of architecture revealed through precedent yields assured convention, and the science of construction implies only empirical optimization.

We came to understand that the experimentation which such a curriculum was intended to foster could not reasonably be nurtured in a context of preconceived rights and wrongs. We assumed that design exercises, while carefully limited and directed, must not be fashioned to yield somehow correct, unitary, or predictable solutions; that there needed to exist for critic as well as student an unpredictability and variability in the process of design and in its results, dependent upon each individual's explorations and related aspirations.

Underlying all criticism, analysis, and evaluation, there was the basic assumption that architecture carries content and meaning, that its content is inevitably expressed, perceivable, and readable, that therefore a work of architecture through its form and materiality is, by definition, analyzable and that the making of architecture must, by definition, incorporate a critical analytical process.

Perhaps the central question in the curriculum which we conceived, the one which seemed to make every exercise the same exercise, had to do with what architectural content might be and how it came to be. While critical analysis could be understood to enable the relationship between form and content, it could not be regarded as the source of it.

For us, that which circumscribed exploration was the enemy, yet we found that the most commonly cited enemies of invention, the preconception, tradition, or even linear logic could, on the contrary, stimulate invention when the design process acknowledged not just a relationship but a reciprocity between form and content, object and idea, and when the instinct to explore found encouragement, a format and the means. (For this characterization of the relationship between object and idea, we are indebted to Michael Graves' "Idea As Model," IAUS 3, Rizzoli.)

We were preoccupied with the generative possibilities inherent in the various forms of graphic abstraction employed by the designer. While we encouraged the use of drawing and modeling as tools capable of extending vision and perception, and while we acknowledged their utility as precise instruments for simulation or dissection, we consistently tended to emphasize certain other opportunities in, for example, a plan, a perspective or a collage which might permit these or any form of graphic abstraction to serve at once as format and as stimulus for an evolving conception.

We came to understand that a reciprocity between object and idea within the process of design meant that, while an idea might stimulate a drawing which would in some measure express it, a drawing—its form, its frame of reference, its materiality, coloration, degree of abstraction, even its inadvertent or mistaken aspects—could, in a reciprocal way, stimulate the designer to initiate, modify, transform, or extend an idea.

In this sense, the designer's media for design served him as a kind of evocative object through which he might advance or redefine his propositions, transcend the limitations of his vision, and present to himself that which, in the absence of such artifice, he could not otherwise imagine—the fortuitous and the unexpected.

In the end, the curriculum which we devised was an immersion in all of the various properties of the architect's media for design, but with a particular emphasis on the role of drawing or model as evocative object. It was intended to initiate and encourage an unpredictable reciprocal relationship between the designer and his design devices, one upon which the genesis and development of an architectural conception could depend. As for the circumstances of our curriculum—its uncertainty about how to begin or proceed, its reactive and opportunistic methods, the evolution of its rationale achieving clarity somewhere near its end—these became an analogue to the terms of the relationship our curriculum aspired to sponsor, implying that the events of a curriculum could also be regarded as evocative objects in the evolution of a conception of another order.

Project Description

As the format for this series of related exercises, students were assigned an abstract context derived from a conventional row house or slot site typology. Specifically, this context was to be a rectangular envelope of space bounded on three of its longest sides (including its base plane) and open at its ends and its top. In addition, it was to be subdivided by two uninterrupted horizontal planes into three distinct spatial layers and was to be further articulated by a line of structure into two longitudinal zones (one thin, the other thick).

In the first of the ensuing exercises, students were simply asked to compose a series of interrelated spaces within the specified con-

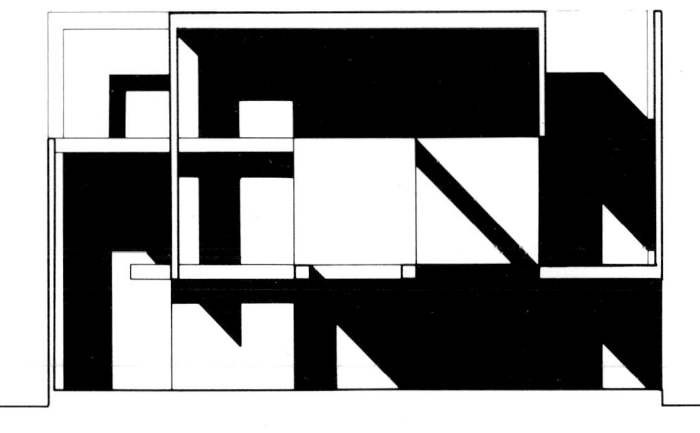

1

2

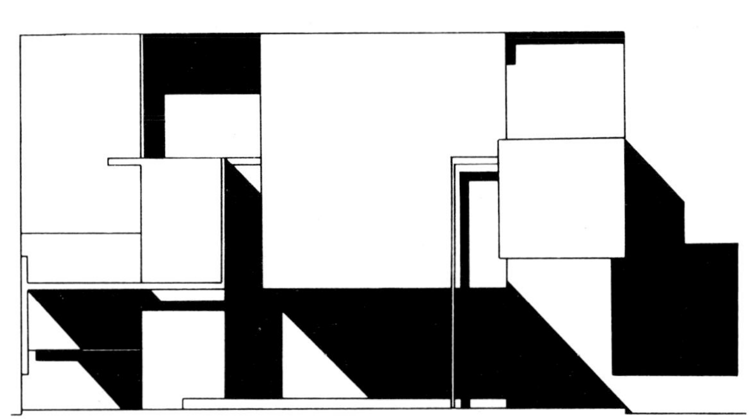

3

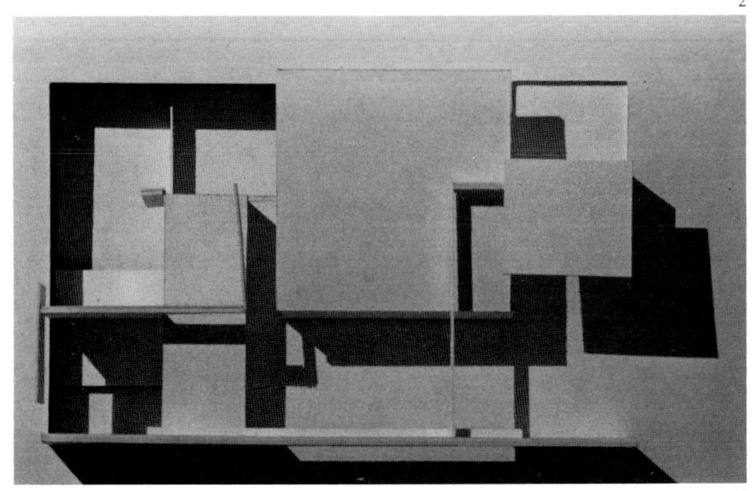

4

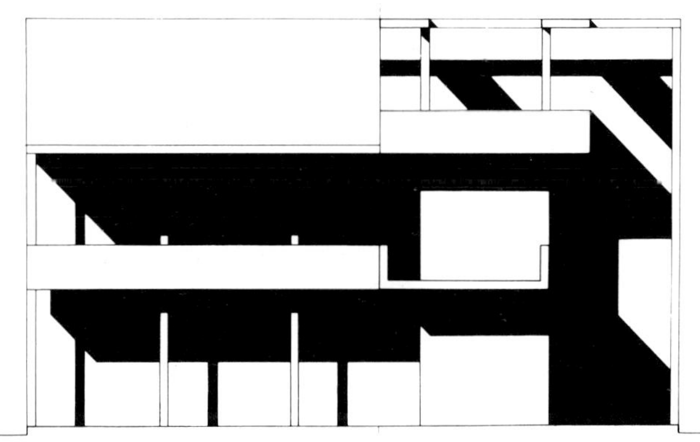

5

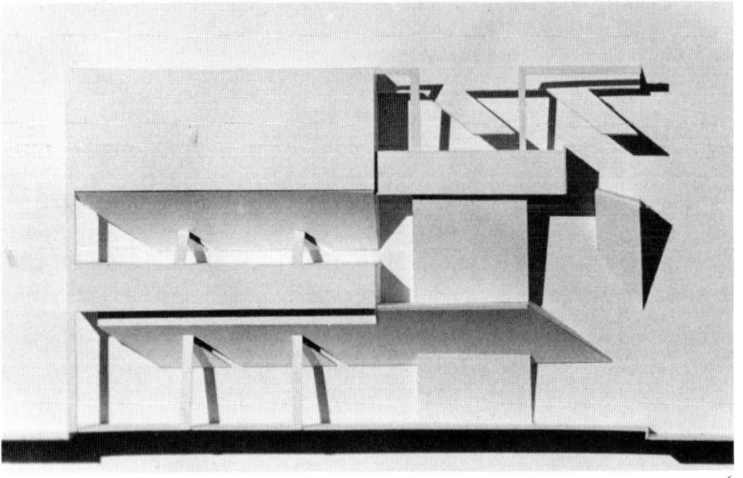

6

1 Sectional Elevation; Kenneth Ong
2 Sectional Elevation; Model
3 Sectional Elevation; Paul Soulellis
4 Sectional Elevation; Model
5 Sectional Elevation; Doug Hocking
6 Sectional Elevation; Model

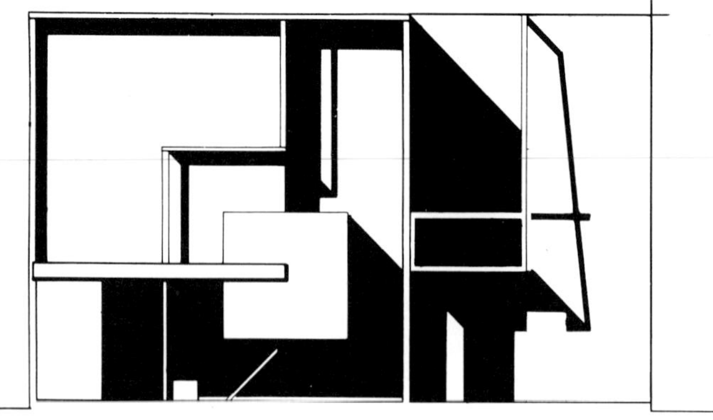
7

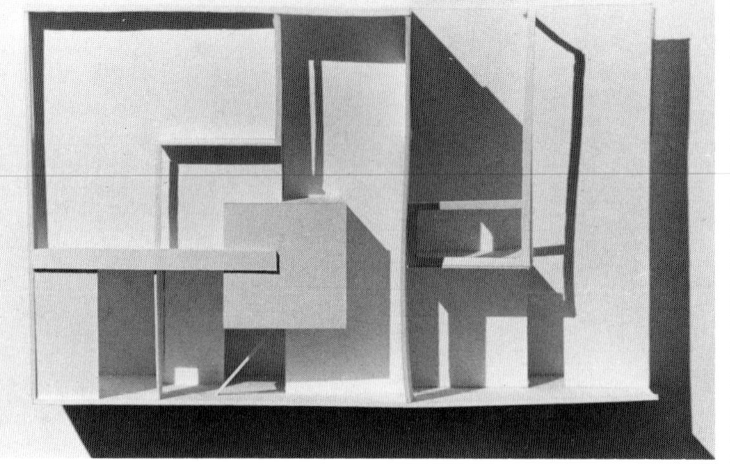
8

text, making one of the spaces clearly dominant. Each composition was to be studied and executed primarily as a cardboard model.

From the results of this preliminary phase, it appeared that the students' initial instinct was to generate space and spatial relationships almost exclusively by means of subtractive operations on the horizontal planes which subdivided the specified container. Obviously, deletions of portions of these planes were inevitable if any spatial continuity through the vertical dimension was to be achieved. Still, the consistent absence of exploration beyond this essential step at so preliminary a stage seemed to suggest inherent limitations of perspective rooted either in the way the exercise was being structured, or in the way it was being studied. We observed that the prescribed cardboard models, fashioned by students to study and portray their compositions, consistently remained literal simulations of the given context, and as a result, tended to predetermine and constrain vantage both in the formation of a conception and in its evaluation. (As simulations, these

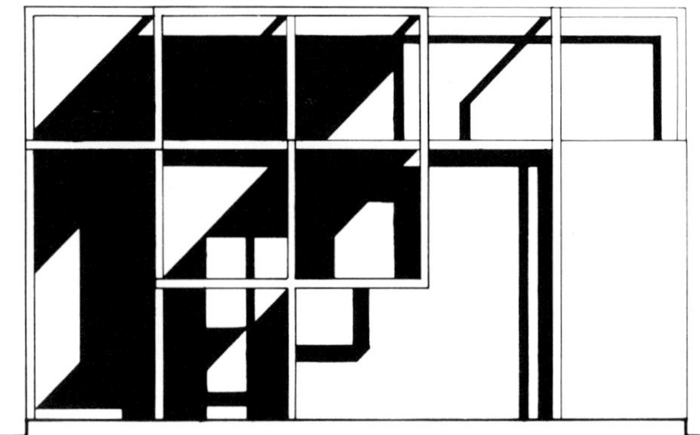
9

10

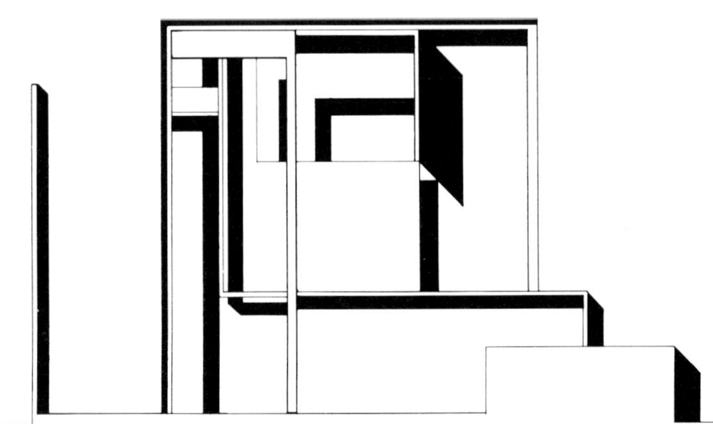
11

12

7 Sectional Elevation; Vivian Kuan
8 Sectional Elevation; Model
9 Sectional Elevation; Marlene Lieu
10 Sectional Elevation; Model
11 Sectional Elevation; Sarah Didvar-Saadi
12 Sectional Elevation; Model

models could only be viewed from above, as plan, or from the ends.)

In response, when students were again instructed to compose a series of interrelated spaces, they were in addition advised to remove one of the longer sides of their models in order to focus on that which might be revealed or stimulated through this otherwise unobservable viewpoint. At this stage as well, they were encouraged to explore and display, within each of their compositions, observable manifestations of point, line, plane and solid as these might relate to the definition of form and space.

Within these results there emerged an extensive variety of exploration. Most had begun to transcend their initial conditioned preoccupation with the given horizontal strata of the container; most displayed signs of an encounter with the third dimension and had at least initiated an exploration into its compositional opportunities; and, in virtually all, space had begun to emerge with space definer as more than a material absence.

The limitations of model as mere simula-

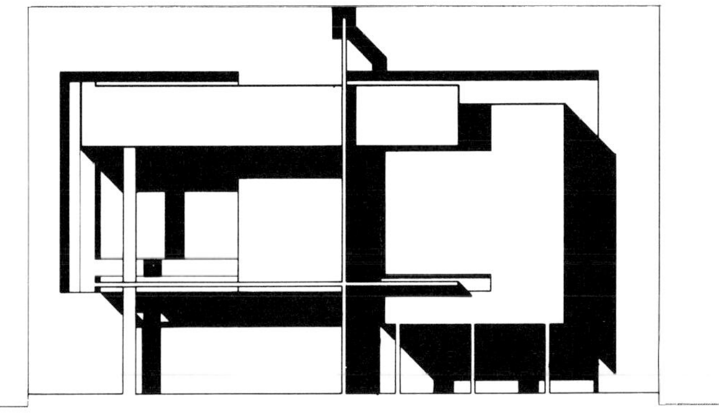

13

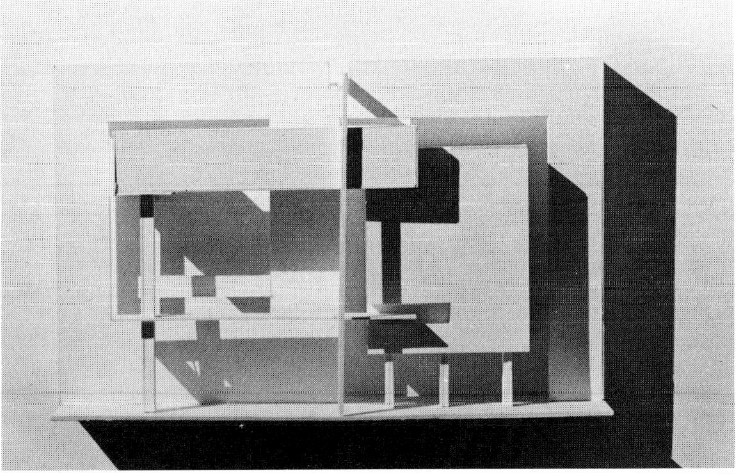

14

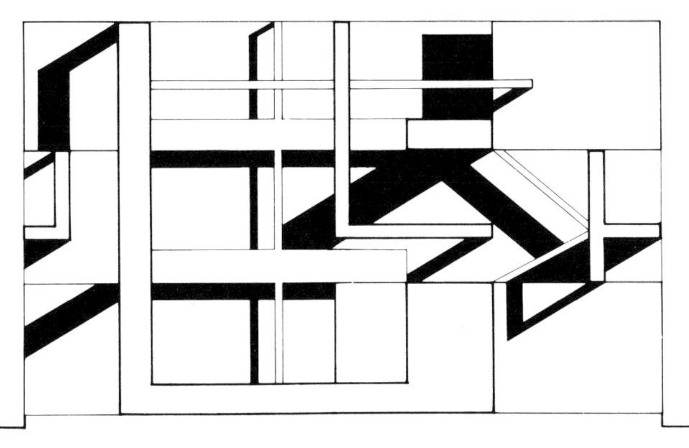

15

16

17

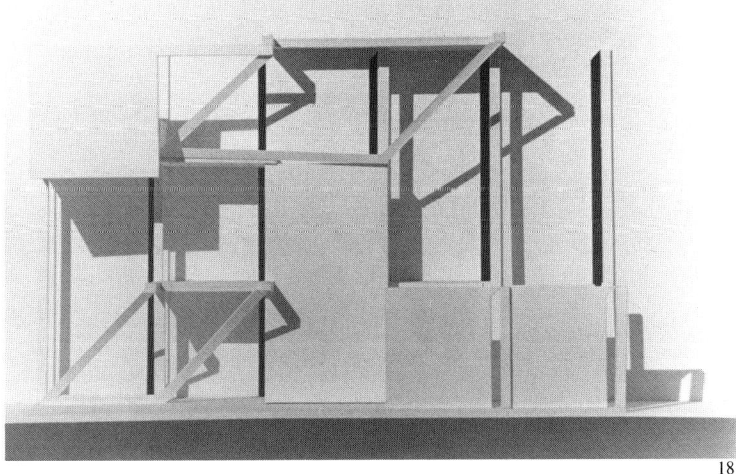

18

13 Sectional Elevation; Jose De La Rosa
14 Sectional Elevation; Model
15 Sectional Elevation; Juan Contin
16 Sectional Elevation; Model
17 Sectional Elevation; William Katz
18 Sectional Elevation; Model

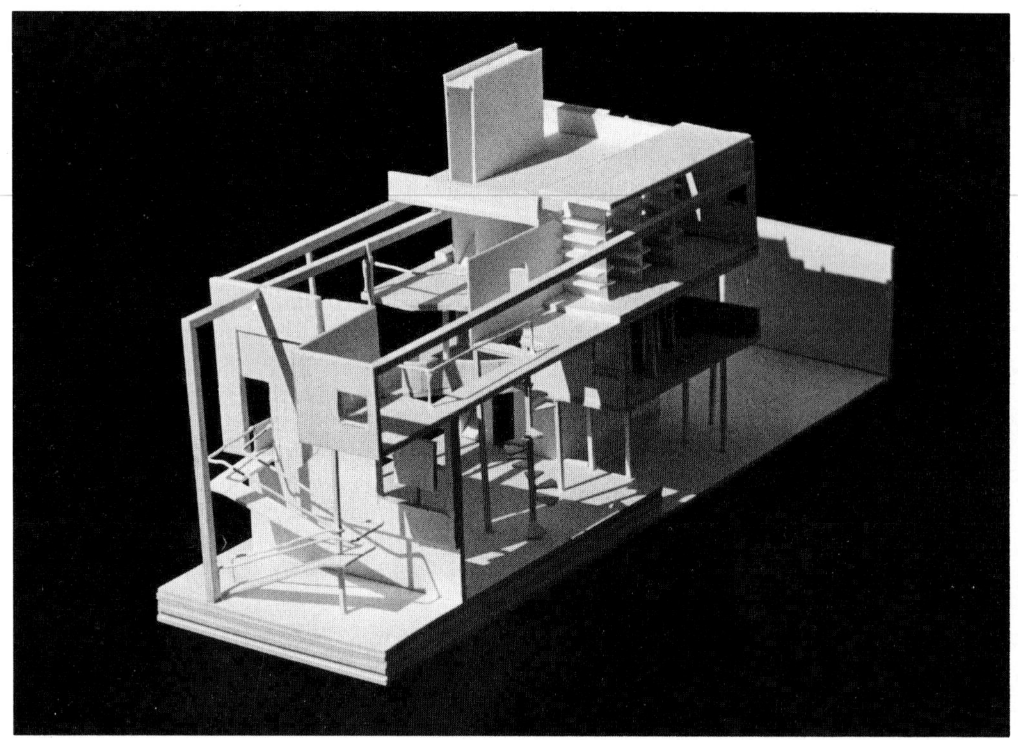

19

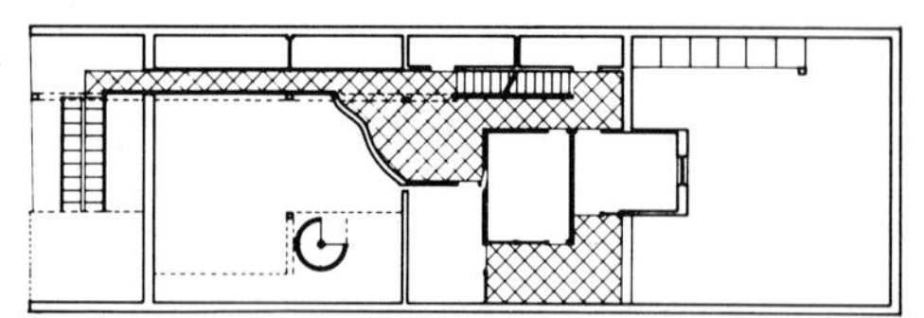

20

21

tor were explicitly overcome when, in the next step, students were asked to transform their most recent compositions into relief models compressing the width of the original context by two-thirds. Then the role of this new model was recast when, on the basis of this transformation, students were asked to recompose what had emerged. This stage of the transformation of the given context appeared to heighten the significance of the containing vertical surface in relation to its horizontal subdivisions, and to substantially advance investigations of planar and spatial relationships through the now abstracted section.

Following a similar logic, students were next asked to construct black and white shadow drawings of their most recent relief models, and to recompose these two-dimensional abstractions on the basis of any new viewpoints (and related ideas) which might emerge.

Finally, students were instructed to compose and construct new relief models based on the results of those previous two-dimensional studies. (Illustrations 1 through 18).

22

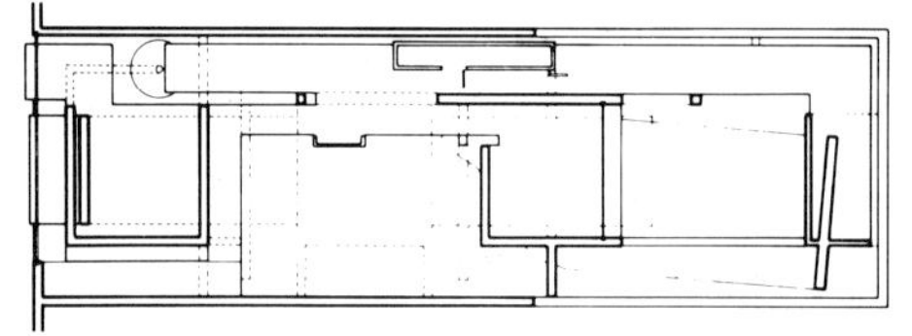

23

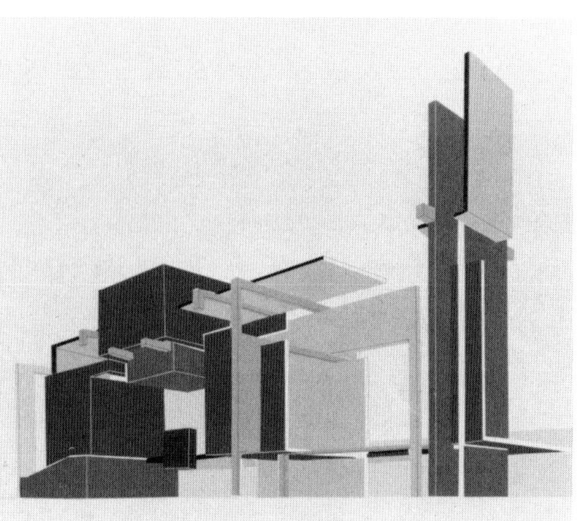

24

19 Travel Society; Model, Liz Herrmann
20 Travel Society; Plan
21 Travel Society; Model
22 Travel Society; Model, Paul Soulellis
23 Travel Society; Plan
24 Travel Society; Perspective

Armed with this orchestrated yet improvisational joint research into the generative and evocative properties of the architect's media for abstraction—and having arrived at some sense of focus in their reflections on form, space and surface in the third dimension—students were then asked to undertake a more synthetic design problem in which function, materiality, structure, orientation, lighting, ventilation, and context were among the issues to be addressed (Illustrations 19 through 31). While this case study was in no way explicitly tied to the studies which preceded it, it was formulated so that similarity of issue and circumstance might encourage a legitimate sense of continuing research, advancing recent insights and lessons while at the same time serving as a format for the application of the fruits of each individual's exploration. ■

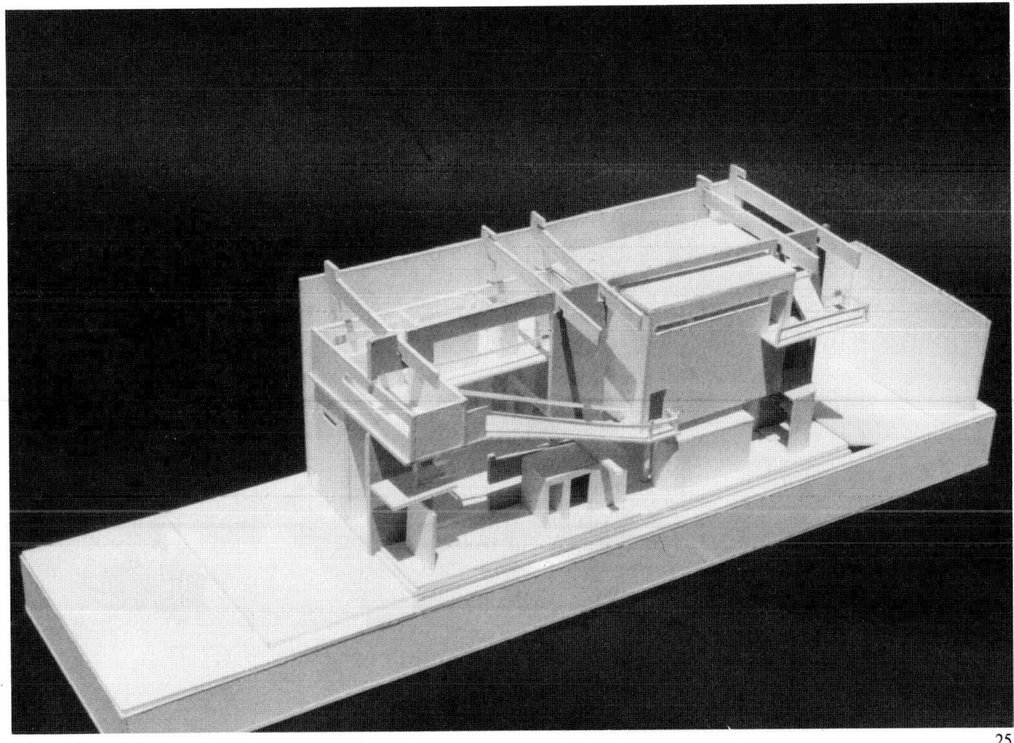

25

26

27

28

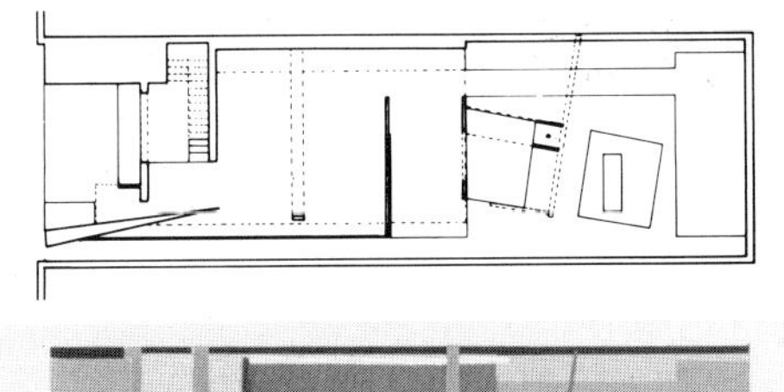

29

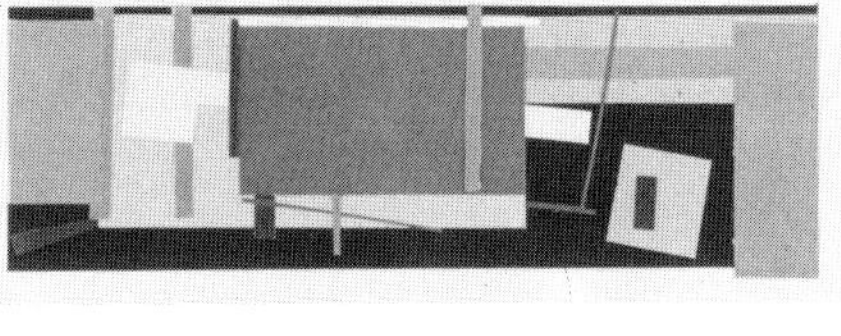

30

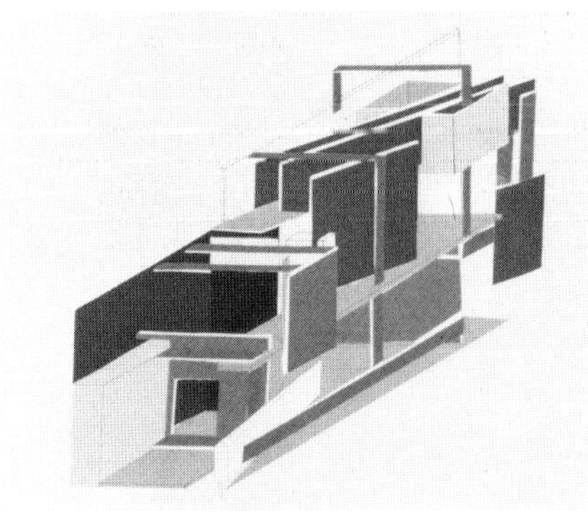

31

25 Travel Society; Model, Jose De la Rosa
26 Travel Society; Model
27 Travel Society; Model
28 Travel Society; Model, Sarah Divadar-Saadi
29 Travel Society; Plan
30 Travel Society; Plan Collage
31 Travel Society; Axonometric

The Bay:

Investigations in the Analysis and Synthesis of an Elevational Phenomenon

Val K. Warke

The analysis and projects illustrated in this section are the recent work of students in the third year studio level at Cornell.

The synthesis of analysis into an architectural design process has always been difficult to effect, despite its being one of the fundamental aspects of the discipline. Pure creativity—the making of something from nothing—has never existed in the arts; it has at most only once occurred anywhere else. Everything one makes originates within a body of knowledge: the collection of 'things' one knows. During the process of making something, additional 'things' may be learned. It is possible that some of these 'things' are known only partially; it is possible that some of these 'things' are known incorrectly. Still, all of what is known assumes a level of truth, or more properly, of verisimilitude, whereby even an 'incorrect' bit of knowledge can lead to a perfectly acceptable result (c.f. Palladio's version of the traditional Roman villa).

The process of making, then, could be best discussed as a process of transformation, the transformation of a given, finite set of elements into one of a virtually infinite set of possibilities. What distinguishes the work of one designer from another, or of one school from another, is a combination of both these aspects: differing bodies of basic knowledge subjected to differing modes of transformation.

The texts and illustrations which follow use the analysis of the repetitive bay in elevation to inform the design of an arcade building, and with the following general purposes:

—to increase the basic pool of the students' knowledge.

—to give the students new means of analyzing existing buildings and projects, thereby expanding their modes of understanding the vertical surfaces in past architecture.

—to provide the students with additional tools for evaluating their own designs and thus to weigh the various options with which they are presented during the process of design.

—to initiate the consideration of new modes of transforming a given object into another object.

It is not the intention of these examples to fix the mode of transformation, in other words to prescribe a design technique which can take elevational bays from any source and—abracadabra—turn them into an 'original' arcade design; in fact, a successful process of analysis, by enlightening one to previously unknown potentialities, often tends to make the design process more difficult—a necessary inconvenience if one wishes to produce a work of architecture which is itself capable of sustaining multiple levels of analysis. Only when used improperly can analysis serve as a prosthetic device.

Moreover, the process of analysis does not obligate the student to produce a design of equivalent inclusivism. It is wrong to think that analysis can solve a work of architecture. The beauty of analysis lies in the fact that, while it can teach you a lot, "if analysis gets in your way," according to William Empson, "it is easy enough to forget it."

Analysis Of A Bay

Since the elevation of a building has traditionally been—especially since the Renaissance—a principal vehicle for conveying architectural meaning, architectural polemic has consequently centered largely upon the art of the vertical surface. However, it was a result of the acceptance of modern architecture's view of the city that the facade lost its preeminent role and much of its capacity for conveying meaning; eventually, architects became less and less adept at producing well-crafted elevations. It is only very recently that changes in architectural and urban sensibilities have led to renewed interest in the potential of the wall.

This exercise represents the investigation of only a fragment of one type of elevation: the bay of the repetitive facade. The pedagogical objectives include the following:

—to discover the extent to which, in superior works of architecture, the bay can be seen as a microcosm of the issues raised by the rest of the building,

—to study the means whereby a repetitive bay system can be used not only to organize a building's elevation, but also, at times, as a means of articulating a building's overall organization,

—to instill an appreciation for the appropriate and consistent development of details in their relation to a design concept,

—to expand the student's repertoire of architectural forms,

—to provoke the usage of new presentation techniques,

—in general, to serve as an initiation into the depths of ostensibly flat surfaces.

The Reversed-Dimension Model

At its most basic level, this model reversed the dimensionality of the original relief: a datum plane is determined, with those elements subtracted from the datum in the original developed as additive elements on the R-D model, and vice versa. Yet it represents far more than simple reiteration, and is, in fact, clearly a design problem. The analytical exercise must inform the layering and formal hierarchies of the R-D model. All formal ambiguities of the original which lead to multiple interpretations must be preserved; however, the dominance of the interpretations (e.g., primary, secondary, etc.) may be reversed.

The pedagogical value of the R-D model lies largely in the manipulation of an historical model. The negation of additive structural elements such as pilasters or rusticated bases, for example, tends to increase the potential for glazed surface area and instantly 'modernize' many of the facades. Ultimately, the result is a mode of transforming a given precedent without resorting to superficial mimicry or tiresome parody.

When one looks inside the mold of a life mask, it is perceived at first as only a bare abstraction of a face, human only in the scale and character of its contours. But when viewed frontally, one's eyes suddenly view this subtractive mold as an eerily accurate representation of a human face. These models could be understood as life masks of the original facade bays, as abstracted representations of the formal essentials of their originals. ■

1

2

Palazzo Pitti

Bartolomeo Ammanati, 1560
Project by Bing-Shing Leung

1 Relief Model
2 Reversed-Dimension Model
3 Elevation
4 Section
5 Plan
6 Proportional Study
7 Proportional Study
8 Proportional Study
9 Framed Fenestration
10 Implied Frame and Infill System
11 Force Transmission
12 Regulating Lines

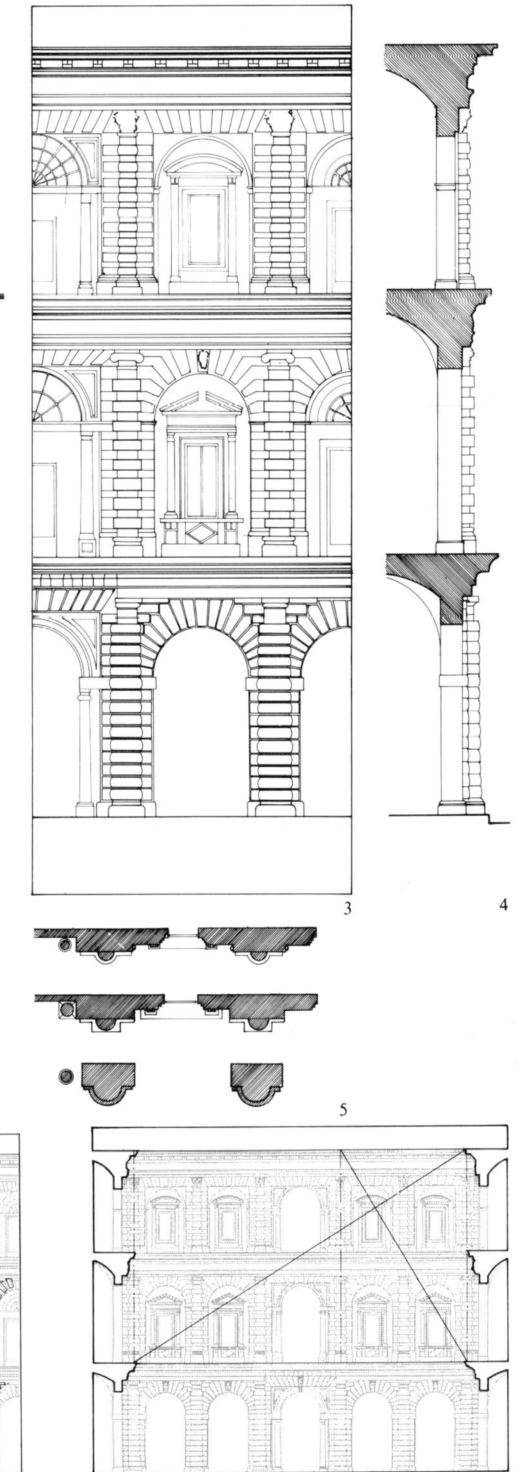

3

4

5

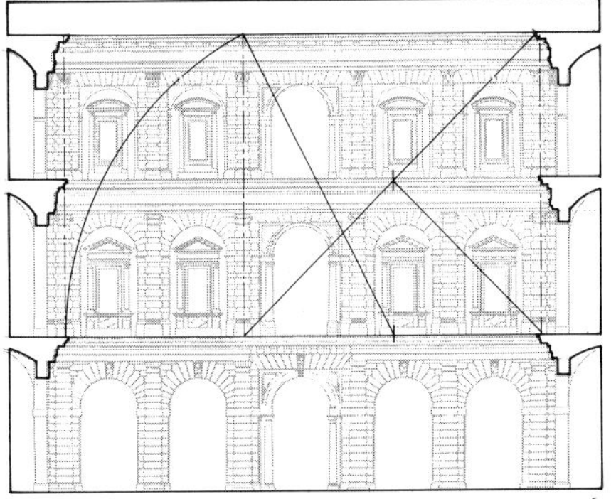

6

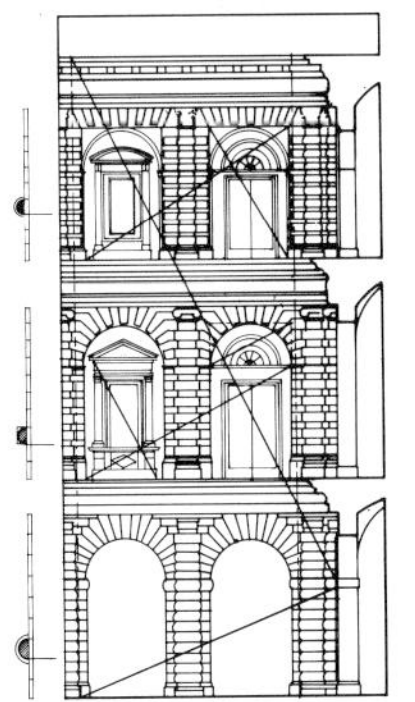

7

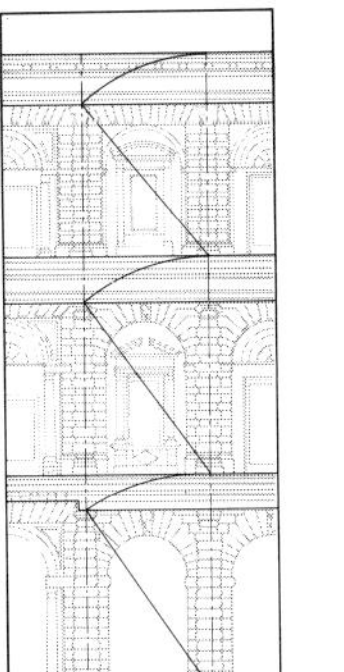

8

9

10

11

12

Doric Cloister, San Ambrogio
Donato Bramante, 1498
Project by Timothy Downing

1 Section
2 Elevation
3 Plan
4 Relief Model
5 Reversed-Dimension Model
6 Context
7 Proportional Study
8 Proportional Study
9 Proportional Study
10 Proportional Study
11 Implied Depth/Perspective

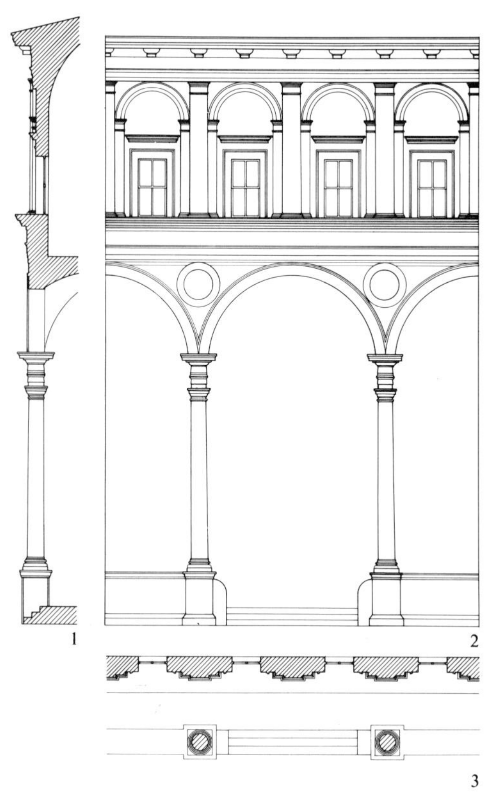

1

2

3

4

5

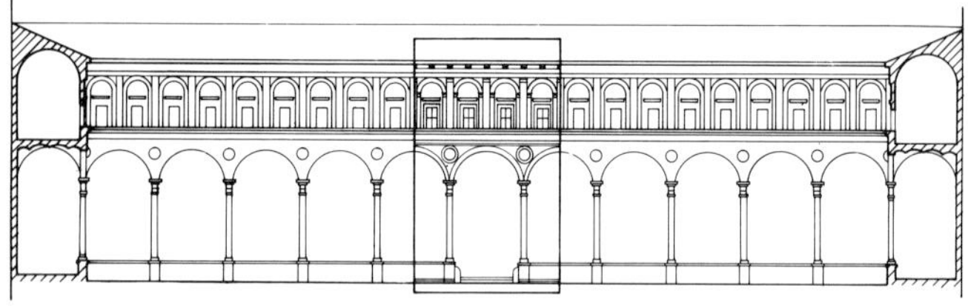

6

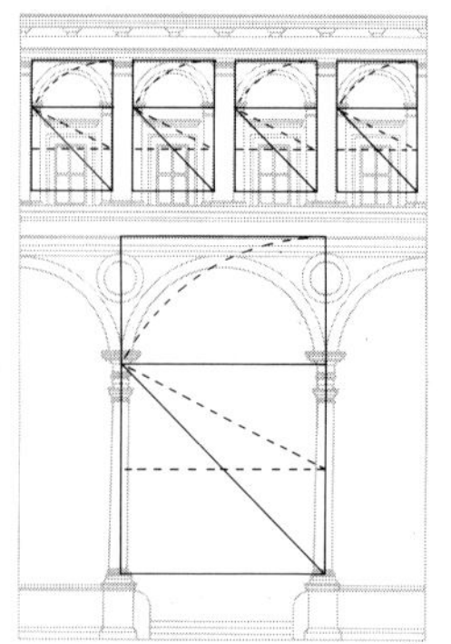

7

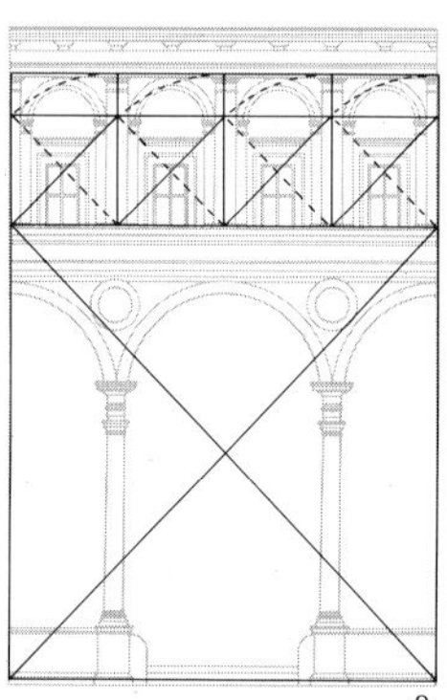

8

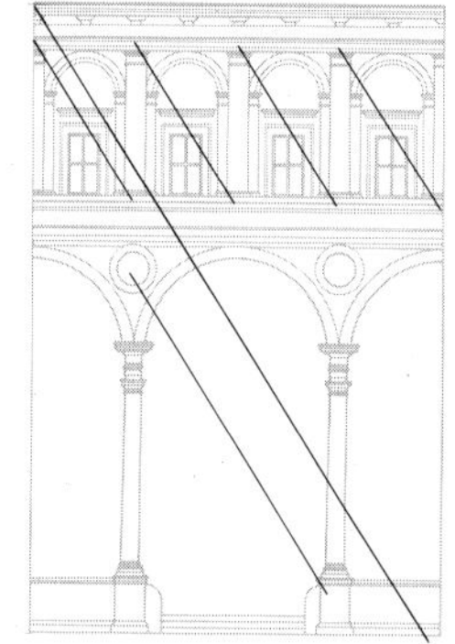

9

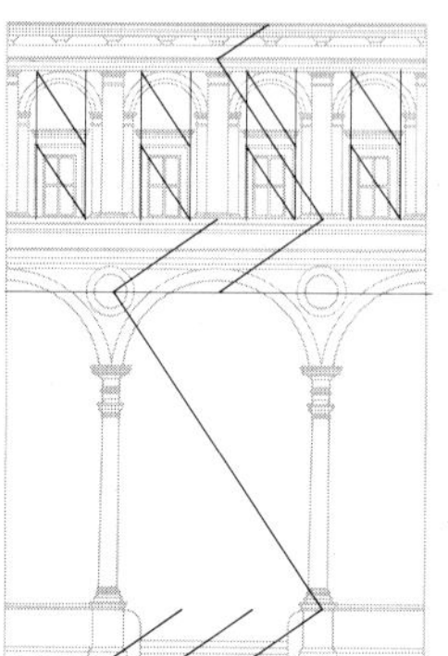

10

11

Palazzo Borghese
Martino Longhi the Elder 1586
Project by Mark Klopfer

1 Relief Model
2 Reversed-Dimension Model
3 Elevation
4 Section
5 Plan
6 Interior/Exterior Facades
7 Big/Little Bays
8 Proportional Study
9 Center to Center
10 Proportional Study
11 Proportional Study
12 Context

1

2

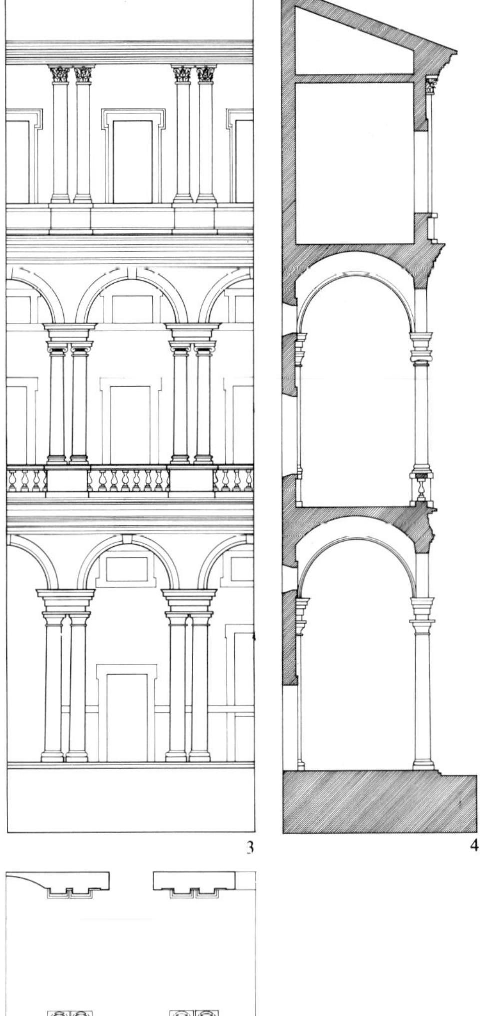

3 4 5

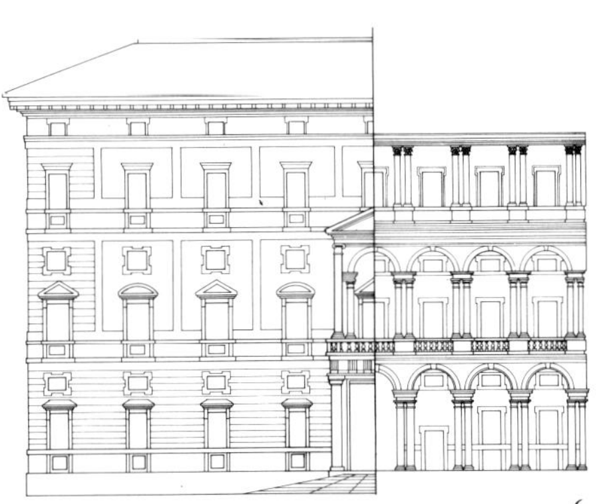

6

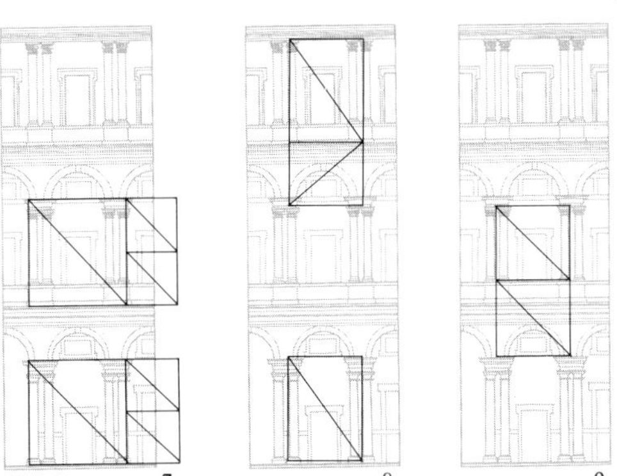

7 8

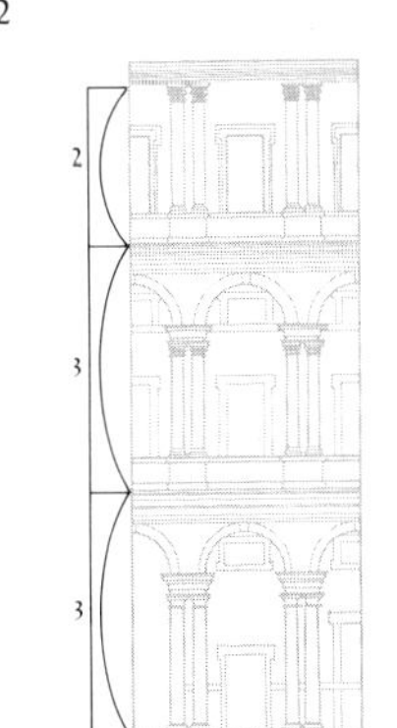

9

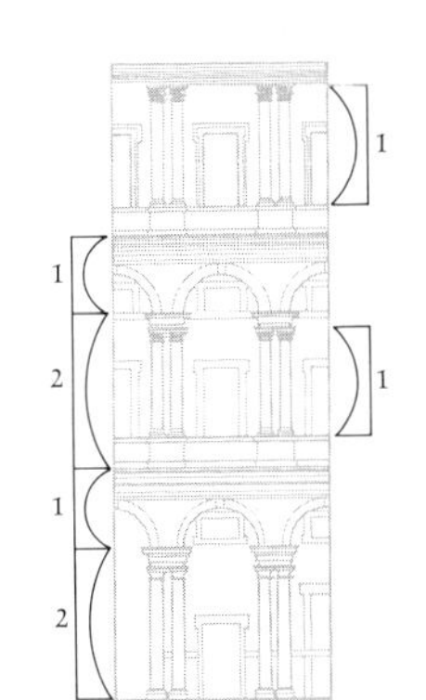

10 11

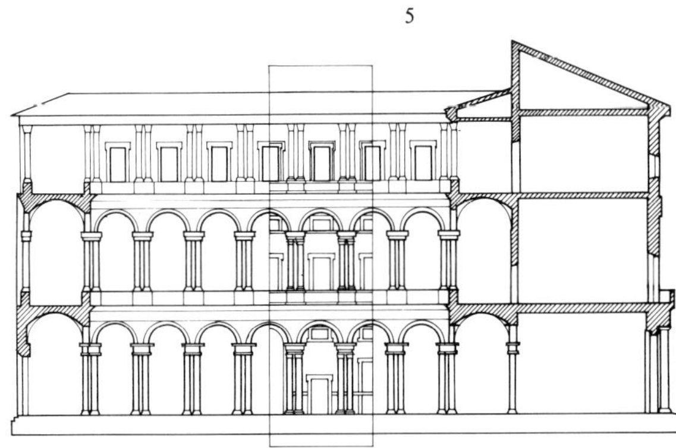

12

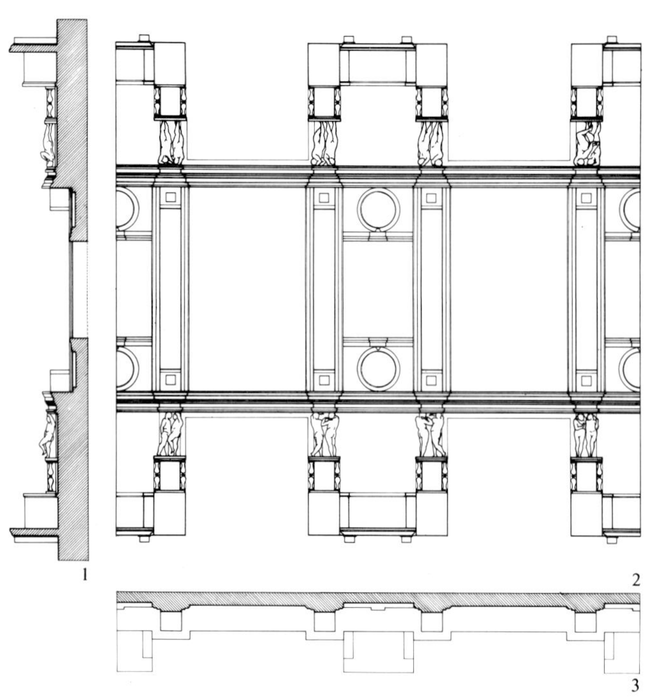

1

2

3

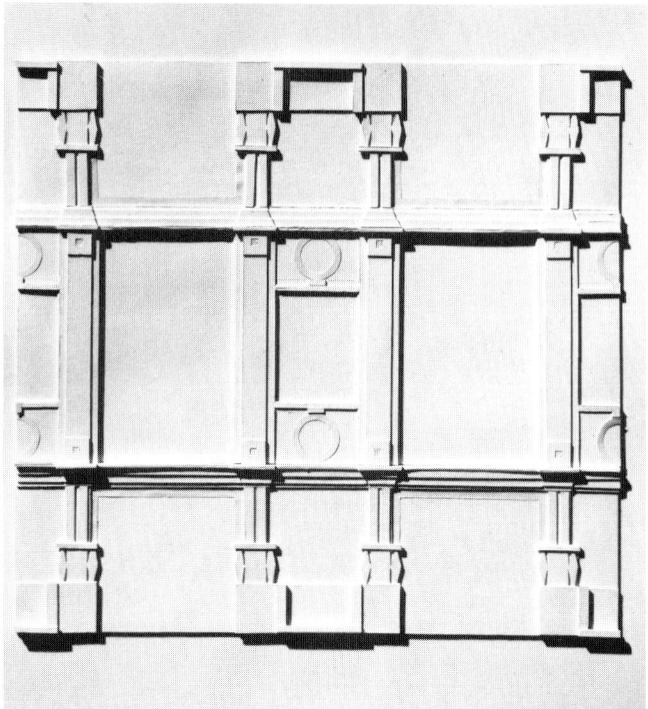

4

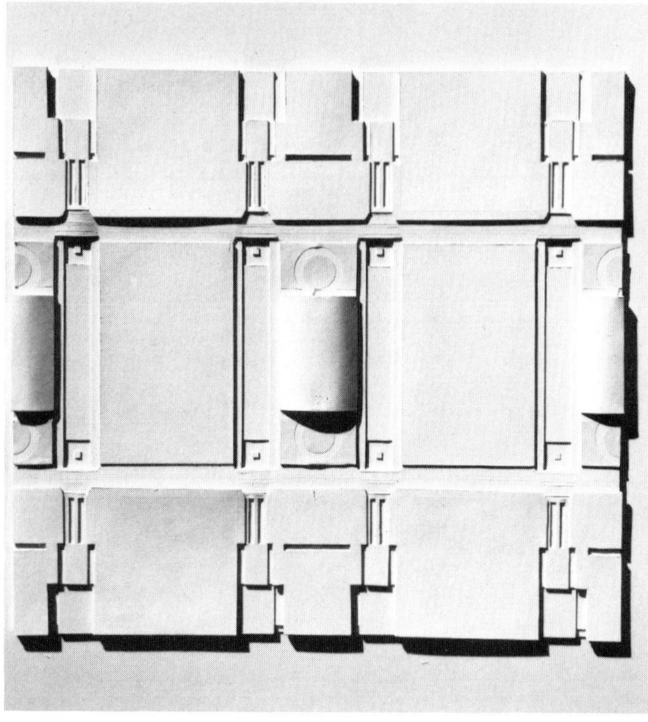

5

Sistine Chapel Ceiling

Michelangelo Buonarroti 1533
Project by Reidun Anderson

1 Implied Section
2 Elevation (Ceiling Plan)
3 Implied Section
4 Relief Model
5 Reversed-Dimension Model
6 Narrow Bay
7 Axonometric; see Michelangelo's project for the tomb of Julius II
8 Framing Elements
9 Scale Relationships
10 Similar Facade: Facade of San Lorenzo, Florence.

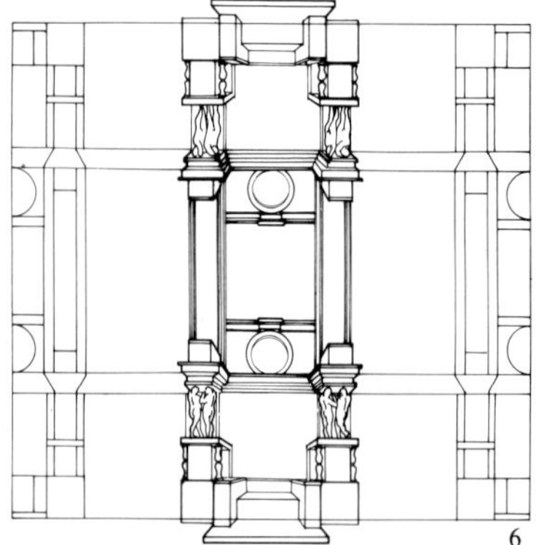

6

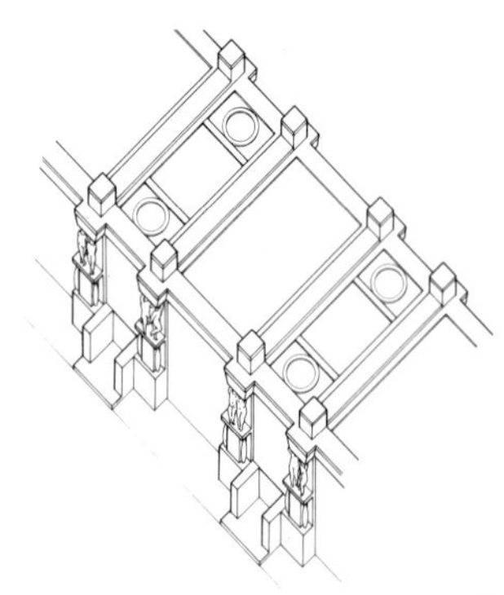

7

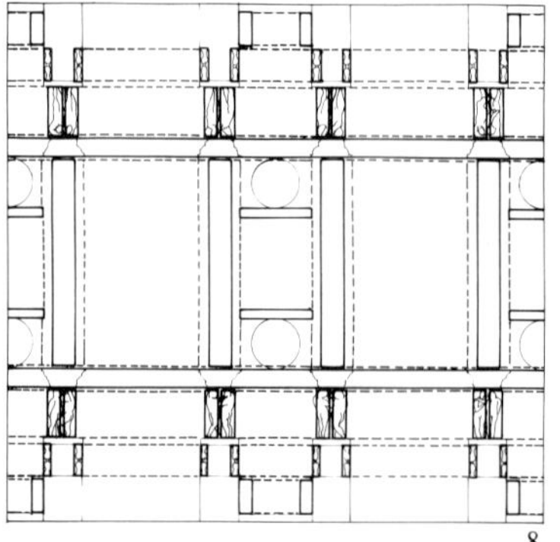

8

9

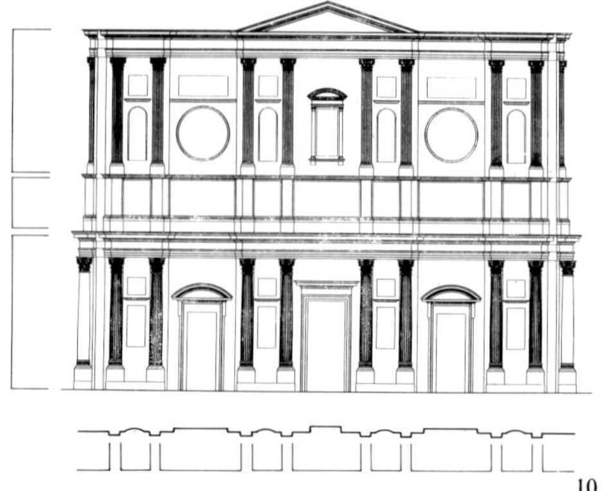

10

1

2

Loggia del Capitaniato
Andrea Palladio 1572
Project by Gabrielle Blackman

1 Relief Model
2 Reversed-Dimension Model
3 Elevation
4 Section
5 Conjectured Plan
6 Scale/Implied Depth
7 Building Types
8 Building Types
9 Building Types
10 Proportional Study
11 Interwoven Layers
12 Ideal/Actual Grid
13 Conjectured Context

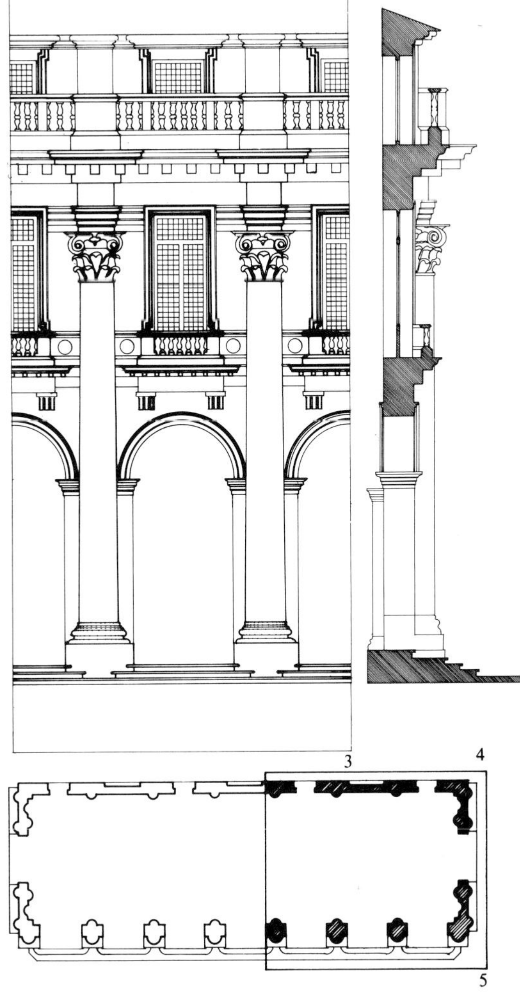

3 4 5

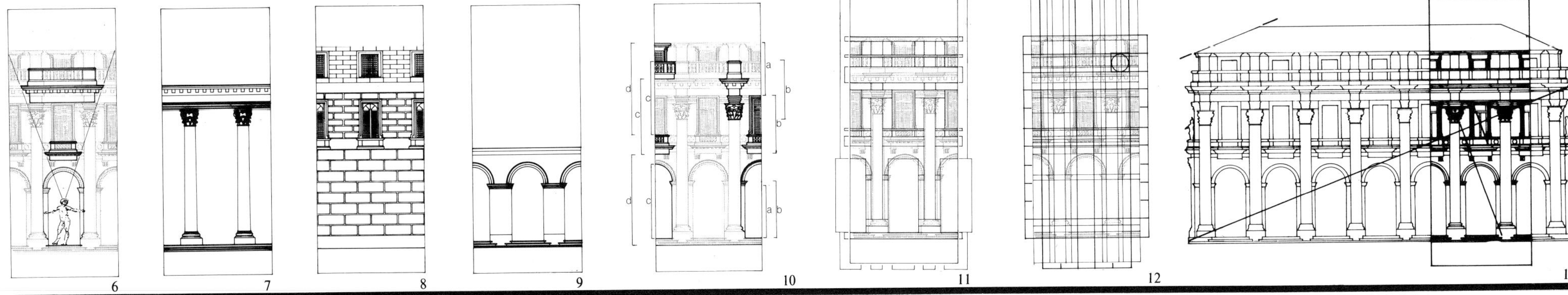

6 7 8 9 10 11 12 13

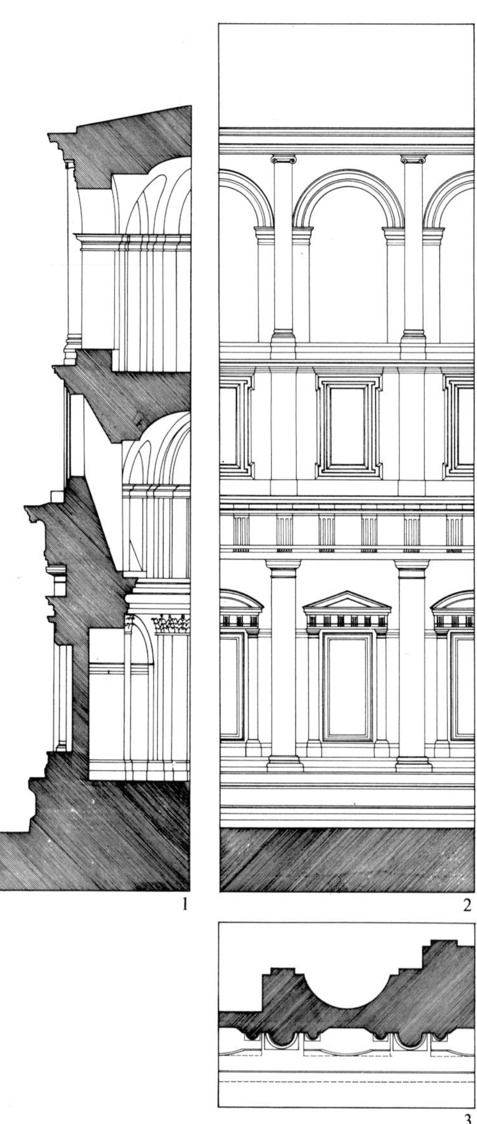
1

2

3

St. Peter's

Antonio da Sangallo the Younger, begun 1505
Project by Ellen Ritter

1 Section
2 Elevation
3 Plan
4 Relief Model
5 Reversed-Dimension Model
6 View
7 Proportional Study
8 Grid
9 Proportional Study
10 Proportional Study
11 Proportional Study
12 Proportional Study

4

5

6

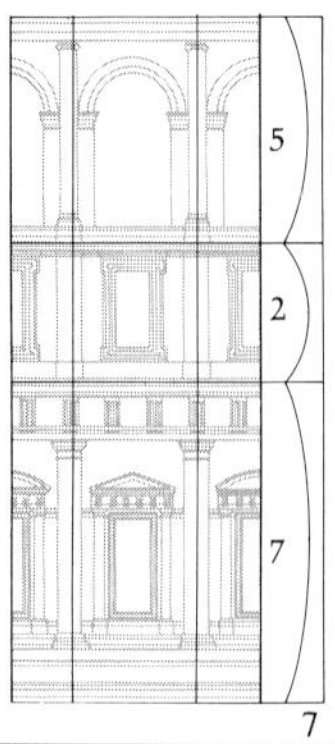

7

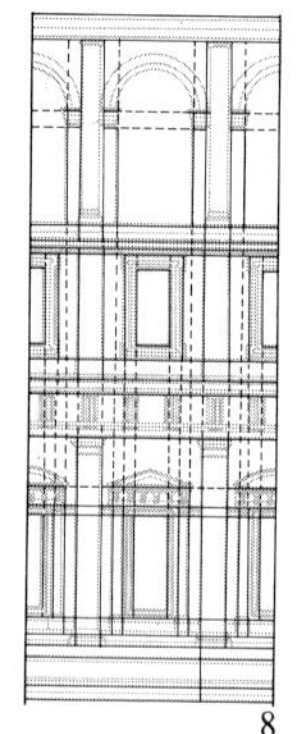
8

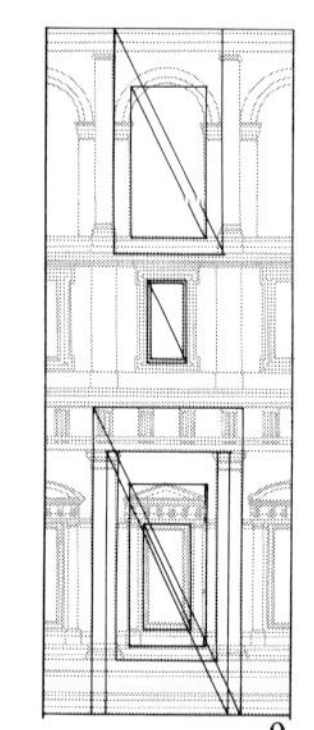
9

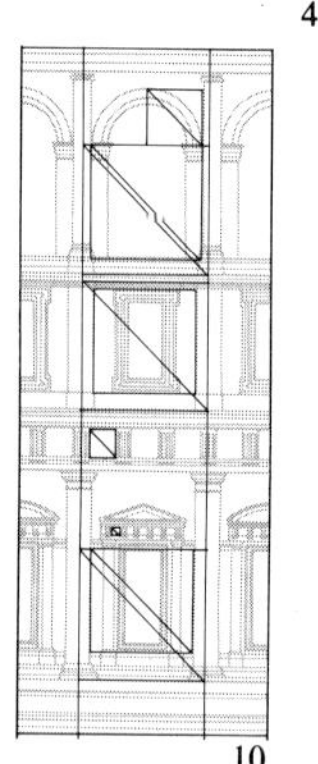
10

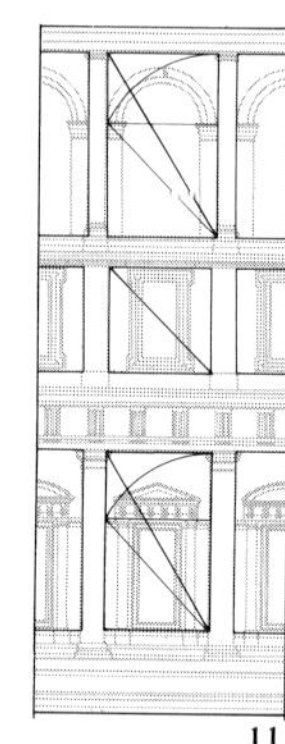
11

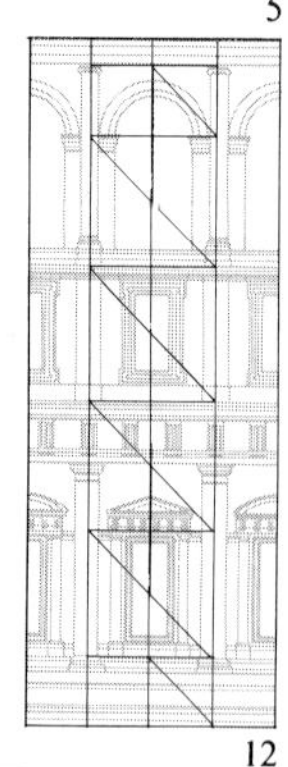
12

1

2

Miracle of a Stillborn Child
Perugino 1473
Project by Jason Ramos

1 Relief Model
2 Reversed-Dimension Model
3 Perspective
4 Elevation
5 Plan/Section
6 Proportional Study
7 Overlay
8 Implied Background
9 Rhythm
10 Perspective and Geometries

3

4

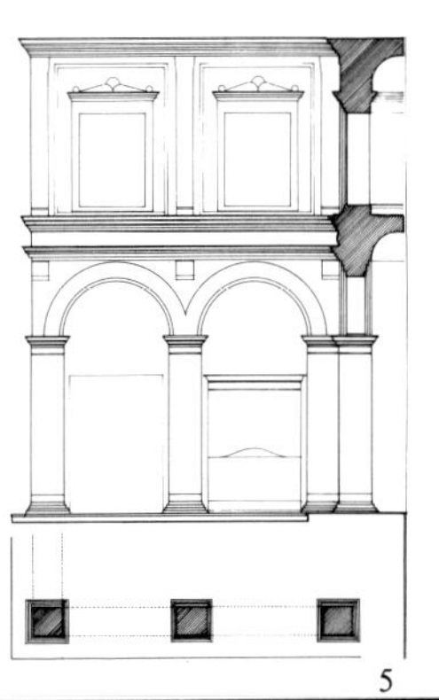

5

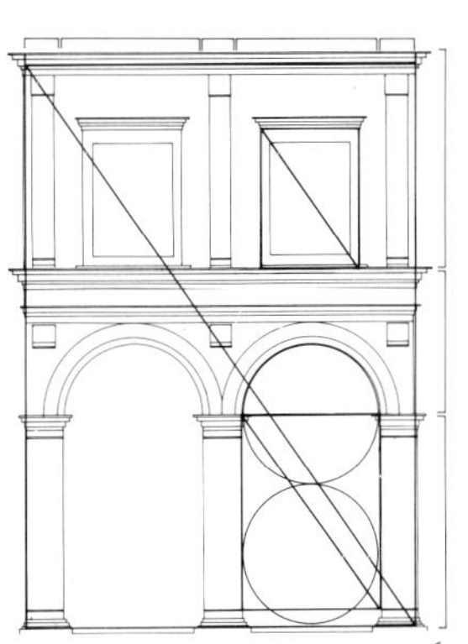

6

7

8

9

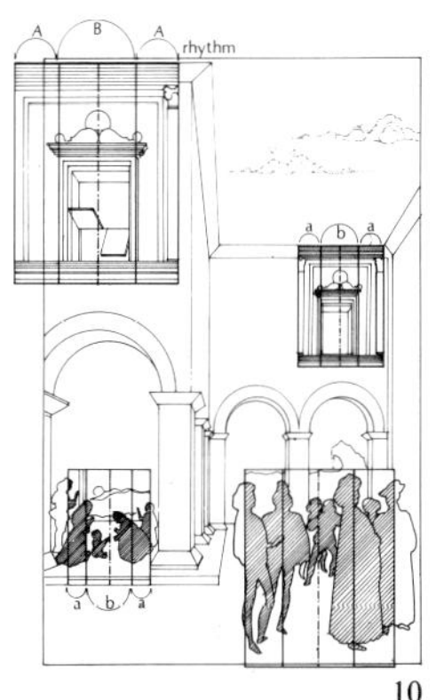

10

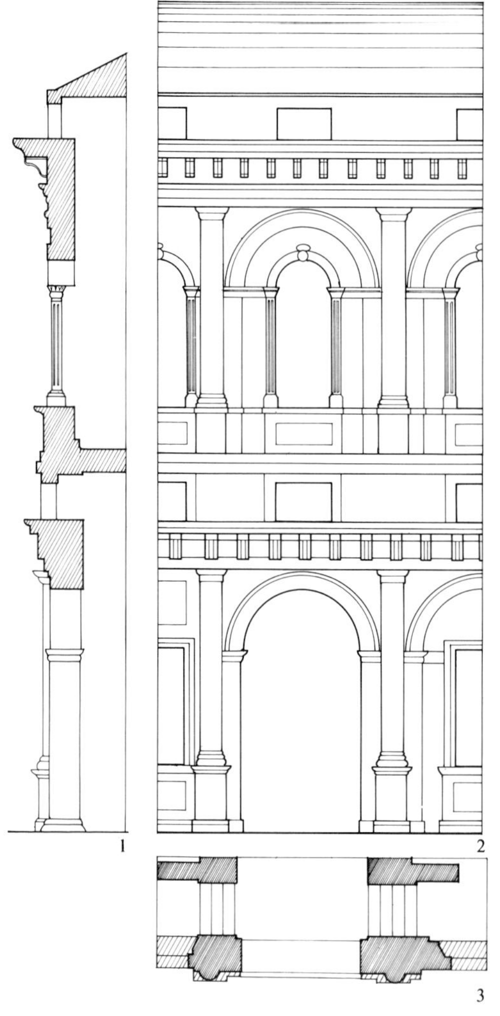

1

2

3

Palazzo Canossa

Michele Sanmichele 1537

Project by Karen Wu

1 Section
2 Elevation
3 Plan
4 Relief Model
5 Reversed-Dimension Model
6 Context Proportional Study
7 Real vs. Implied Rhythm
8 Proportional Study
9 Proportional Study
10 Proportional Study
11 Context

4

5

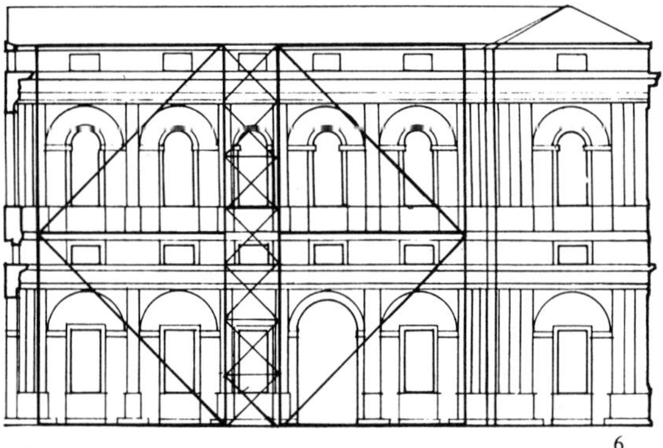

6

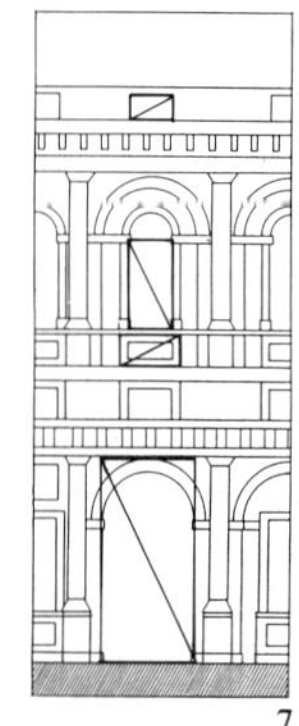

7

8

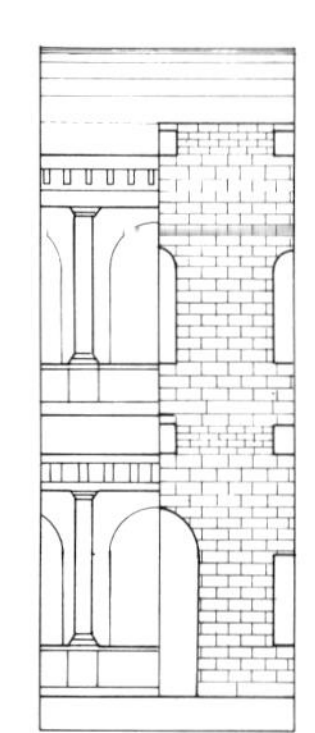

9

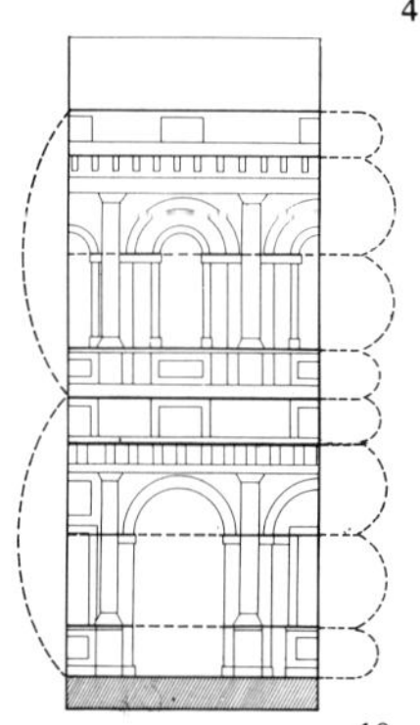

10

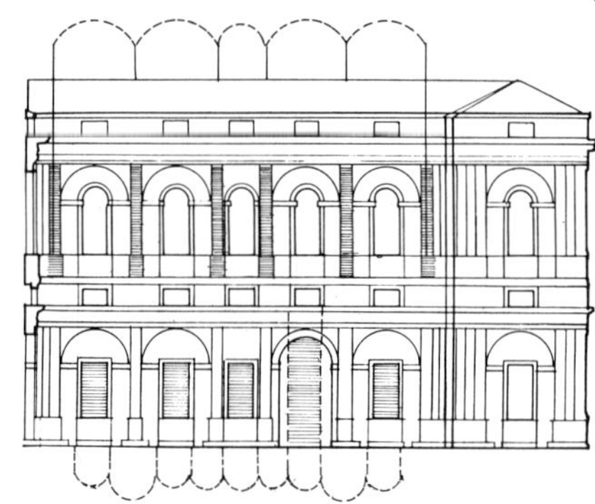

11

1

2

Palazzo Bevilacqua

Michele Sanmichele 1532

Project by Sharon Chung

1 Relief Model
2 Reversed Dimension Model
3 Elevation
4 Section
5 Plan
6 Proportional Study
7 Proportional Study
8 Proportional Study
9 Openings
10 Implied Structure
11 Inversed Layering
12 Implied Perspectives
13 Context

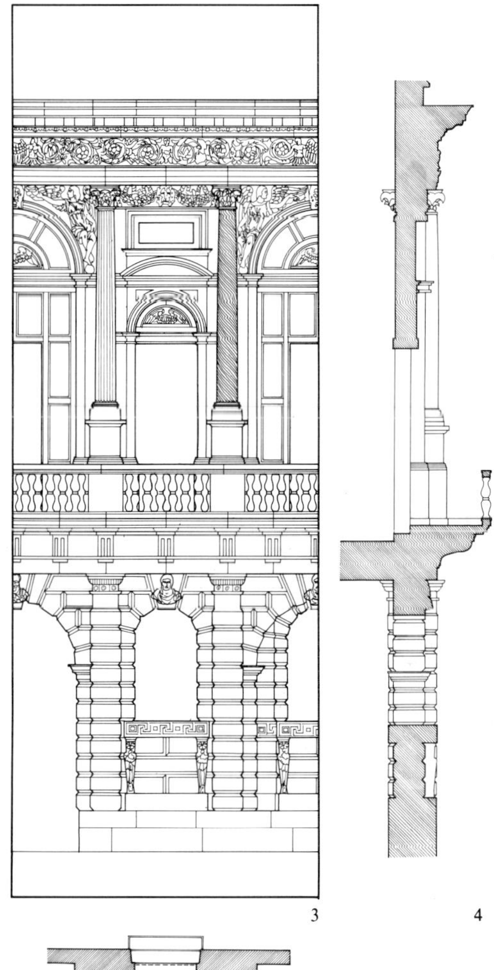

3 4

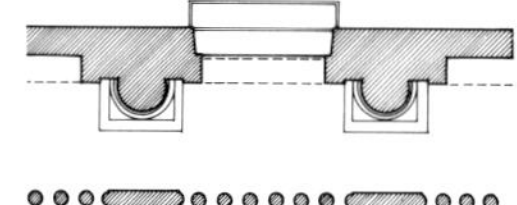

5

6 7

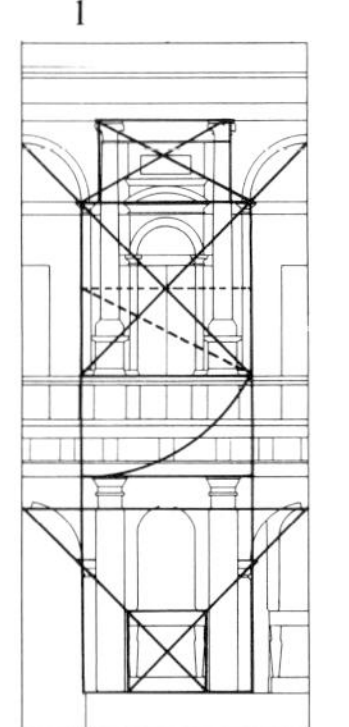

8

9

10

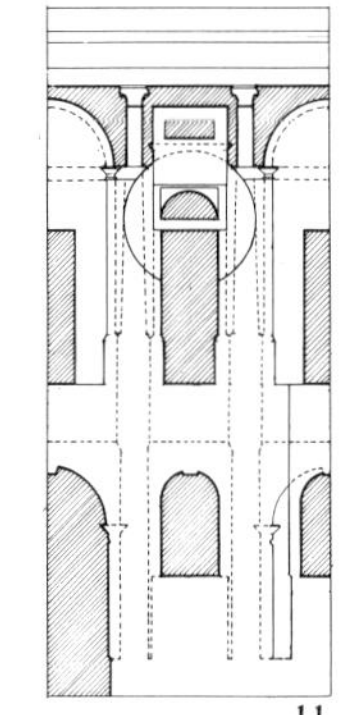

11

12

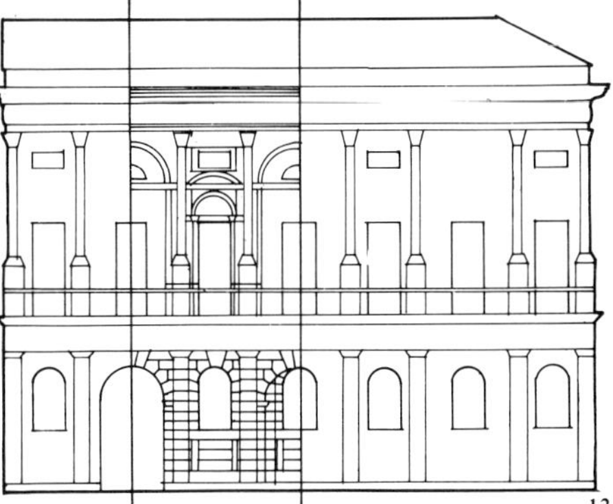

13

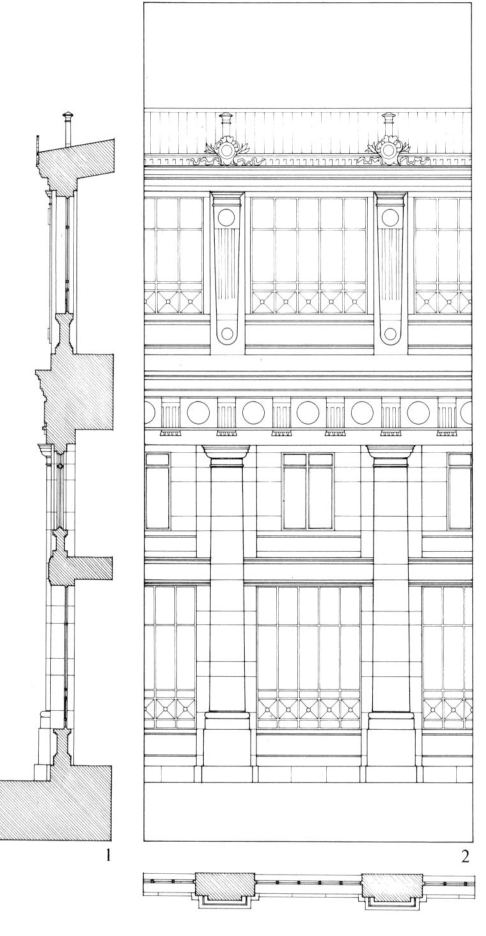

1 2 3

Station on the Gurtellinie of the Alser Strasse

Otto Wagner 1897
Project by Jeffrey Holmes

1 Section
2 Elevation
3 Plan
4 Relief Model
5 Reversed-Dimension Model
6 Proportional Study
7 Proportional Study
8 Structure
9 Column Analysis
10 Proportional Study

4

5

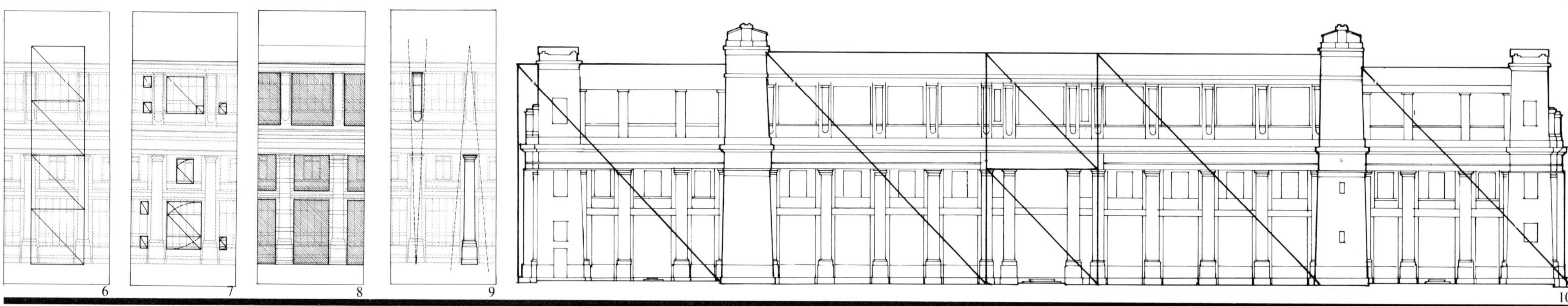

6 7 8 9 10

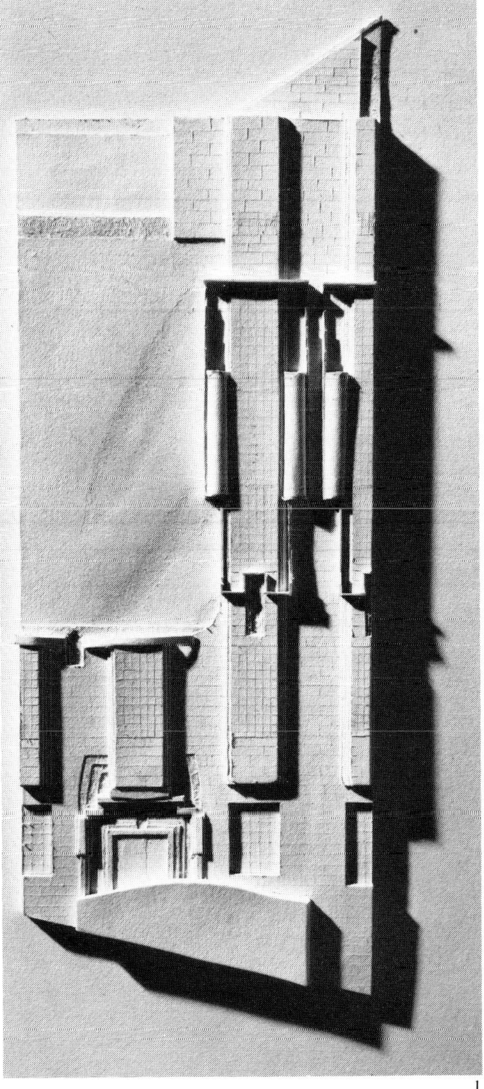

1

2

Glasgow School of Art

Charles Rennie Mackintosh
1896
Project by Patrick Daly

1 Relief Model
2 Reversed-Dimension Model
3 Elevation
4 Section
5 Plan
6 Rhythm
7 Geometries
8 Axes
9 Geometries
10 Surface Elements
11 Proportions
12 North Elevation

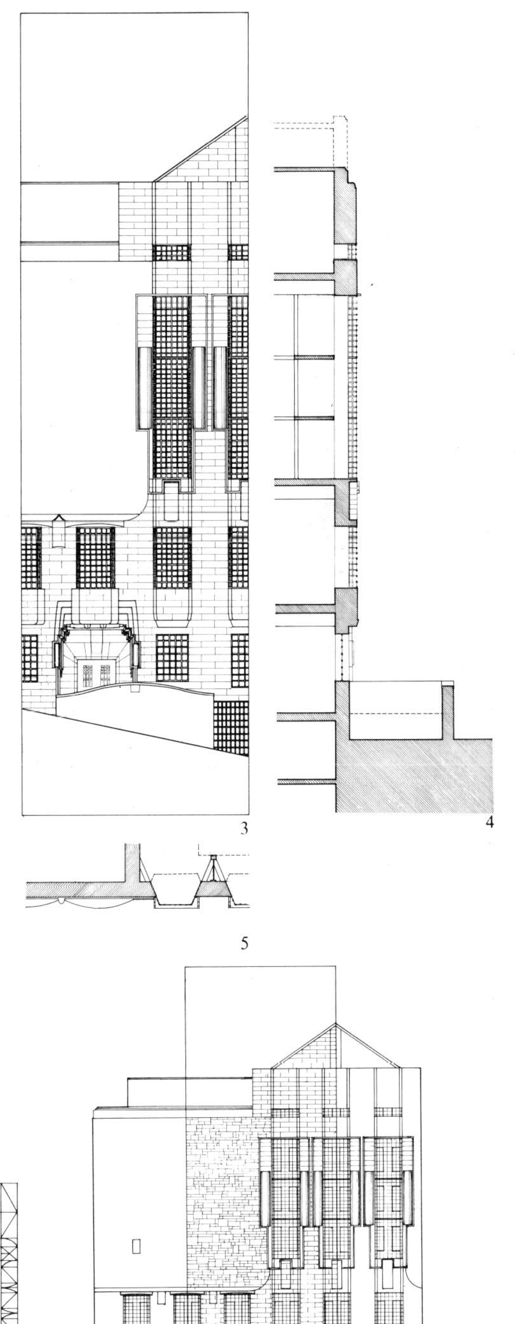

3 4 5

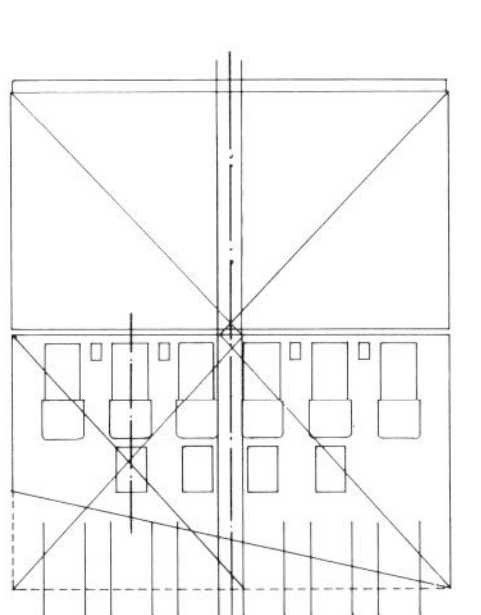

6

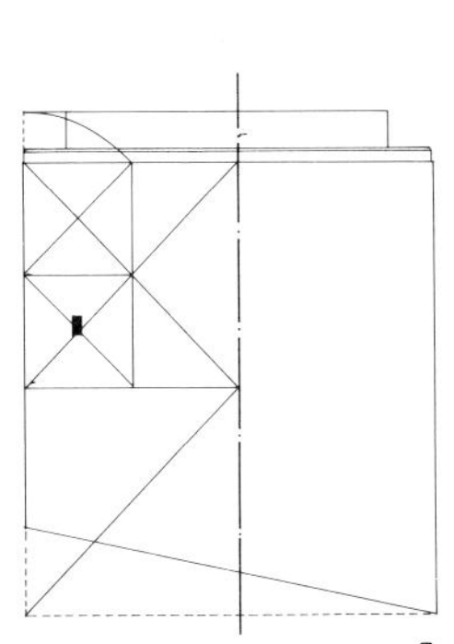

7

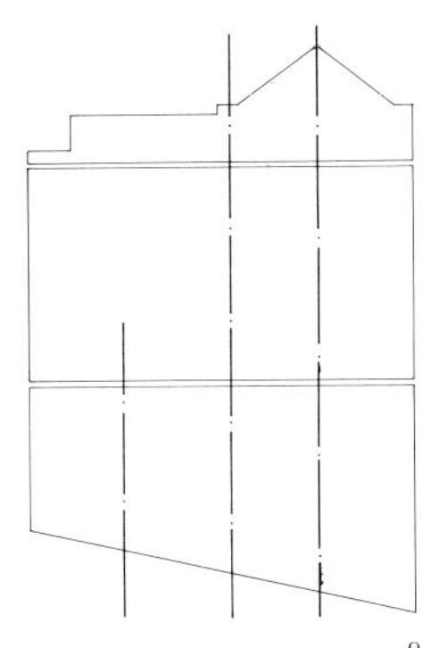

8

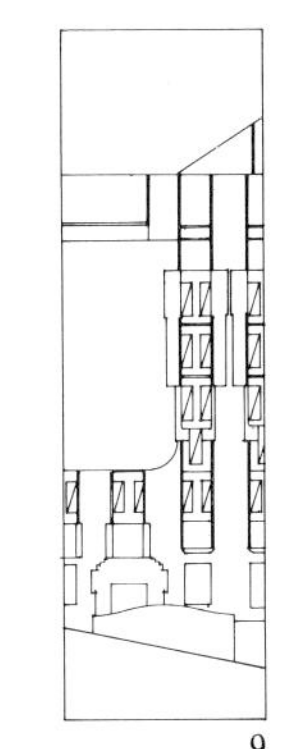

9

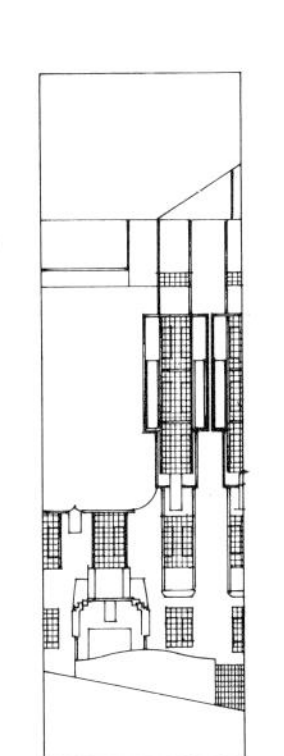

10

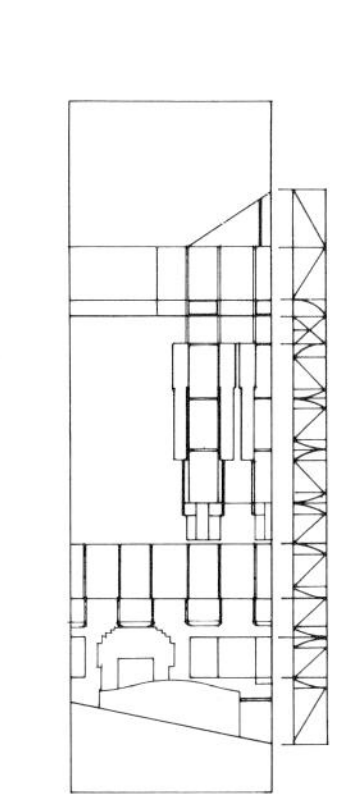

11

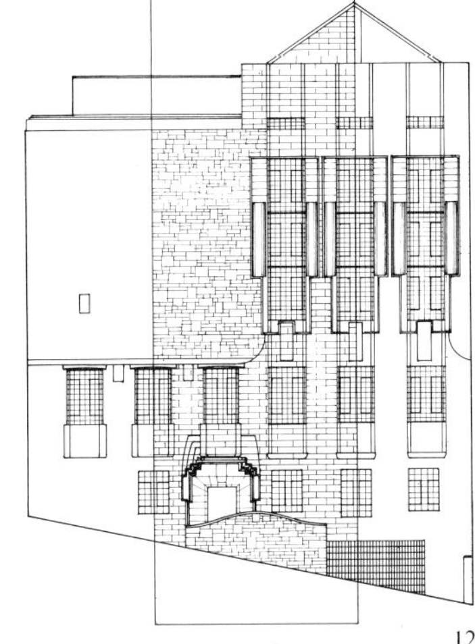

12

The Boston Opera Arcade and Tower
Critic: Val Warke

The history of Arcade and Passage buildings is concerned primarily with notions of extruded sections and concatenated interior elevations. This exercise, therefore, offers the student an opportunity to continue to 'plumb the depths' of relatively flat surfaces, an investigation begun in the analysis of the Bay.

The urban requirement of the new Opera Arcade, located between Washington Street on the east and Tremont Street on the west, is to connect the Boston Opera House and the Roxy Music Hall with the Boston Common. Since the new arcade will function as the major pedestrian passage between the Washington Street shopping district and the Boston Common, it will be, in effect, two buildings: a person on the Common should be able to interpret the building as a vestibule to the theaters and shopping districts beyond; while a person on Washington Street must be able to interpret the building as a gateway to the park, and six or eight times during the summer as a lobby to the grand exterior theater.

1 Ground Floor Plan; Jason Ramos
2 Detail of Interior Bay
3 Longitudinal Section
4 Detail Bay; Phil Kim
5 Transverse Section; Jason Ramos
6 Ground Floor Plan; Phil Kim
7 Second Floor Plan
8 Longitudinal Section

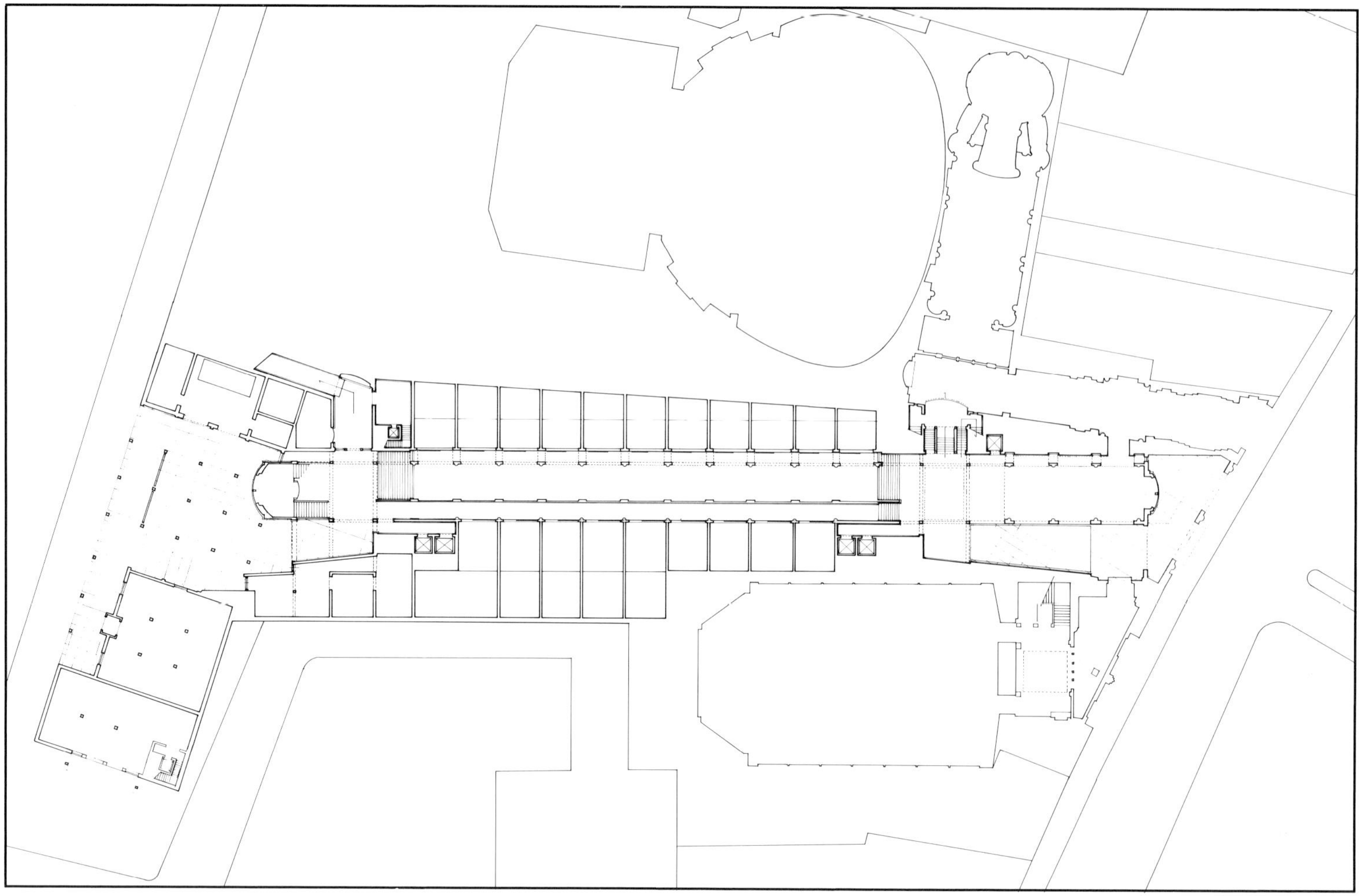

1

2

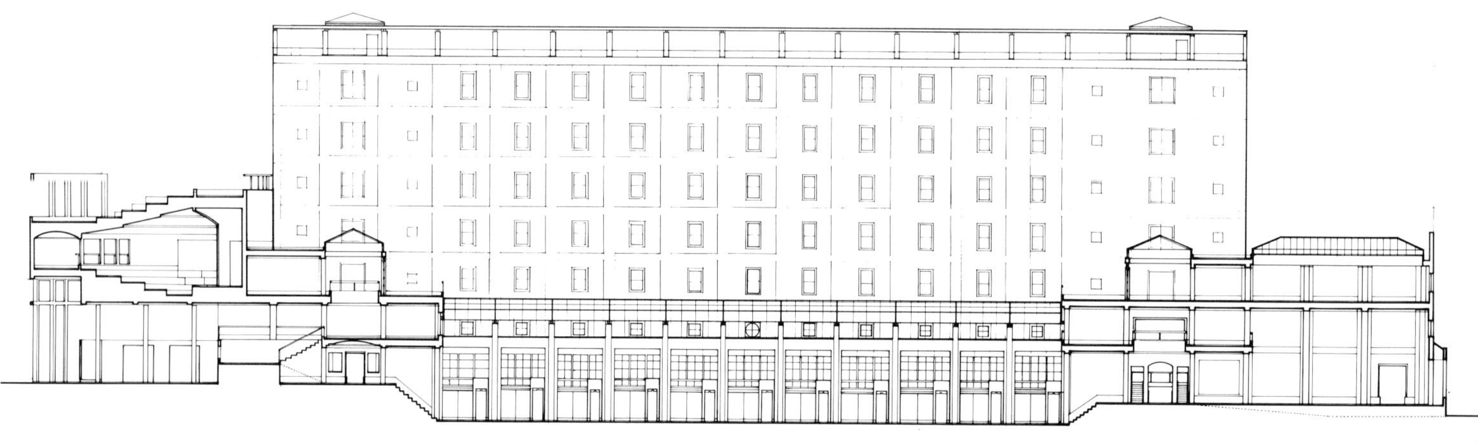

3

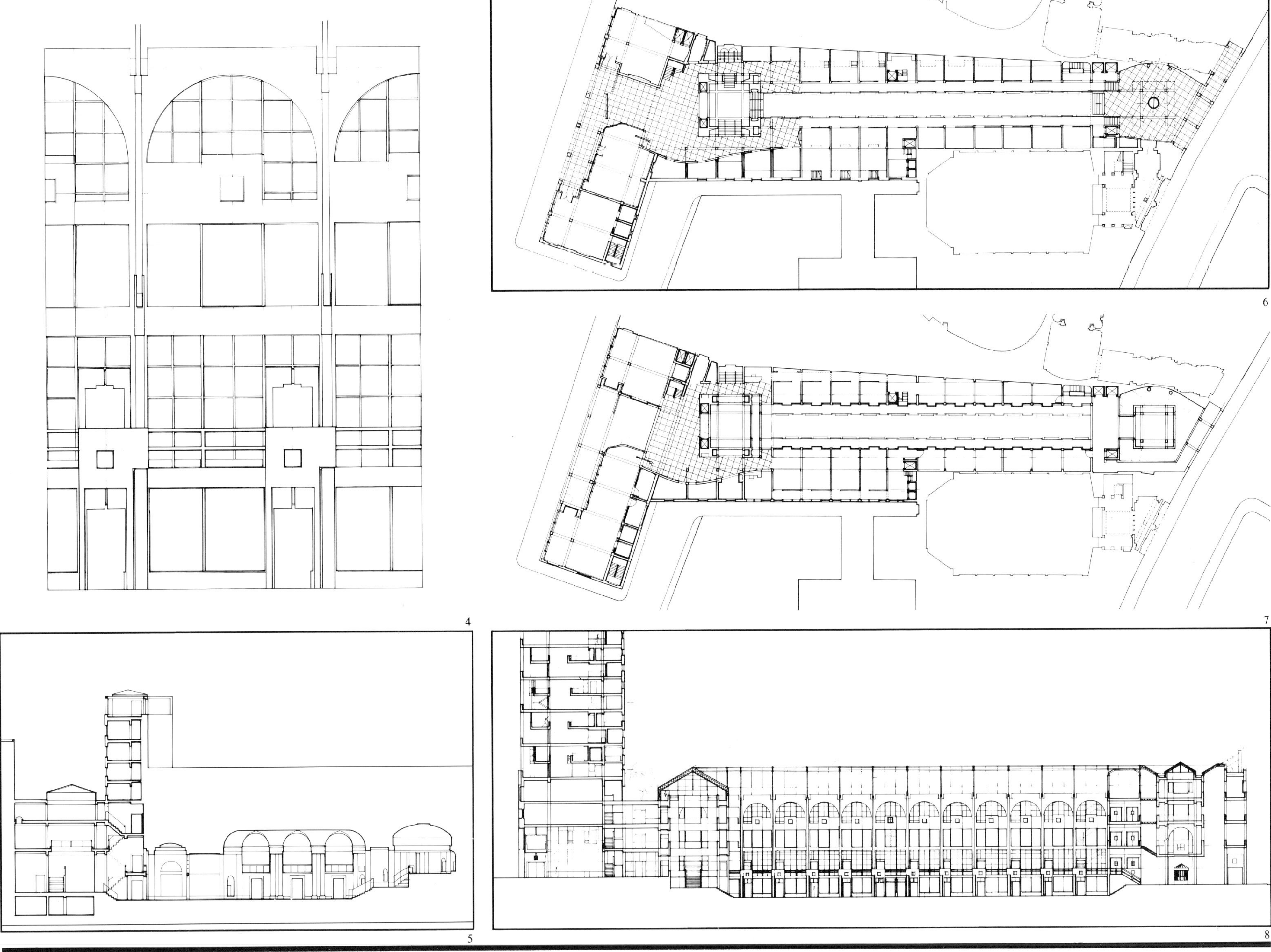
6
7
4
5
8

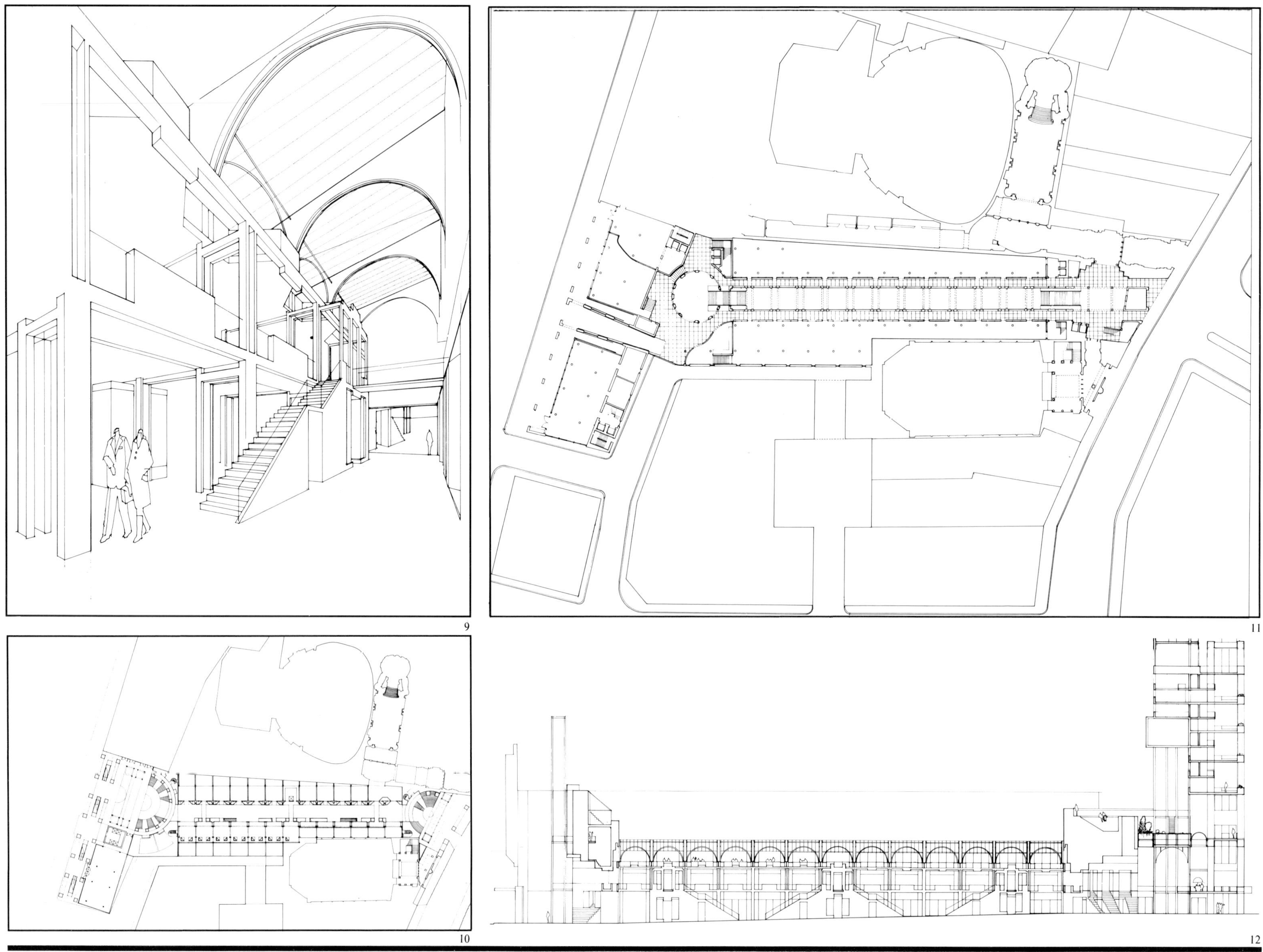
9
11
10
12

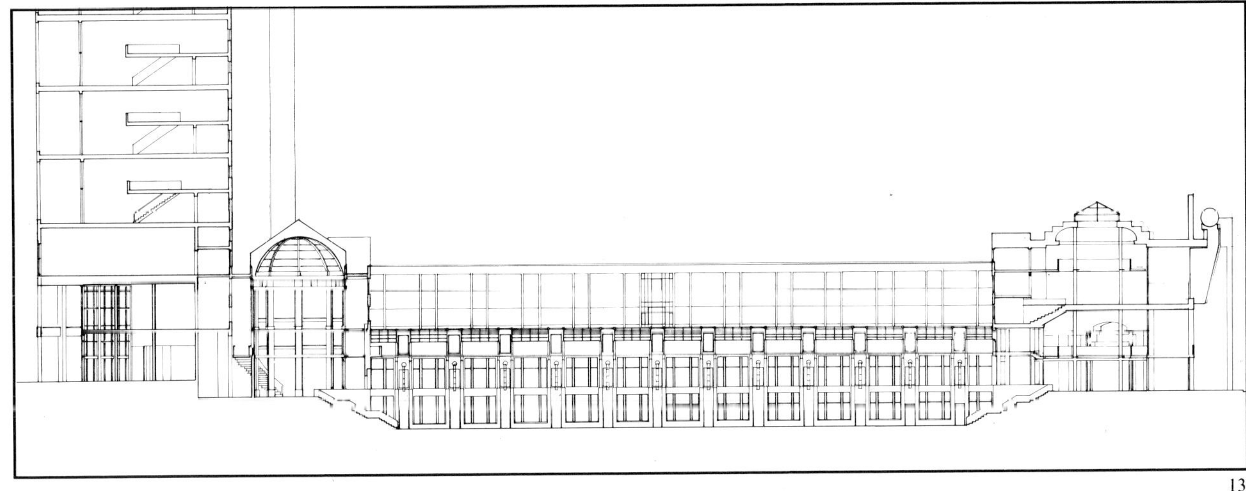

13

14

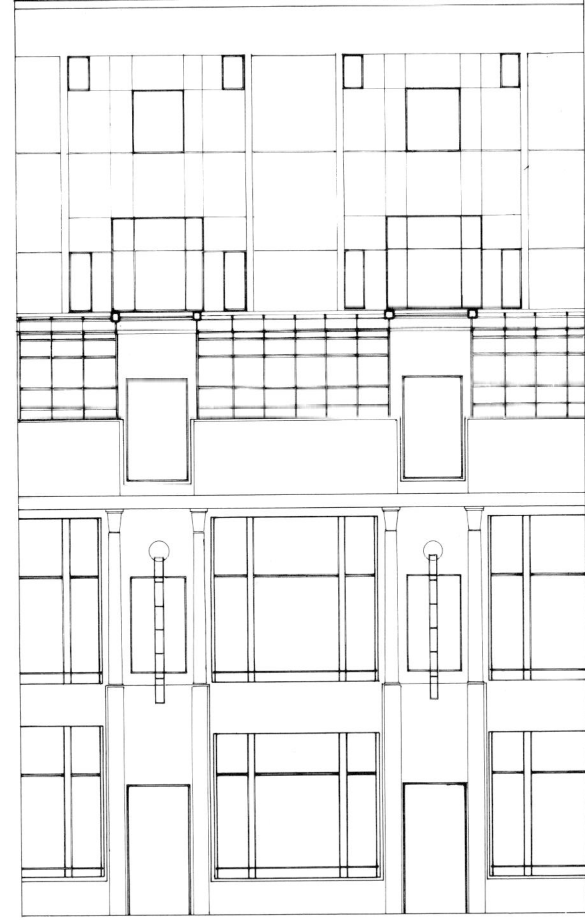

15

9 Perspective View; Carol Hsiung
10 Ground Floor Plan
11 Ground Floor Plan; Patrick Daly
12 Longitudinal Section; Carol Hsiung
13 Longitudinal Section; Patrick Daly
14 Tremont Street Facade
15 Detail of Interior Bay
16 Cross Section Through Arcade

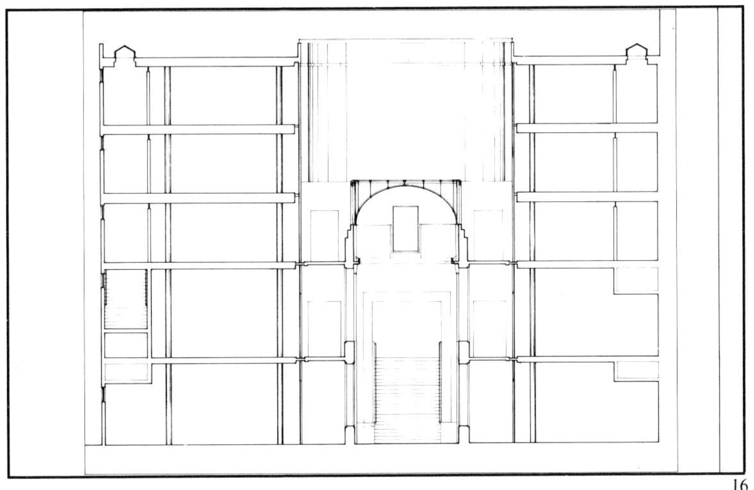

16

Galleria Numismatica, Rome

Located in the Bianchi region of Rome, this gallery displays a collection of coins, bills, and international monies. Initiated and developed in Rome, the project alludes to neighboring buildings including Sangallo's Antica Zecca, Borromini's Oratorio dei Filippini, and Peruzzi's Palazzo Massimo. Using the manufacture of money as a metaphor, the project addresses the issue of two-dimensional, two-sided vertical surface. The addition of this "wall" mends the damage caused by 19th century road construction, recalls Baroque facade development, and reinstates Renaissance planning ideas in this formerly Florentine quarter of Rome. Perspective views, framed by narrow Renaissance streets, such as Via Giulia and Via Paola, generate the gallery's curved surface, which defines the Piazza D'Oro facing S. Giovanni dei Fiorentini. The Ponte Sisto fountain, reintroduced onto Via Giulia in this piazza, appears to pin the delaminating, curved museum to the existing urban fabric. Circulation inside the gallery occurs between these constituent layers.

Alan Brown

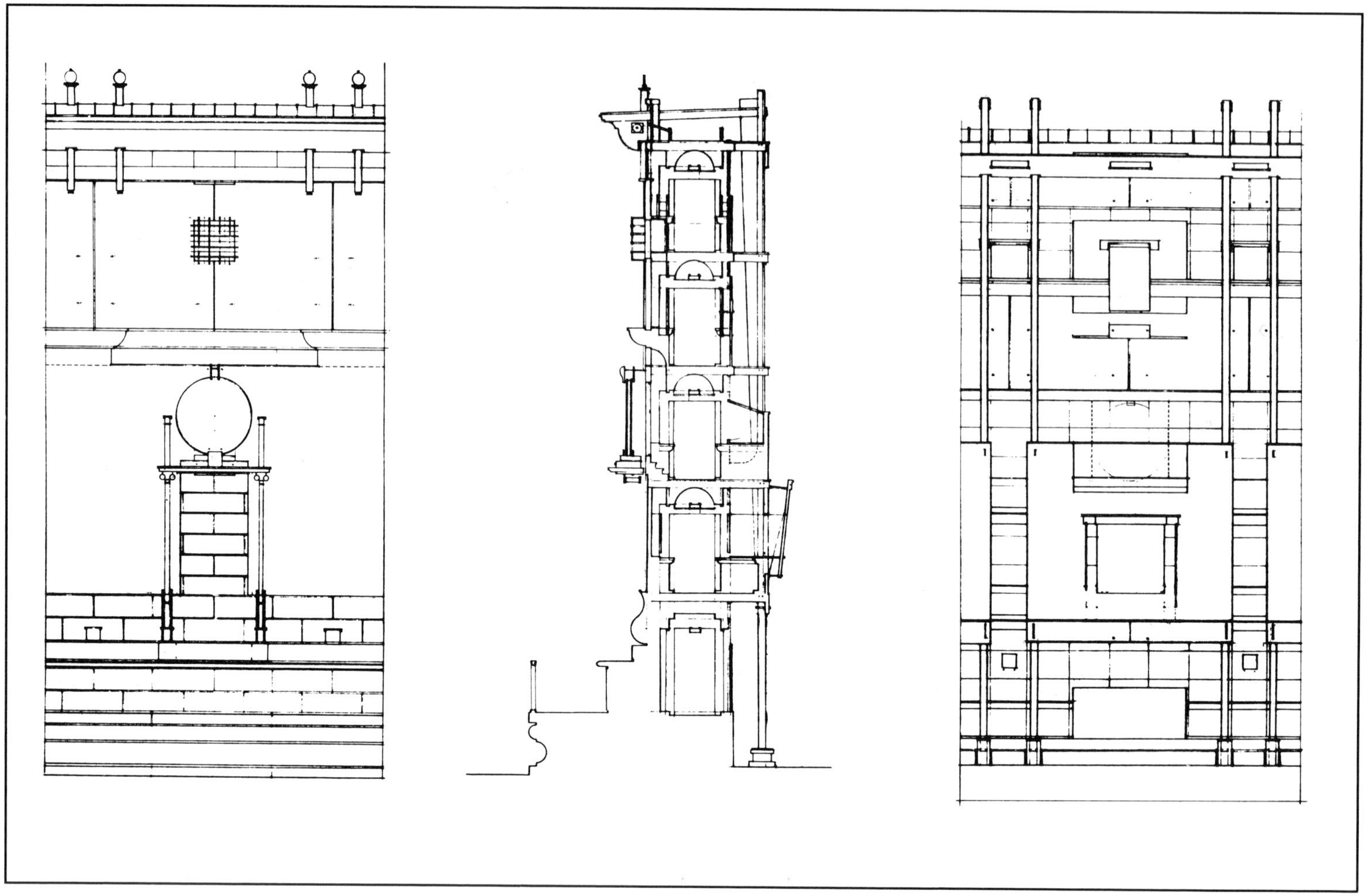

2

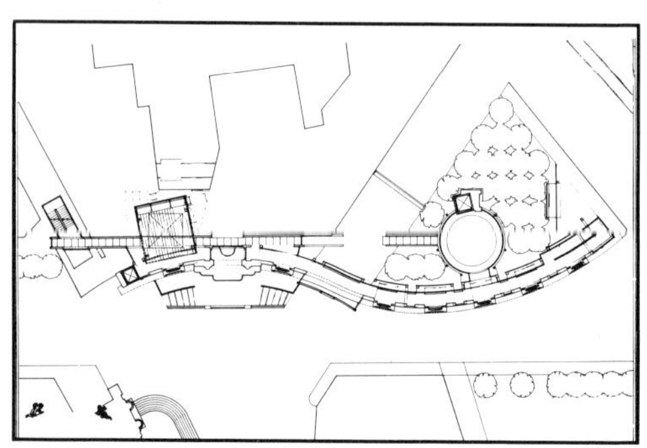

1

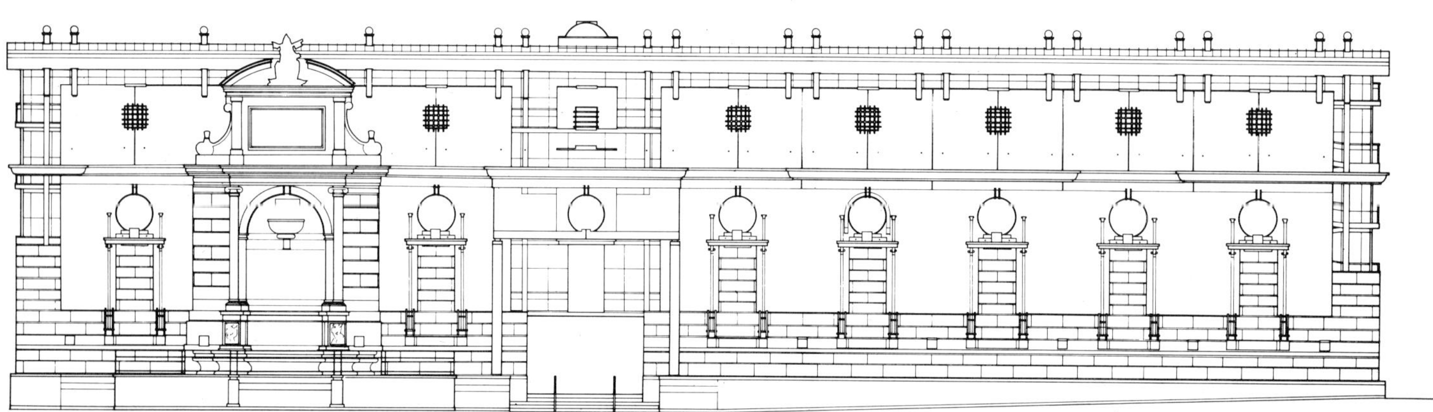

3

1 Galleria Numismatica, Rome; Site Plan; Alan Brown
2 Detail of Front and Back Bay with Section
3 Front Facade
4 Axonometric View
5 Photo Montage
6 Photo Montage
7 Photo Montage
8 Photo Montage

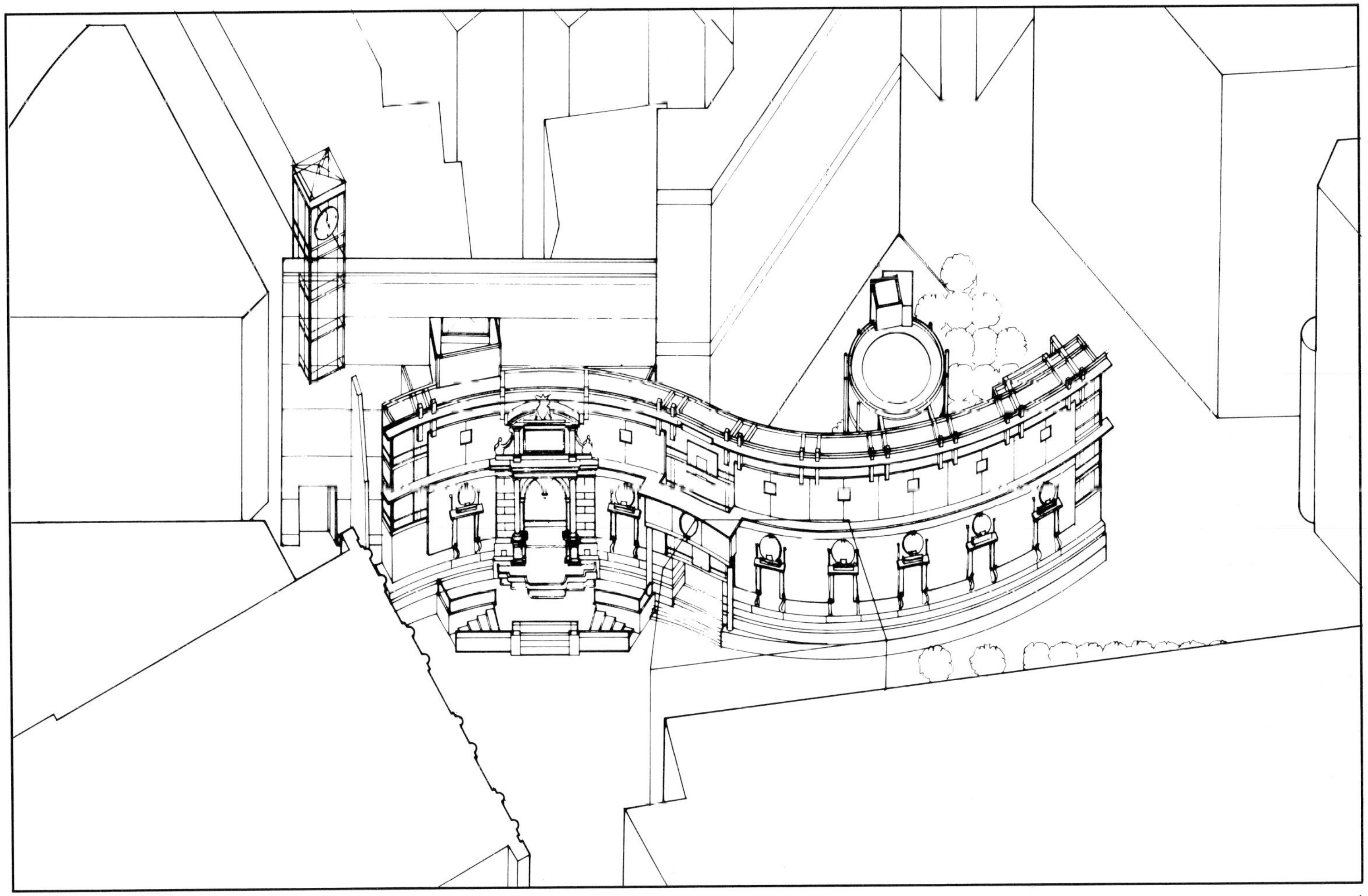

4

5

6

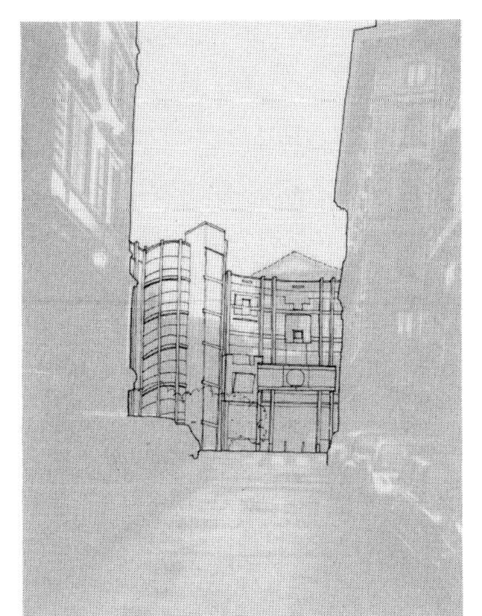

7

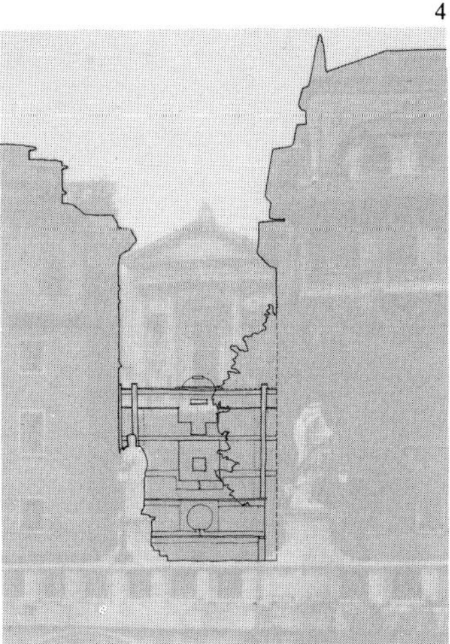

8

The Opera Arcade and Tower

Much of what animates and distinguishes Architecture lies in levels of ideas beyond the 'parti'. It is the province of this thesis to explore how the elements of a given building type, the arcade, lend character, scale, and image to space, and how their canvas, the vertical surface, orchestrates, animates and informs both exterior and interior.

The Arcade and its associated programatic accoutrements; shops, eateries, office space and apartments are employed to realize the site's potential as an expansion of the Boston Opera House and is developed to give the Opera a more substantial presence in the city.

Daniel Kaplan

1 The Opera Arcade and Tower; Tremont Street Facade, Daniel Kaplan
2 Ground Floor Plan
3 Interior View of Arcade
4 Longitudinal Section

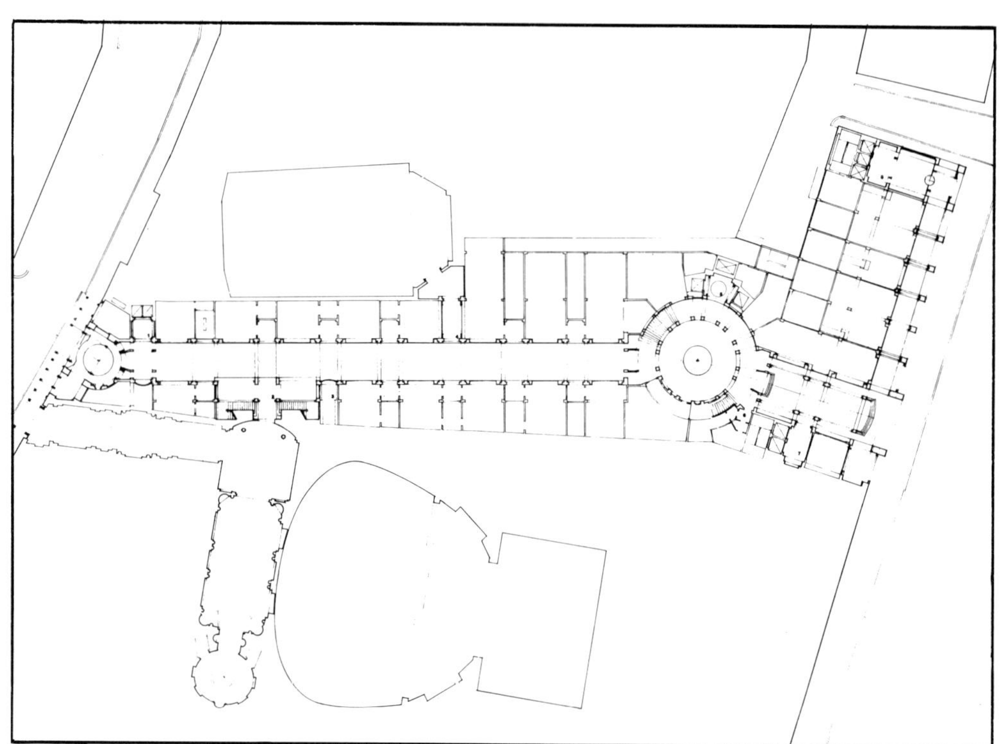

2

3

1

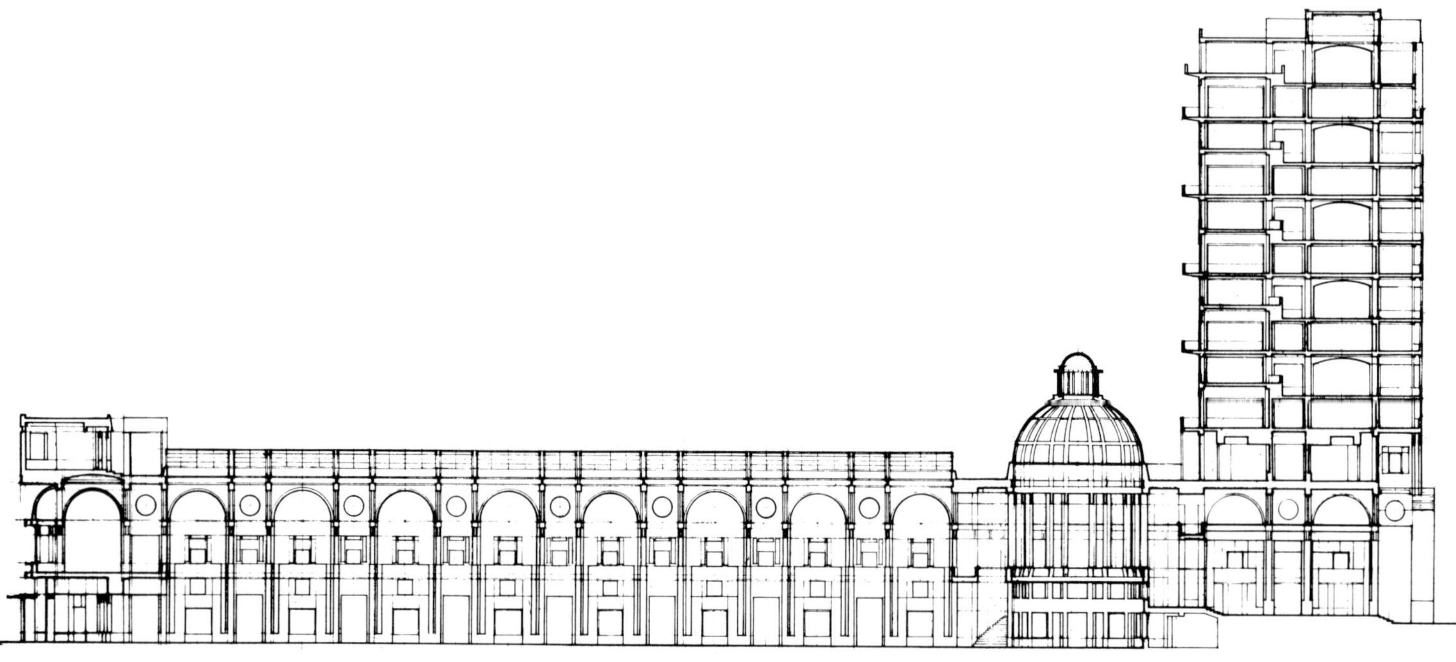

4

United States Embassy, Brasilia

The city of Brasilia, envisioned as a progressive new capital, symbolic of the aspirations of South America's largest nation, was also an audacious and controversial experiment in modern urban design on a large scale. This project for the United States Embassy in Brasilia is an experiment in the city of modern architecture, using Brasilia as the clearest paradigm of large-scale urban design. Situated on an open plot 200 meters south of the central monumental axis, at the northern edge of of the city's 'embassy zone,' the embassy compound includes a chancelery/office building and an ambassador's residence.

Charles D. Eldred

1 United States Embassy, Brasilia; Third Floor Plan, Charles Eldred
2 North Elevation
3 Longitudinal Section
4 Cross Section

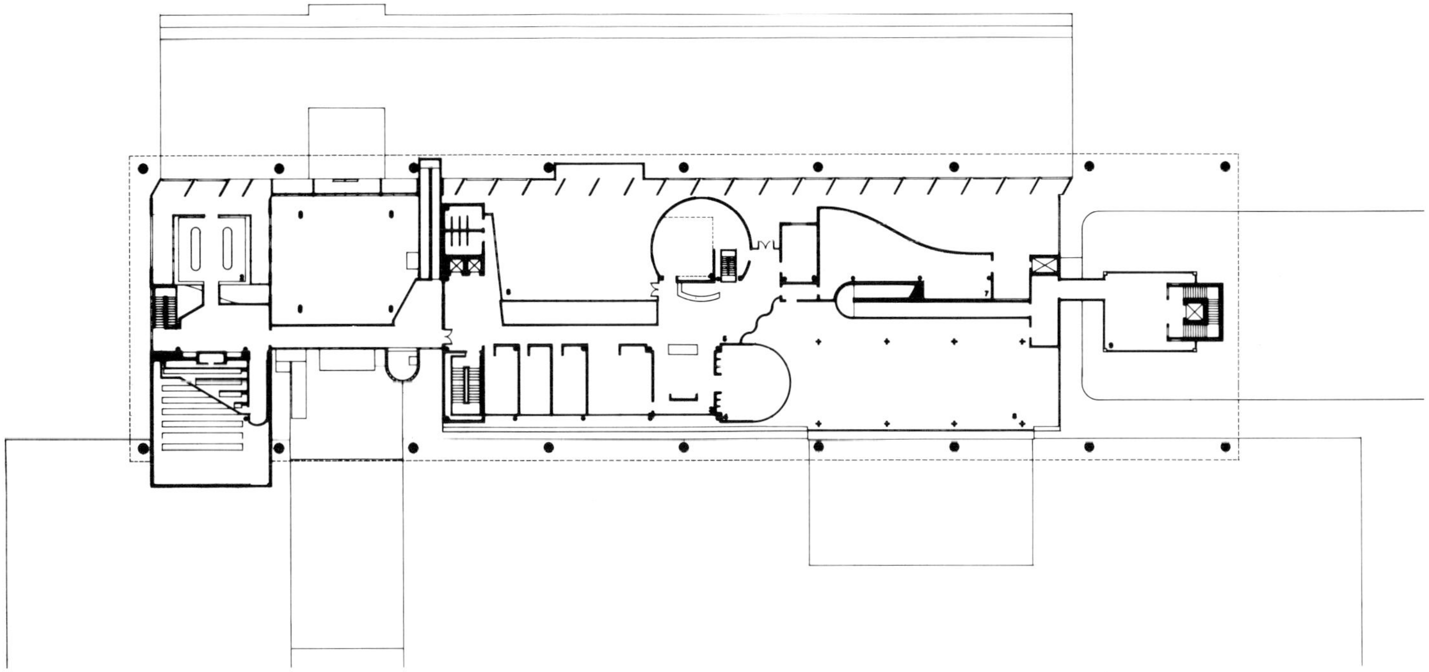

1

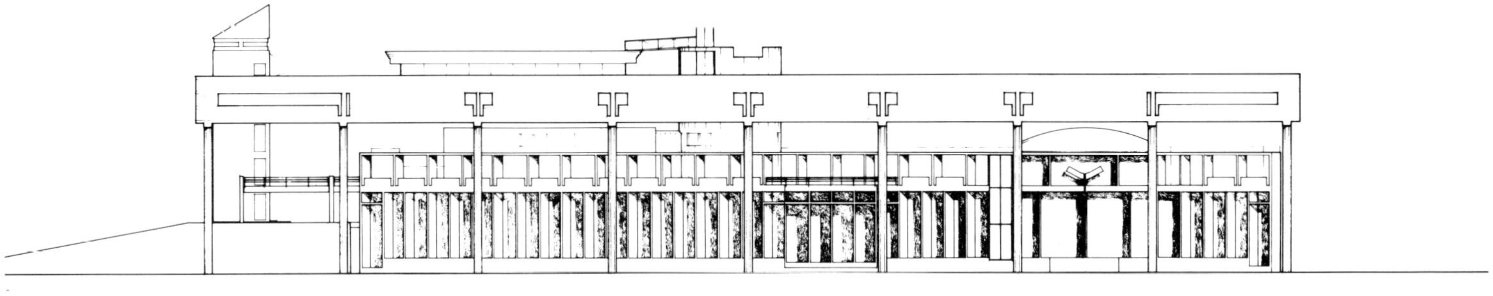

2

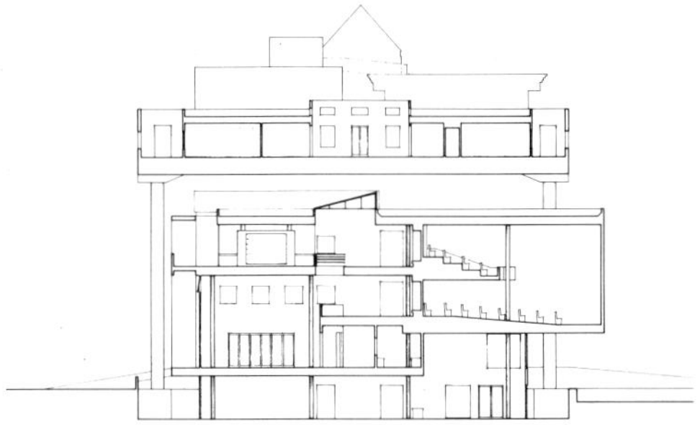

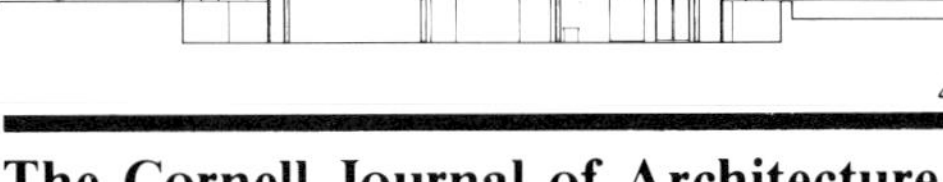

4

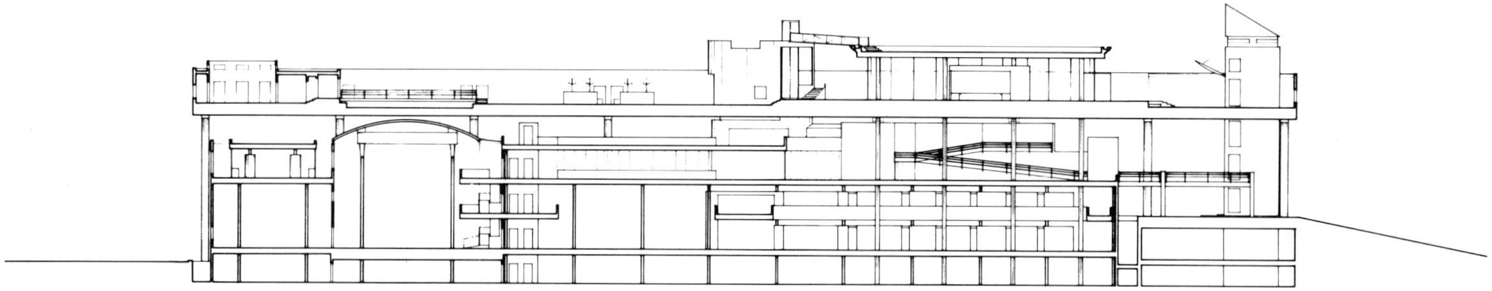

3

Museum & Institute for Film/ Cinema

The relationship between cinema and this institute lies in the tradition of dialogue between similar 3-dimentional and 2-dimentional pursuits. The lineage of interaction between the stage set and its 2-D counterpart provides not only the sustenance of a great deal of modern cinematography but a scenario for the process of this investigation. The virtues and limitations of pictoral imagery and evolving space in film have informed the unfolding of the exaggerated perspectival constructions and guided sequence in a manner which exploits the difficulty of satisfying divergent urbanistic intentions.

Marianne Kwok

1 Museum & Institute for Film/Cinema; Site Axonometric; Marianne Kwok
2 Plan
3 Section
4 Section
5 Compositional Studies
6 Compositional Studies
7 Compositional Studies
8 Compositional Studies
9 Frontal Axonometric
10 Collage; Stair to Second Level
11 Collage; View of Auditorium Entry
12 Collage; View from Catwalk

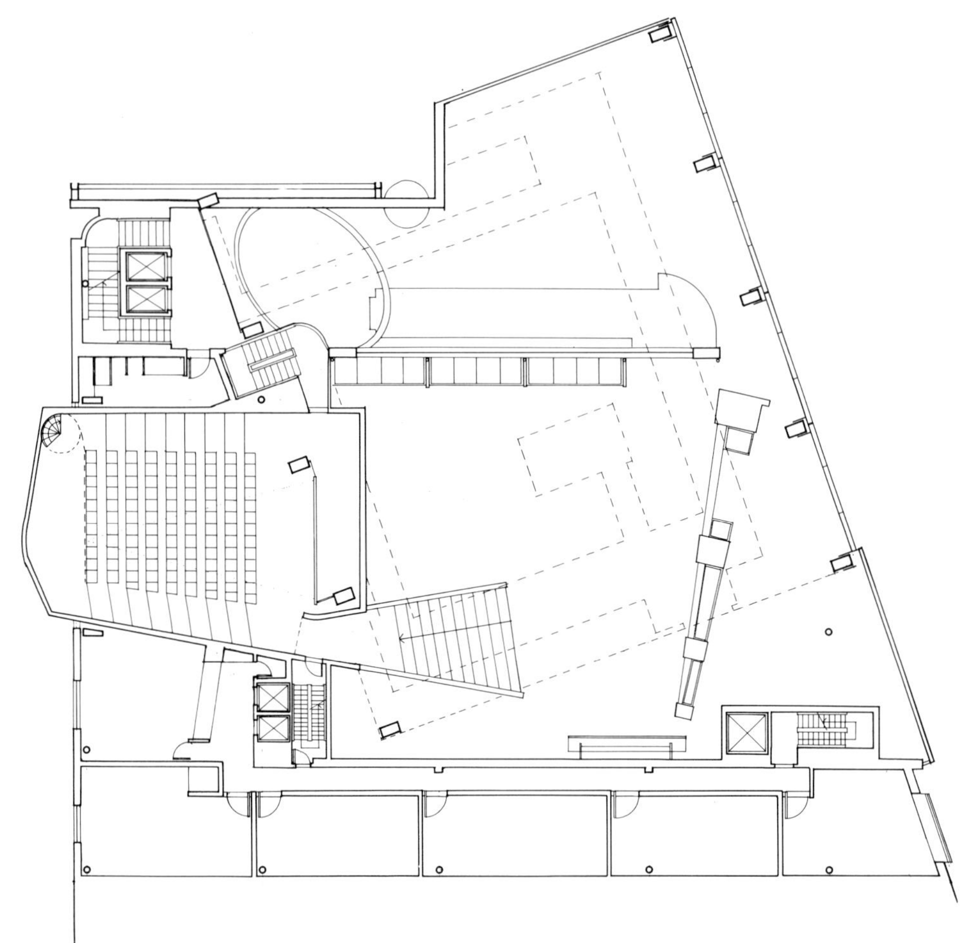

2

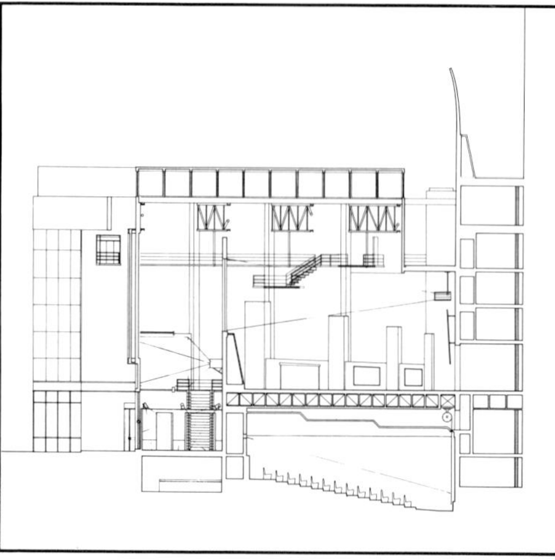

3

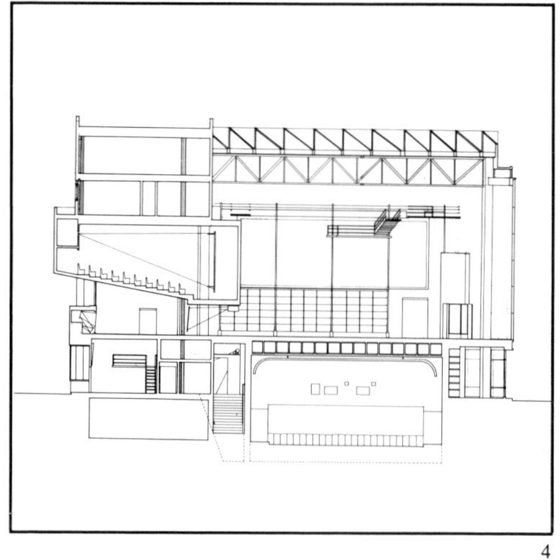

4

1

5

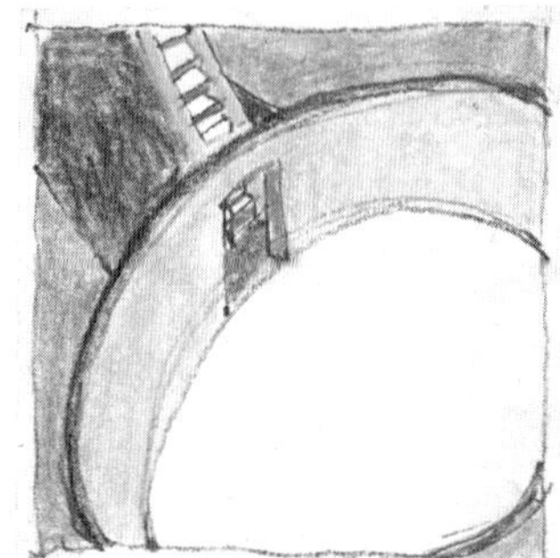

6

7

8

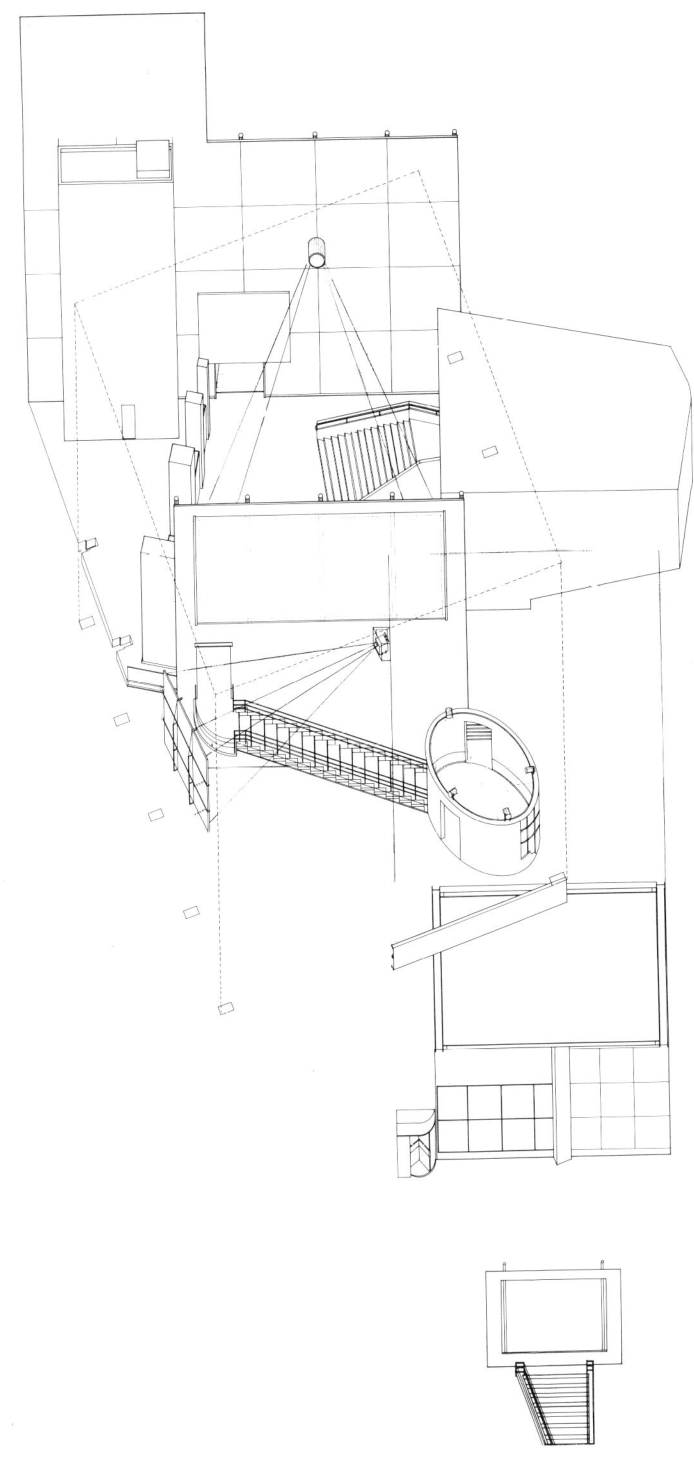

9

10

11

12

Television Broadcasting Studio and Museum

The site for this project is located at the edge of Boston's Theater District, two blocks east of the Commons and the Financial District. It is situated at the juncture of the city's major grids, influenced by ethnic circulation from Chinatown, south of the site, and various other city sectors. Certainly one popular image of a television station today is that of an isolated machine located along some highway or tucked away in a mountainside. Programmatically, this building involves transforming this traditional image of private enterprise into a place where the public may observe the production of live television events. By placing the building in an urban theater district context, more constraints are established in terms of the way the internal vocabulary of the studio theater can express itself relative to the existing classical theaters nearby.

Clifford Chang

1 Television Broadcasting Studio and Museum; Ground Floor Plan, Clifford Chang
2 Perspective View
3 Stuart Street Elevation
4 Longitudinal Section

2

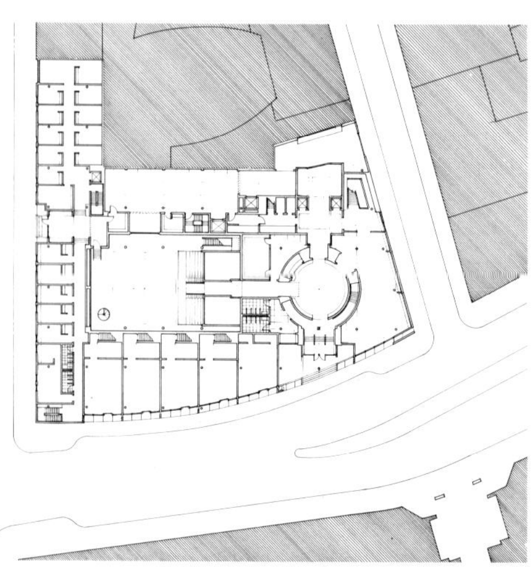

1

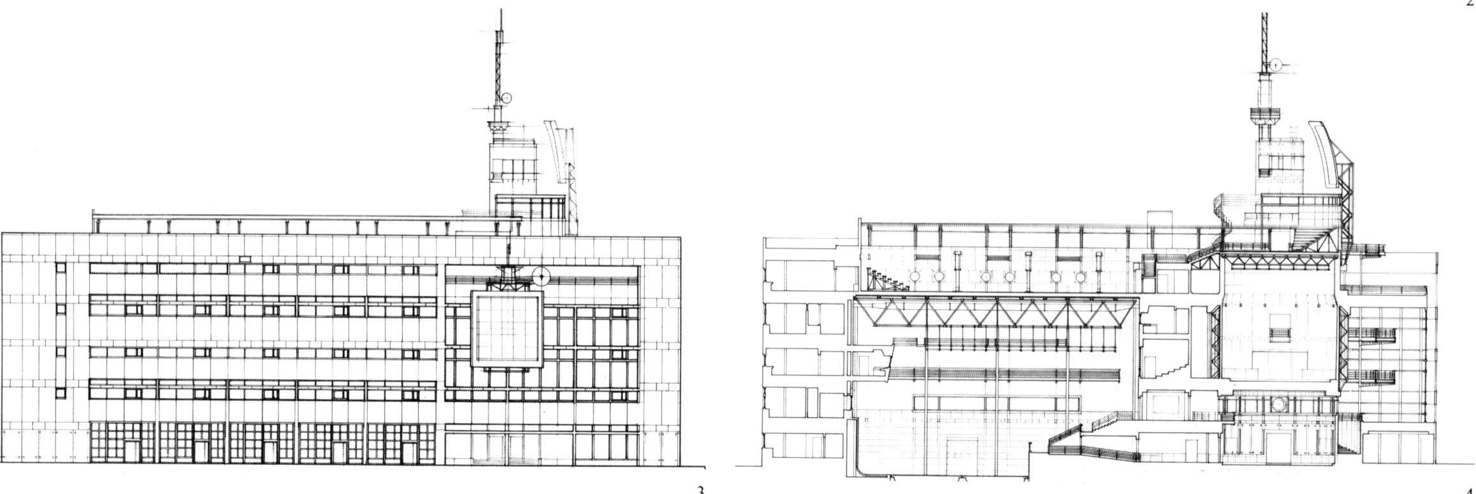

3

4

Essex County Courthouse

This thesis proposes to examine both architectural and contextual issues inherent in the design of a particular building type. The thesis pairs a federal building–a courthouse, which necessarily dictates the recognition and inclusion of imagery, symbolism, and popular iconography associated with the architecture of social democracy, as well as a certain amount of social responsibility physical stature and architectural character–with a green town common or 'mall' that is an important part of the public domain and under the auspices of the nineteenth-century architecture within which it resides. As a result, a conflict arises between the need for both public and private accommodation. The primary objective is to examine the courthouse as building type, integrate the building with site and community, and finally to explore issues of context within the content of American vernacular architecture in the late twentieth-century.

Laura Weiss

1 Essex County Courthouse; Second Floor Plan; Laura Weiss
2 Longitudinal Section
3 North Elevation
4 Cross Section through Courtroom
5 East Elevation
6 Longitudinal Section through Courtroom
7 South Elevation

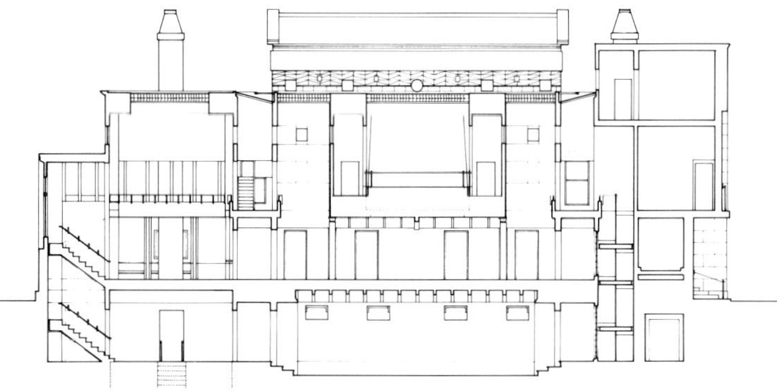

2

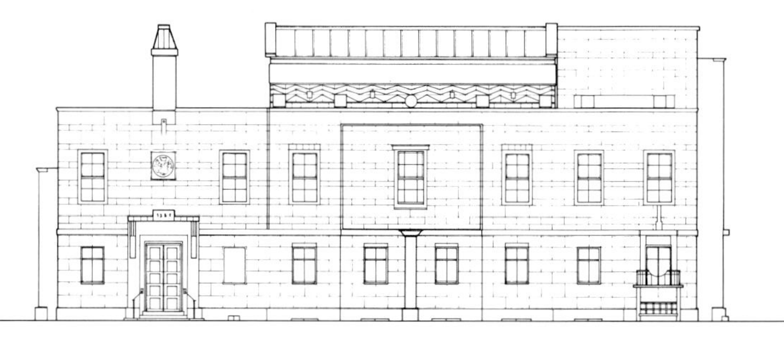

3

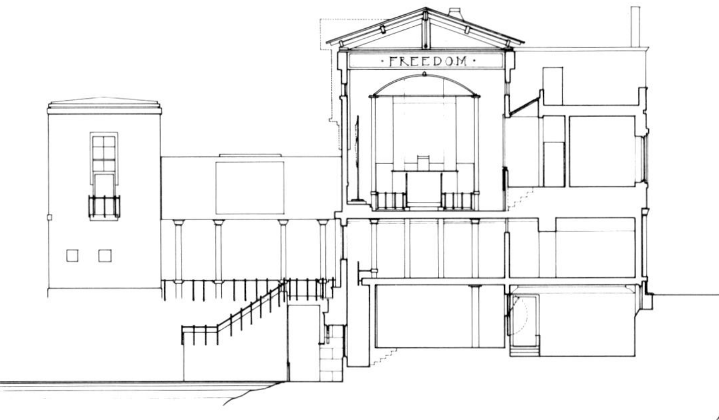

4

5

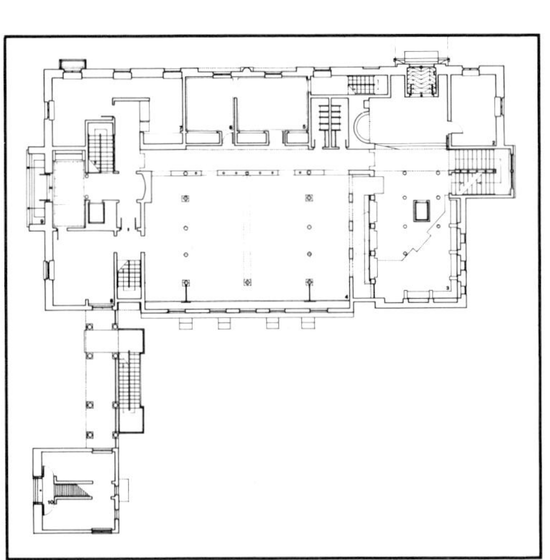

1

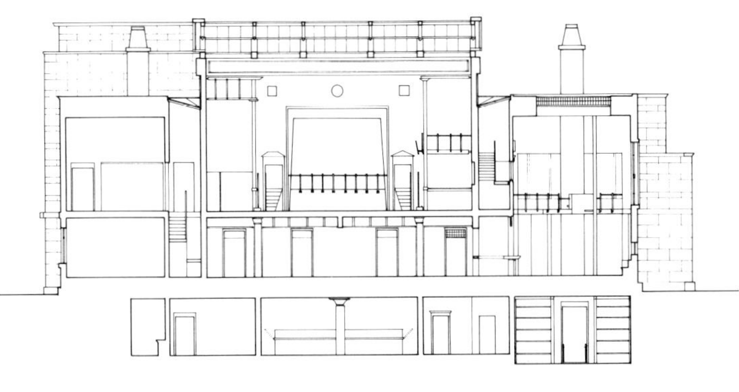

6

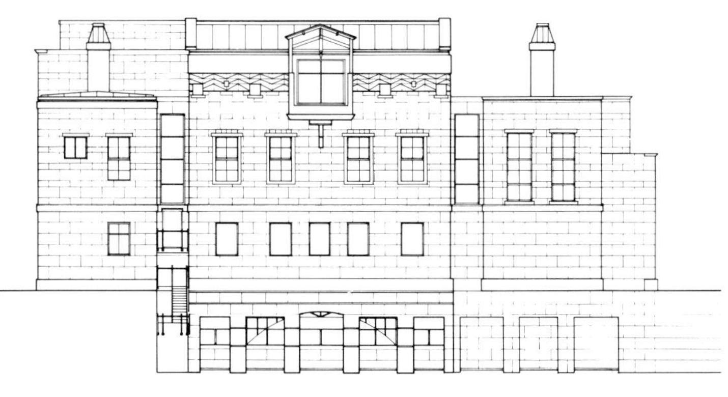

7

Jacqueline/Picasso–A Museum...

The impact of painting on architecture has usually been founded on formal properties. However, one could go beyond that by being able to extract a metaphysic from a collection of paintings, thereby adding a new dimension to the formal issues.

In the specific collection of Jacqueline Picasso, the paintings are more than paintings: they are the representation of a character, the symbol of a life in common, the private property of an individual who died a little while ago... but they are still the paintings of Picasso. The museum is therefore more than a museum: it is a memorial, a private domain, a haunted house... but it is still a museum, where an investigation of the perception of surface examines the dialogue between painting and architecture. This reciprocity between the mediums blurs their spatial distinction and expands their perceptual limits.

Rania Matar

1 Jacqueline/Picasso–A Museum; Site Plan; Rania Matar
2 North Oblique Elevation
3 West Oblique Elevation
4 North/East Elevation
5 Collage; North/East Elevation
6 Third Floor Plan
7 Ground Floor Plan
8 Fourth Floor Plan
9 Collage; View from Entry
10 Collage; Gallery
11 Collage; Gallery
12 Collage; Gallery
13 Collage; Gallery
14 Longitudinal Section
15 Cross Section

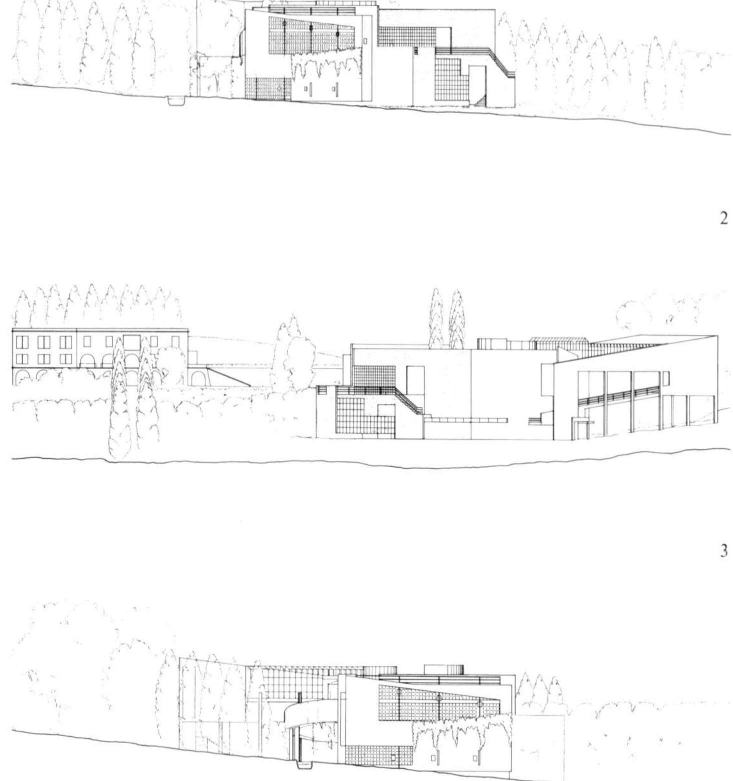

2

3

4

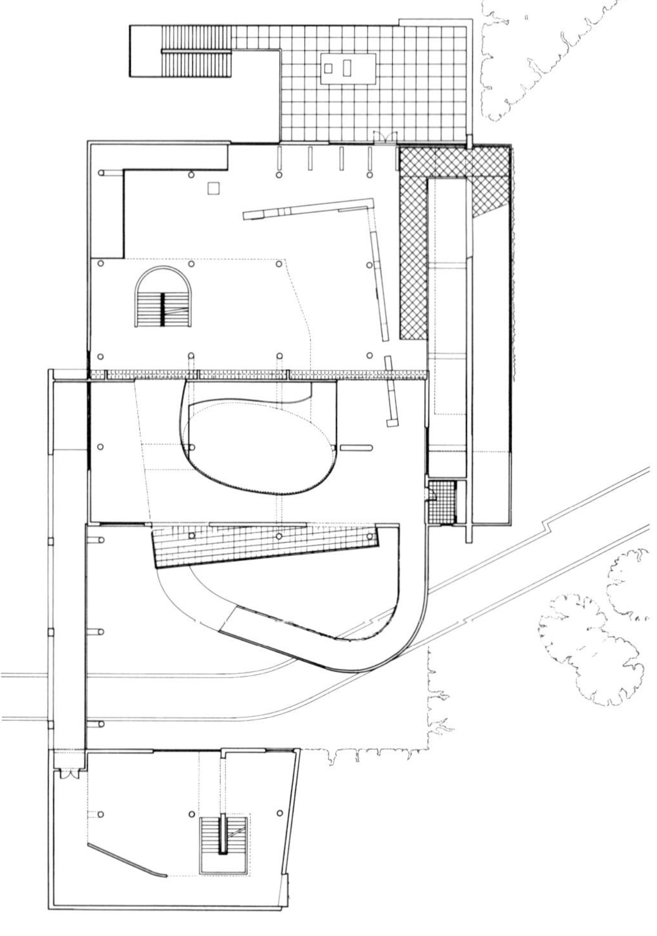

6

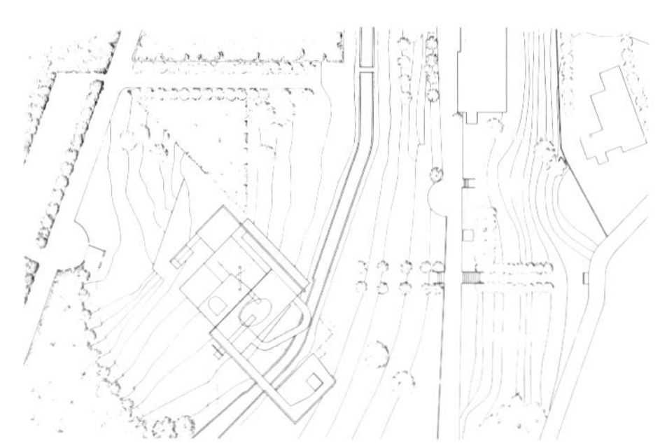

1

5

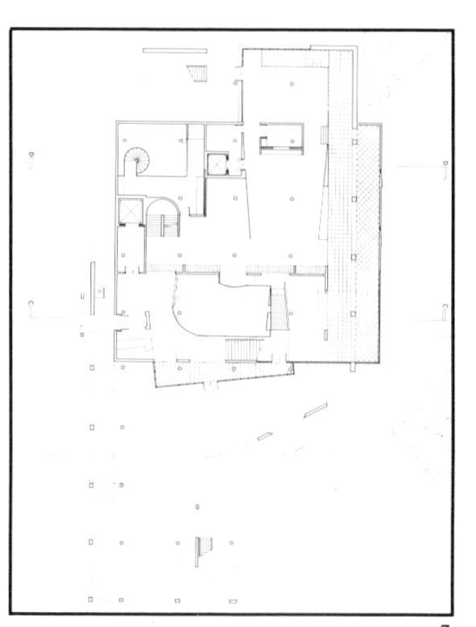

7

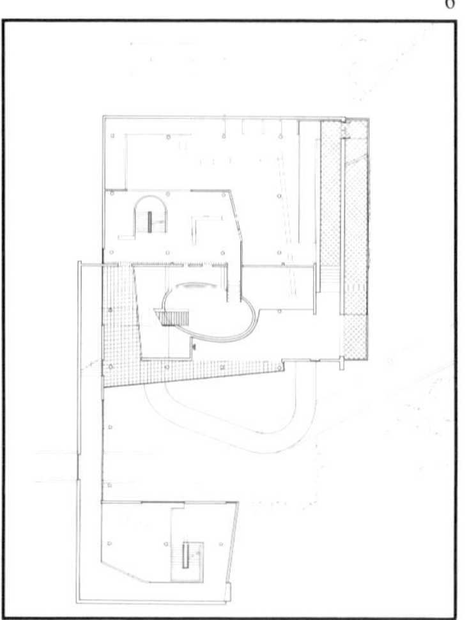

8

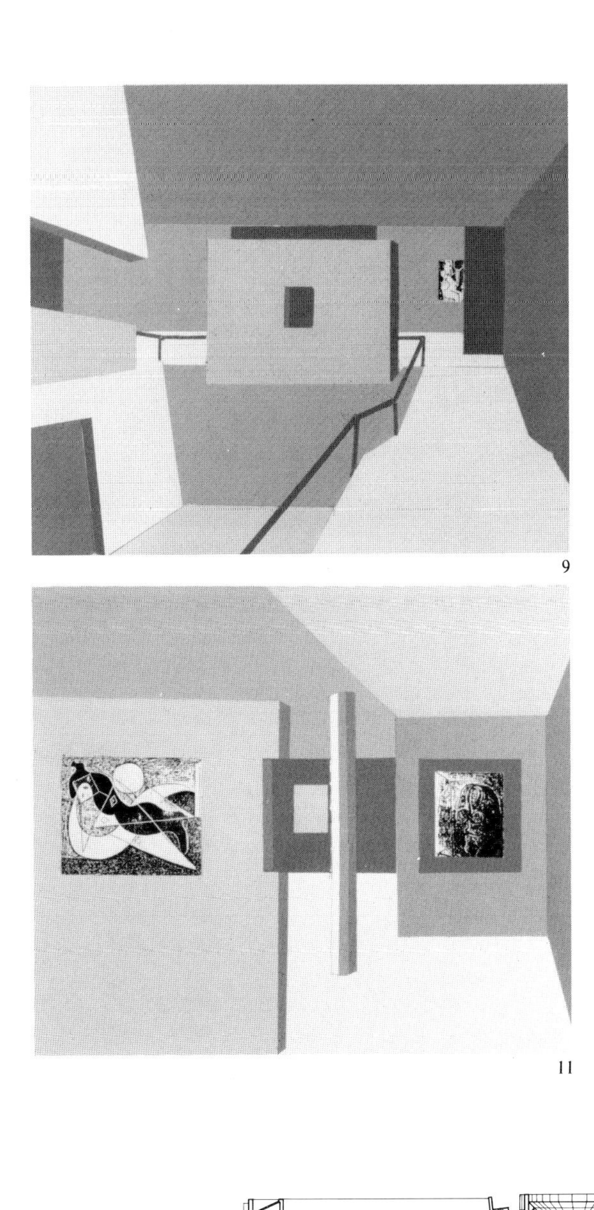

9

11

10

12

13

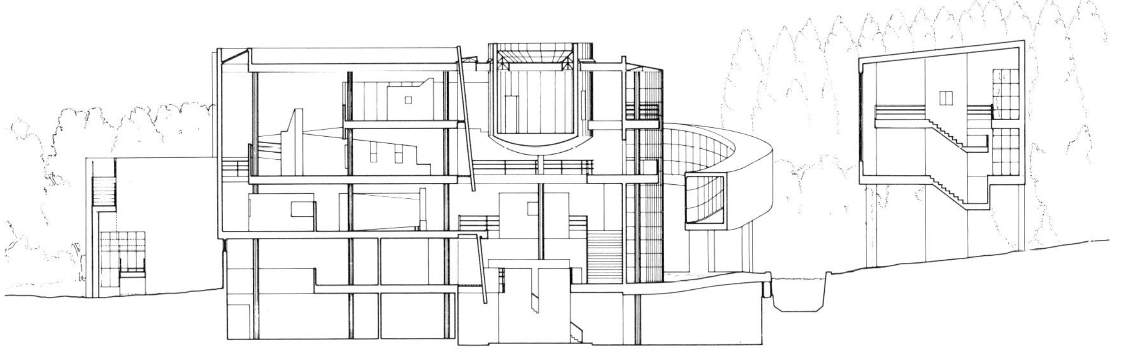

14

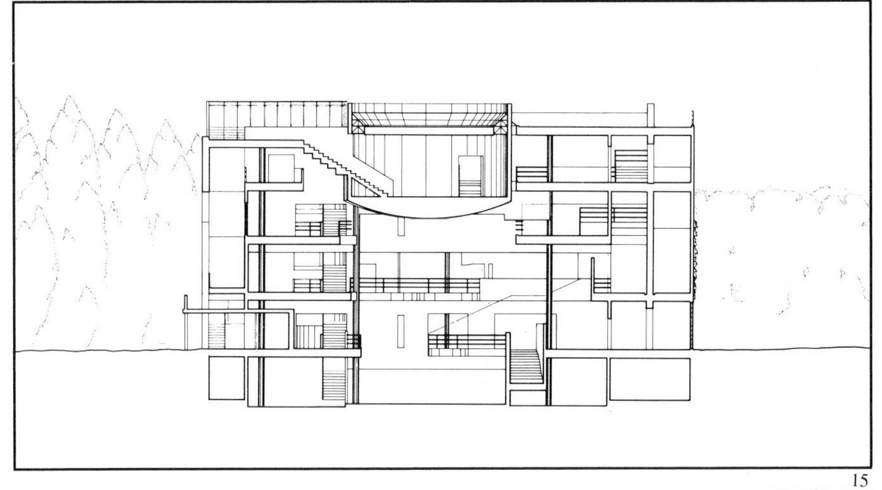

15

Footnotes

The Skull and the Mask

1 Nikolaus Pevsner, *Outline of European Architecture* (London: Pelikan, 1958), p. 285.
2 H.P. Berlage, *Gedenken uber Stijl*, quoted in R. Banham, *Theory and Design in the First Machine Age* (New York: Praeger, Holt, Rinehart, Winston, 1959), p. 141.
3 Kenneth Frampton, "Critical Regionalism."
4 Roland Barthes, "The New Citroen," reprinted in R. Barthes, *Mythologies* (New York: Hill and Wang, 1972), p. 88.
5 Siegfried Giedeion, *Space, Time and Architecture* (Cambridge: Harvard University Press, 1963), p. 423.
6 Le Corbusier, *Towards a New Architecture* (London: The Architectural Press, 1927), p. 31.
7 See Michael Dennis, *Court and Garden* (Cambridge: MIT Press, 1986).
8 *Ibid*
9 Banham, *European Architecture*, p. 20.
10 Peter Collins, *Changing Ideals in Modern Architecture* (Montreal: McGill-Queens University Press), pp. 286-287.
11 For a discussion of the rhetorical uses of the Column and the Frame see Colin Rowe, "Chicago Frame," reprinted in *Mathematics of the Ideal Villa and Other Essays* (Cambridge: MIT Press, 1976).
12 H.R. Hitchcock, and Philip Johnson, *The International Style* (New York: Norton), pp. 40-49.
13 Robert Venturi, *Complexity and Contradiction in Architecture* (New York: MOMA, 1966), p. 71.
14 One hardly imagines Stanford White being asked, "Where's the glass line?"
15 Le Corbusier, *Oeuvre Complète 1910-29* (Zurich: Les Editions d'Architecture, 1964), p. 128.
16 While the tendencies I have described are surely widespread, it would be wrong to assume that all modern architecture falls into the categories I have enumerated. Mies' work in America and Kahn's architecture after the Salk Center certainly do not fall into these categories.
17 See Patricia Waddy, Unpublished manuscript, "Transformations of Plan and Section," Syracuse University, 1985.
18 Richard Etlin, "Les Dedans: J. F. Blondel and the System of the House," *Gazette des Beaux Arts* (April 1978), p. 140.
19 See Anthony Vidler, *The Writing on the Walls*, (Princeton: Princeton Architectural Press, 1986).
20 Marc-Antoine Laugier, *An Essay on Architecture* (Los Angeles: Hennessey & Ingalls, 1977), Translation of the edition of 1753.
21 Gottfried Semper, *Der Stil* (London: 1853).
22 Joseph Rykwert, "Gottfried Semper and the Problem of Style," *Architectural Design Profile: On the Methodology of Architectural History*, edited by D. Porphyrios (London: 1981), p. 12.
23 Rosemarie Bletter, "Gottfried Semper," biography in the *Macmillan Encyclopedia of Architects* (New York: 1982), 4: p. 27.
24 Ibid.
25 Ibid.
26 John Summerson, "A Case for the Theory of Modern Architecture," *RIBA Journal* (June 1957), p. 309.
27 Ibid.
28 Christopher Alexander, *Notes on the Synthesis of Form* (Cambridge: Harvard University Press, 1964).
29 Karsten Harries, "On Truth and Lie in Architecture," *VIA 7* (Cambridge: MIT Press, 1984), p. 55.
30 Charles Jencks, *The Language of Post Modern Architecture* (New York: Rizzoli, 1977), p. 115.
31 See William Jordy, "The Symbolic Essence of the Modern European Architecture of the 20's and 30's and Its Continuing Influence," *JSAH* (October 1963).
32 John Ruskin, *The Seven Lamps of Architecture* (New York: Farrar, Strauss & Giroux, 1981), p. 37.
33 See Christian Norburg-Schultz, *Intentions in Architecture* (Cambridge: MIT Press, 1963).
34 In the case of S. Andrea, the pilaster insets occupy a plane that is literally recessed behind the surface of the wall to which they are 'applied'. Does this make Alberti a Mannerist?
35 The trabeations of Michaelangelo's Capitoline Palaces, probably reinforced with iron, are yet another of his 'Mannerist' gestures, whereas the *serliana* window more closely recognizes the nature of compressive structure. See James Ackerman, *The Architecture of Michelangelo*, (Chicago, University of Chicago Press, 1986), p. 155.
36 John Macsai and Paul Doukas, "Expressed Frame and the Classical Order in the Transitional Period of Italy 1918-1939," *Journal of Architectural Education*, (Summer 1987).
37 Berthhold Lubetkin, "Highpoint Number Two," *Architectural Review*, (October, 1938), p. 176.
38 Alan Colquhoun, "Form and Figure," *Essays in Architectural Criticism* (Cambridge: MIT Press, 1981), pp. 190-191.
39 Ibid., p. 193.

Palladian Variations

1 This paper is a revised version of a lecture delivered in the fall of 1984 at Cornell University and at the University of Texas at Arlington, spring 1984.
2 Robert Venturi notes that certain classical buildings display the same decorative structure on the inside as on the outside, thereby creating a connection of consistency. See Venturi, *Complexity and Contradiction in Architecture* (New York: MOMA, 1966), p. 71.
3 See Ruskin, *The Seven Lamps of Architecture*; also Harries, "On Truth and Lie in Architecture," pp. 47-58.
4 Bruno Zevi.
5 G.C. Argan, *The Renaissance City* (New York: Braziller, 1969), p. 30.
6 W. Hegemann, *Facades of Buildings* (London: Benn, 1929), p. 9.
7 Paolo Maretto, *L'Edilizia Gotica Veneziana* (Venezia: Filippi Editore, 1978), p. 71 (my translation).
8 Colin Rowe and Robert Slutzky, in Transparency II, *Perspecta*, 13, 14, noted the overlapping of readings between center and edge in the Venetian Palace type.
9 R. Wittkower, *Architectural Principles in the Age of Humanism* (New York: W.W. Norton, 1971 edition).
10 Wittkower, pp. 89-97.
11 Ibid., p. 92.
12 Ibid., p. 95.
13 Ibid., pp. 94-95.
14 Ibid., p. 90.
15 Ibid., note, p. 95.
16 Staale Sinding-Larsen, "Palladio's Redentore, a Compromise in Composition," *The Art Bulletin XLVII*, 1965, p. 422, note.
17 Ibid.
18 Ibid.
19 J.Rykwert, "Palladio: Chiese Veneziana," *Domus* (609, 1981), p. 28-31.
20 See William McDonald, *The Pantheon* (Cambridge: Harvard University Press, 1976), p. 92.
21 See Wittkower, op. cit.; Peter Murray, *Renaissance Architecture* (New York: Abrams, 1971); James Ackerman, *Palladio* (Hammondsworth: Pelican, 1966).
22 Wittkower, *Architectural Principles*, p. 85. He continues, "The disquieting effect of this arrangement was observed and put on record in the 18th century when Temanza lamented that the corners had been weakened though these were just the points which should show the greatest strength. But this is precisely what Palladio here intended to do. In no other buildings did he attempt an equally deliberate break with established classical conventions."
23 Ackerman, *Palladio*, p. 112.
24 Ibid., "...the change in the outer bays is suggested in the plan; it corresponds to a more restricted dimension of the interior spaces behind these bays."
25 Sinding-Larson, "Palladio's Redentore."
26 Some scholars have argued that the emphasis on the two storey division at the corner was made to knit the building into its context. This theory in no way contradicts my observation. See Ackerman, *Palladio*, p. 112; Murray, p. 307; and Caroline Constant, *The Palladio Guide* (Princeton: Princeton Architectural Press, 1985), pp. 74-75.
27 Wittkower, *Architectural Principles*, p. 84.
28 Ibid., p. 93.
29 Ibid., p. 85.
30 Ibid., p. 92.
31 This interpretation was suggested to me by Bernard Mallat.
32 See Ackerman, Wittkower, and Constant, op. cit.
33 Ackerman, *Palladio*, p. 112; Ackerman mentions that Palladio worked on the Palazzo Valmarana at the same time he was working on S. Giorgio.

Voluminous Walls

The initial investigation of St. Peter's was undertaken while a Fellow at the American Academy in Rome, 1980-81. The author wishes to thank Laura Martin for her assistance in the construction of the model, Henry A. Millon for sharing his insights about St. Peter's, and Christian Otto, Elwin Robison and the editorial staff of the Cornell Journal of Architecture for their comments which were especially helpful in the development of this article.

1 Colin Rowe, *The Mathematics of the Ideal Villa and Other Essays* (Cambridge: MIT Press, 1976), p.11.
2 See Micheal Dennis, *French Hotel Plans* (Cornell University, Ithaca, NY: Department of Architecture Studio Publication, 1977).
3 See Steven K. Peterson, "Space and Anti-Space," *Harvard Architectural Review*, Vol. I, Spring 1980 (Cambridge: MIT Press, 1980).
4 For a comprehensive history of St. Peter's, see James S. Ackerman, *The Architecture of Michelangelo*, Vols. I & II (London: A. Zwemmer Ltd., 1961).
5 It is perhaps ironic that Sangallo's elaborate wooden model for St. Peter's is housed in one of these spaces.
6 Romaldo Giurgola and Jaimini Mehta, *Louis I. Kahn* (Boulder, CO: Westview Press, 1975), p. 90.
7 A similar reciprocity of section can be found at a smaller scale in Bramante's *Tempietto*, where the altar of the upper chapel is hollowed out to allow light to penetrate the lower chapel.
8 For a discussion of detached inner linings, see Robert Venturi, *Complexity and Contradiction in Architecture* (New York: Museum of Modern Art, 1966), pp. 76-89.
9 Aalto, in fact, consistently delineates his sections by depicting only the internal volumes being shaped, thereby stressing the autonomy of the interior space. See Demetri Porphyrios, *Sources of Modern Eclecticism* (London: Academy Editions, 1982), p. 20. Yet, Aalto remains one of the few modern architects whose manipulation of the section approaches that of the plan.
10 A similar situation is found at the Palazzo Farnese in Rome where a small court along the side wall of the palace permits light to flood the middle landing of the main staircase. Likewise, the desire to maintain the outer volume of the structure results in the facade

extending past the court as a punched screen wall.

Viennese Facades

1 See also footnote 4.
2 Otto Wagner, *Die Baukunst unserer Zeit* (Vienna: 1979), pp. 44-45. Reprint of the Vienna 1914 edition.
3 Curtain-walls were first used in Chicago. The term 'curtain wall' has probably been formulated with respect to Semper's theory of clothing.
4 Gottfried Semper does not follow Vitruvius' thesis that wood construction is the basis for stone construction. He also rejects Laugier's primitive hut as a model for architecture. In Gottfried Semper's view, the carpet as a vertical partition becomes one of the primary archetypes of architecture. It becomes the *Urform*, the basic form of spatial subdivision. The wall *(Wand)* then is clothed with such a 'garment' (*Gewand*). The textile art with its principles becomes the base of all ornament in architecture. He maintains that architecture in its primeval condition was 'clothed' (*bedeckt*) and by saying so he gives logical priority to ornament over structure. For more about the significance of the clothing theory in Semper's aesthetic views, see Heinz Quitzsch, "Die Aesthetischen Anschauungen Gottfried Sempers."
5 Otto Wagner, *Die Baukunst unserer Zeit,* p. 52.
6 Adolf Loos, "Die Potemkinsche Stadt," *Ver Sacrum* (1898). English translation in Benton & Sharp, *Architecture and Design 1890-1939.*
7 Adolf Loos, "Ornament und Verbrechen," first published in *Cahiers d'Audjourd'hui*, 1913.
8 Adolf Loos, "Architektur," first published in *Der Sturm*, December 15, 1910.
9 See the excellent analysis of Adolf Loos' building for Goldman & Salatsch on the Michaelerplatz by Hermann Czech & Wolfgang Mistelbauer, *Das Looshaus* (Wien: Verlag Locker & Wogenstein, 1976).

Sources and Credits

Illustrations courtesy of the following; reprinted by permission:

The Skull & the Mask

1 De Capo Press (1975), A. Morancé (1926, 1927)
2, 3 Reinhold Publishing Corp. Inc.
4, 6 Fondation Le Corbusier
5 Audemas Piguet and Victor Norman & Partners
7 Zanichelli Editore
8 Prentice Hall Inc.
9 Electa Editrice S.R.L.
10,11 *The Four Books of Architecture*
12 Princeton Architectural Press
13 Architecural Review and Dell & Wainwright

Palladian Variations

1, 27, 29, 66, 69, 70, 75 Alec Tiranti Ltd.
2 Sir Bannister Fletcher, *Romanesque Europe*
3-6, 11, 12 *Edifices De Rome Moderne,* Paul Letarouilly
7, 17, 20, 28, 30-36, 38-48, 53-57, 59-65, 67, 68, 71-74 Thomas Schumacher
8,9 Il Milione Edizione
10 B.T. Batsford Ltd.
13-15 Istituto Poligrafico e Zecca dello Stato
16 Marsilio Editore
18 *Storia delle l'Arte Italiana*, Adolpho Venturi
19 MIT Press
21-26 Stamperia di Venezia
37, 49 Centro Internazionale di Studi di Architectura A. Palladio, Vicenza
50, 58 *The Four Books of Architecture*, as drawn by Isaac Ware
51 Braziller
52 James Ackerman

The Interior Facade

1 *Romanesque Europe*
2 *Edifices De Rome Moderne,* Paul Letarouilly
3-6,10 Lee Hodgden
7, 8, 28 The Museum of Modern Art
9 Casa Editrice Neri Pozza
11 Country Life, Tower House
12 Scala S.A.S.
13, 14 Retoria: Y. Futagawa & Associated Photographers
15-17 Princeton Architectural Press
18 Arnoldo Mondadori Editore S.P.A.
19 Birkhauser Verlag Basel
20, 21, 24, 29, 32, 33 Fondation Le Corbusier
22 *Picasso*; William Boeck and Jaime Sabartes
23 *Juan Gris*; Juan Antonio Gaya Nuño
25-27 Da Capo Press
30 Macmillan Publishing Co., Inc.
31 St. Martin's Press Inc.
34 Instituto Di Studi Romani Editore
35 Academy Editions
36, 37, 39, 40 By courtesy of the Trustees of Sir John Soane's Museum
38 Officina Edizioni

The Voluminous Wall

1-4 James Ackerman
5, 17 Phaidon Press Ltd.
6-11, 13, 31, 35 *The Vatican and the Basilica of St. Peter's,* Rome; Paul Letarouilly
12 Harry Abrams
14 *Storia delle l'Arte Italiana*, Adolpho Venturi
15, 16, 18, 32, 33, 36, 39 Spence Kass
19 Penguin Books Ltd.
20-22 Courtesy of the Trustees of Sir John Soane's Museum
23-30 Verlag fur Architektur Artemis
34 City Art Museum of St. Louis
37 Progressive Architecture
38 Fondation Le Corbusier
40 Giulio Einaudi Editore

Viennese Facades

11 William S. Heinman Imported Books
12, 13, 18, 22 Werner Goehner
14, 16 Residenz Verlag
15 Herman Bohlas Nachf
17 Ferdinand Berger & Sohne OHG
19, 21 Edition Tusch Buch-und Kunstverlag
2 Oesterreichischer Bundesverlag
23 - 27 Löcker Verlag
Köstlergasse 3 drawings by Anne Philps
Looshaus drawings by Alan Berman
Portois & Fix drawings by John Reed
Schottenring 23 drawings by James Mahoney
Zacherlhaus drawings by Doug Look
Ankerhaus drawings by Louis Chien
Wienzeille 40 drawings by John Koga
Wienzeille 38 drawings by Sibel Ksantugrul
Rennweg 3 drawings by Samart Suepianthiam
Artaria Haus drawings by Laura Rohrbach

The Plight of the Object

1 Philippe Dotremont Collection, Brussels
2, 3, 5-7, 9, 11 Scala S.A.S.
4 Vallecchi Editore
8, 30, 31, 46 Val Warke
10, 32-34, 36-43, 45 Drawings by Timothy Downing
12, 13, 22, 23 Electa Editrice
14-20 Harry Abrams Inc.
21 Penguin Books Inc.
24, 27, 28 Rizzoli International Publications, Inc.
25, 29 MIT Press
26 Fondation Le Corbusier
35 Oxford University Press, Inc.
44 AB Tidskriften Byggmaastaren

Handsome Faces

The following teaching assistants for first year design were critics for the student work presented in this article:
Pamela Butz
Mark Cleary
Francesca Franchi
Merhdad Hadighi
Jeffrey Klug
Tom Sammons

The Cornell Journal of Architecture would like to acknowledge an error in the omission of the name of Michael Dennis from studio projects done under his supervision that appeared in Journal 2. His contribution to the Urban Design Studio has been significant, and we apologize for this oversight.

Every effort has been made to eliminate all errors in this Journal and to give credit where credit is due. We apologize to any person or organization who has or that has not been properly represented in this Journal.

Acknowledgements

We would like to thank all of the authors for their extreme patience, cooperation, and support.
We are also indebted to the following people for making this issue possible: Dick Lovley and Dick Gingras at Cornell Graphic Services; Barbara Gingras and Susan Brohard at Cayuga Press; Dorothy Pasternak and Marty Crowe for copy editing; Joan Heffernan for manning the typewriter above and beyond the call of duty; Rose Perfetti for her sense of humour and access to every room in Sibley Hall; Donna Stevens for managing our accounts; Andrea Talmadge for handling all of our "crises;" Amy Opperman Cash for her advice and her laserprinter; Judy Holiday for allowing us to stay in Pergatory and Barbara for interceding; and our only full time staff member--the Sanyo® TAS 3000.
A very special thanks to Scott Grooms for his technical ability, advice, and dedication.
And lastly, for all of those people who gave so unselfishly. . . you'll never know your contribution.

Address correspondence to:

Editor
The Cornell Journal of Architecture
143 East Sibley Hall
Cornell University
Ithaca NY 14853-6701

Printing: Finger Lakes Press, Auburn, NY
Binding: Riverside Book Bindery, Rochester NY
Photographic Services: Grooms Reprographics, Lansing NY;
Triaxon, Ithaca NY
Composition: Cayuga Press, Ithaca NY;
In-house Apple® Desktop Publishing system
Cover: 100 Warren L.O.E.
Text: 80 Vintage Velvet
Edition: 4500
Typeface: Times Roman